ORDINARY LIVES AND GRAND SCHEMES

EASA Series

Published in association with the European Association of Social Anthropologists (EASA)

Series Editor: James G. Carrier, Senior Research Associate, Oxford Brookes University

Social anthropology in Europe is growing, and the variety of work being done is expanding. This series is intended to present the best of the work produced by members of the EASA, both in monographs and in edited collections. The studies in this series describe societies, processes and institutions around the world and are intended for both scholarly and student readership.

ORDINARY LIVES
AND GRAND SCHEMES

AN ANTHROPOLOGY OF EVERYDAY RELIGION

Edited by

Samuli Schielke and Liza Debevec

berghahn
NEW YORK · OXFORD
www.berghahnbooks.com

Published in 2012 by

Berghahn Books

www.berghahnbooks.com

© 2012, 2016 Samuli Schielke and Liza Debevec
First paperback edition published in 2016

Library of Congress Cataloging-in-Publication Data

Ordinary lives and grand schemes : an anthropology of everyday religion
/ edited by Samuli Schielke and Liza Debevec.
　　p. cm. — (EASA series ; 18)
ISBN 978-0-85745-506-2 (hardback) — ISBN 978-1-78533-199-2
(paperback) — ISBN 978-0-85745-507-9 (ebook)
1. Religious life. I. Schielke, Joska Samuli. II. Debevec, Liza.
BL624.O74 2012
204—dc23

　　　　　　　　　　　　　　　　　　　　　　　　　　　2011052024

British Library Cataloguing in Publication Data

A catalogue record for this book is available from the British Library

ISBN: 978-0-85745-506-2 (hardback)
ISBN: 978-1-78533-199-2 (paperback)
ISBN: 978-0-85745-507-9 (ebook)

Contents

Introduction

Samuli Schielke and Liza Debevec

A key issue for the anthropological study of religion – especially of large world religions with long-lasting textual and institutional traditions – has been how to account for the complex duality of religion as an everyday practice and a normative doctrine. The problem is evident and well-known. If we ask people to explain how they understand belief, ritual, life and death, and if we look at the way such issues are presented and debated by experts, institutions, authorities and traditions of learning, we commonly gain an image of a specific religious tradition as a comprehensive metaphysical, moral and spiritual order. In such an order, the key problem is how to provide justifications and explanations, how to draw lines – in short, how to maintain the coherence of a religious world-view. If, on the other hand, we ask people about their specific concerns, experiences and trajectories, and if we look at the way people live lives of which religious beliefs and practices constitute a part, we gain an image in which religion is a highly immediate practice of making sense of one's life, coming to terms with fear and ambivalence, all-present at times and absent at other times, very sincere in some moments, and contradictory in other moments. In such a practice, the key problem is how to navigate a course of life, and coherence and order are less of an issue.

There is quite some debate about whether and under what conditions 'religion' is a sustainable anthropological category (see, e.g. Asad 1993). And while our specific concern is with traditions and practices which are generally recognized as religious in some way, many of the themes of this book might be transferred to political ideologies, human rights discourse, and other powerful ways of making sense of the world (see Marshall, this volume). Our concern, however, is not with the question as to what is or is not religion (a question which is historically and culturally contextual and therefore has no general answer), but rather with accounting for a feature that appears to be characteristic of many of the most powerful religious traditions and practices around the world: they have a strongly normative character, offering compelling ways to act, to live, to be and to perceive the world – and yet how people actually live religious lives appears to be a very different business.

Numerous solutions have been suggested to deal with this difference, some of them blunt, others subtle. One very influential solution has been to take the articulation of normative doctrine as the primary field of religion, and to look at the practical enactment (and non-enactment) of that doctrine as a secondary one, a watered-down 'popular' version of religion proper. This solution has been increasingly questioned in the past two decades, and there is wide recognition in the fields of anthropology and sociology of religion that we have to look at the ways religious beliefs on the one hand inform people's subjectivities, and on the other hand allow people to make sense of their experiences and anxieties. In short, it has become clear that there is little use in distinguishing between religion proper and religion popular, be it in terms of institutions vs. laymen or in terms of doctrine vs. enactment. If there is such thing as religion proper, it involves all these.

And yet the hierarchy of a primary and secondary field of religion lives on. When we, the editors of this volume, met at a conference in 2007, our research on Muslims who see themselves as believers but live lives that are impious at times, was instinctively identified as dealing with 'popular religion' by many colleagues. Why were the kinds of religiosity we studied popular? Intrigued by this we decided to organize a panel on the subject at the EASA biannual conference in 2008 to pursue the question about what exactly it is that makes popular religion popular. The more we pursued the question during the panel, however, the clearer it became that we had to rethink the problematic altogether. This volume presents the outcome of that rethinking, suggesting that the persistence of the notion of the popular in spite of its well-known shortcomings points out at a gap in the anthropological approaches to religion, a gap that is located exactly in that moment where daily practice and grand schemes come together. And they often come together in contradiction as people navigate a complex and inconsistent course of life partly by evoking a higher moral, metaphysical and spiritual order.

Building on ethnographic studies from various locations and from different religious traditions around the world, we argue for a view that takes this everyday practice (in the sense developed by Michel de Certeau) of religion as the starting point, looking at actual lived experiences and their existential significance for the people involved. Grand schemes constitute one part of this experience – in fact a highly important one, and their significance lies precisely in their grandness, in their being posited above and outside the struggles and manifold paths of daily life. Doing so, they can be evoked, they can offer guidance, and they can be employed in the use of power. But all of this is only possible through the actual little practices of evoking authority, searching guidance, exercising power – practices that are always also informed by the lifeworld they are embedded in, 'the knowledge whereby one lives a life' (Jackson 1996: 2). Herein lies the often amazing power of persuasion that religious traditions can have. And herein lies also the plural, complex and essentially unsystematic nature of religion as lived practice.

With this book, we do not claim to offer anything even distantly approaching a general vision of religion and everyday experience. But we do suggest that the elusive nature of religion as part of a complex ordinary life can be better understood through the notion of the everyday and through an existential, phenomenological perspective that grants primacy to the complexity and openness of practices and experiences.

From the Popular to the Everyday

The question about the relationship of grand schemes and ordinary life became an issue for anthropology after the World War II as anthropologists, moving forward from an academic tradition once primarily focussed on 'primitive' and 'small-scale' societies, increasingly came to look at global power relations and industrial societies. Doing so, they also slowly began to develop an interest in established world religions like Christianity and Islam. It is in this context of a widening focus of the ethnographers' outlook on the world that the relationship of people's immediate practices and stories with grand systemic, economic and ideological frameworks first became a key analytical problematic.

It was in this time that Robert Redfield, a Chicago School sociologist, came up with analytical directions to pursue the problematic that have remained influential until our day (Redfield 1960a; 1960b). Redfield tries to understand the society and culture of small village communities, and he argues that these communities can never be understood on their own terms as cultural isolates. Peasant communities especially, Redfield argues, are heavily dependent on the political, religious, economic, educational and other influences of the metropolitan centres, an influence that makes them what they are, but in which they never have a full share. To account for the way all communities are influenced by and dependent upon each other, albeit in an unequal way, Redfield describes the dominant culture of the urban centres and high civilization as 'the great tradition', and the dependent culture of the villages as 'the little tradition'. (Redfield 1960a: 146)

Redfield's articulation of great and little traditions inspired a generation of scholars to conceptualize the differences, transformations and exchanges of – especially religious – traditions. One of the most influential (and most problematic) proponents of this line of study has been Ernest Gellner (1981) who develops a holistic view of Islam as 'the blueprint of a social order' that consists of two clearly distinct variants, interdependent but always distinct and often antagonistic: a central, orthodox, intellectual, potentially modernising 'great' variant and a peripheral, heterodox, ecstatic, traditional 'little' variant.

Gellner's vision, influential though it has been, was contested from the beginning on by ethnographies that offered a more nuanced look at Muslims' religious lives without resorting to such sharp dichotomies (see, e.g. Gilsenan 1982). In past decades, it has become widely accepted in the anthropology of religion that the notions of great and little tradition, and of official and popular religion, are problematic by default because they are based on an implicit recognition of a hierarchy. Meredith McGuire (2008: 45–46) points out that such notions are based on a distinction between a proper realm of 'real' religion, and a secondary realm of (semi-) religious practices and beliefs that are seen to be something less than the real thing. Doing so, they take for granted hierarchies of class, gender, expertise, political power and access to public that should better be made the focus of study. The fact that deviation thus understood has often been appreciated, even celebrated as a moment of popular resistance (see, e.g., Fawzi 1992; Scott 1990) does not change the core hierarchy involved.

Furthermore, the distinction of great and little traditions offers a dichotomous image of the pure religious doctrine of the specialists vs. the syncretistic practice of the ordinary people which is more often than not empirically wrong. The power of religious establishments to systematically discipline their followers is, in fact, a rather modern phenomenon (McGuire 2008: 41). And in our time, many of the most powerful movements promoting rigorous anti-syncretism – such as the revivalist movements in Islam, Pentecostalist churches in Christianity, and indigenous religious movements resisting the pressure of missionary religions – are largely carried out by people without formal religious education and at times in open confrontation with religious establishments (Gifford 1998; Bowie 1999; Bowie 2006; Hirschkind 2006b; Laffan 2007). Religious establishments in turn – notably the Catholic and Orthodox churches – are often intimately involved in promoting and organising religious practices which they frame as 'popular' (see Mesaritou, this volume).

But if the answers inspired by Redfield's work have been proven wrong, the question he phrases is still worth asking. At the time of its emergence, the notion of great and little traditions seemed to solve a key problem: How to account for the way ideas travel, transform and become part of people's lives? How can we account for people's belonging to traditions, living complex lives and evoking great powers and grand schemes in a way that does justice to their unity in everyday practice?

One solution has been presented by Catherine Albanese (1996) who argues for an understanding of the popular in relation to religion that is not based on a hierarchical model but instead takes popularity in the sense of very wide circulation and (typically electronic) mediation. While this approach to religion as part of popular/mass culture may prove itself useful where priests turn to stars and rites of initiation are recorded on video in a way to look like a telenovela (van de Port 2005; 2006), we still lack an approach to those many things in everyday life that are not (or not primarily) linked to the mass mediation that defines the analytic value of 'the popular' in this context. In fact, much of what is commonly described as 'popular religion' is not mass mediated and often not even known to a wide audience: devotional practices and objects, saints veneration, healing, divination, festive culture, etc. These are often highly personal practices, and sometimes secretive or socially marginal. They require a different kind of account.

It is therefore helpful to turn to the large body of literature that develops approaches to the complexity of religious practice that do without the notion of popularity and without hierarchical models of the proper and the secondary. We should take the popular seriously as an emic category that, inspired by Christian theology, nationalism, folklore studies, the social sciences, etc., has become a very powerful notion in service of claims to orthodoxy and authority around the world. Yet when it comes to issues of syncretism, travelling ideas, different styles of religiosity, and the place and significance of religious practice and concepts in people's life experiences, different approaches are needed.

In their edited volume *Syncretism/Anti-syncretism,* Charles Stewart and Rosalind Shaw (1994) develop an approach that can be helpful when we try to think about the daily significance of grand schemes not as something ready and separate from daily life, but as something that is continuously in construction. Religious beliefs and practices do not simply mix with other traditions, cultural models, and ideologies; more than that, their development and articulation, their growth and decline, emerge from a lived engagement with a multitude of ideas, expectations, pressures and possibilities. This engagement does not necessarily take the form of a friendly and inclusive syncretism – Stewart and Shaw show that it can also take the form of anti-syncretism, a demand for purification for the sake of an untainted authenticity. Religious synthesis, Stewart and Shaw argue, is essentially a practical, political matter, and therefore essentially contested (1994: 2; see also Meyer 2006; Feuchtwang 2001). For us, this opens the question about the work involved when people try to find and establish new or authentic bases for life and action. To look at attempts of organising life and universe is also to look at the uncertainty and complexity of life that people try to thus put into order. Finally it is to look at what happens to life as people try to do such ordering.

In this regard, the issue of ritual has inspired some very interesting and useful approaches that deserve closer attention. One very interesting approach to the relationship of ritual and doctrine has been offered by Talal Asad (1986) who argues that the attempts by anthropologists (especially Gellner) to define what Islam is have all been unable to come up with a satisfactory solution because they have looked at the religion of Muslims in a fragmentary fashion, split into separate entities defined by region or class that have very little to do with the way Muslims see their religion. Instead, Asad suggests, we need to look at Islam as a discursive tradition that is constituted by the way Muslims make reference to their textual sources (the Qur'ân and the authoritative traditions of the Prophet Muhammad), debate them, and try to reach a coherent normative sense of correct practices, their aims and shapes.

Asad's intervention has been followed by a veritable wave of anthropological research that shows that Muslims are engaged in debating and enacting their religious tradition in a way that makes a hierarchy between proper and popular religion irrelevant (Bowen 1993; Salvatore and Eickelman 2004; Hirschkind 2006a; Osella and Osella 2008). The question of orthodoxy, in consequence, becomes a political one: orthodoxy is nothing else than the capability to credibly claim to represent the true, correct reading and practice of a tradition – a position that is subject to change and contestation. Orthodoxy is thus never given, and cannot be made the starting point of the anthropological study of a religious tradition.

This is a very fruitful approach which probably could be made to work in regard to other religious, quasi-religious and non-religious traditions as well: Christianity, Marxism, the human rights discourse and academic standards of scientific research could probably all be shown to have a similar sense of discursive connectedness to founding persons and texts, a living tradition of debate, a concern with correct practice, an outlook towards a history and a future, and an aim to reach normative coherence. But as a solution to the problem of accounting for the relationship of grand schemes and lived practice, Asad's notion of tradition is only a partial one. This becomes evident when we look at one of the most influential works inspired by Asad: Saba Mahmood's (2005) study on the Muslim women's piety movement in Cairo, Egypt.

Looking at the way women of the piety movement try to make their own pious, God-fearing attitude, Mahmood argues that bodily practices such as praying and weeping are not merely instruments of indoctrination but core elements of a sense of the relationship of the body and the virtues of a Muslim, informed by a discursive tradition. Pursuing to enact that relationship, the women in the movement are not being simply oppressed nor are they making choices of the autonomous, liberal kind. Instead, they are working to fulfil a sense of personality that they see as the right one by the power of the tradition they belong to.

Mahmood presents a convincing critique of feminist and liberal notions of freedom and volition that compels us to enquire what senses of embodiment and volition people have, rather than just assuming a predefined ideal. This approach becomes problematic, however, when we try to take it back to its original field of empirical enquiry: the lives of people who want to be good believers. Even when people are seriously engaged in trying to fulfil a certain moral ideal of themselves (and this is not always the case), this does not yet allow us to understand how such attempts actually inform their lives, and for what reasons they resort to them. In practice people may refer to such perfectionist ideals not in order to reach perfection, but in order to make at least some sense of the imperfections and complexities of their lived experience (Jackson 1996; 2005).

In their book on Jaini ritual, Caroline Humphrey and James Laidlaw (1994) develop an interesting approach on ritual that specifically looks at the intentions and meanings involved in engaging in ritual. They provide a useful working definition of ritual (in contrast to performance) as a modality of action characterized by an objective, external quality granted to it by those involved in the ritual. This is an understanding of ritual that can help us a step further to understand the peculiar relation of lived practice and grand schemes: the particular logic of performing a ritual entails that the act of ritual is granted some kind of independent existence outside and above the person performing it, and yet it only gains its significance because it is being performed by somebody with an intention. If we think with Humphrey's and Laidlaw's notion of ritual, the apparent perfection and factuality of grand schemes turns into a pragmatic condition of action. By being granted coherence and objective power, they become things that people approach, use and do. This allows for a high degree of ambiguity and leeway when it comes, for example, to the perfectionist nature of ritual obligations and moral ideals. Falling short of them does not make them less valid, and their being clearly different from how people actually live does not make them less useful as sources of guidance.

Albanese, Stewart and Shaw, Asad, Mahmood, and Humphrey and Laidlaw all offer useful directions to think about religious practice in a way that is not based on a hierarchy of proper and secondary religion. Why is it so difficult, then, to do without at times calling practices, ideas and traditions 'popular' when they seem to be characterized by an unruly and ambiguous relation to religious texts and authorities? It seems that these approaches, each with their specific focus, still leave open a question which continues to attract the shorthand notion of popularity (for a discussion of this problem from a historical perspective, see Cabral 1992). That question, we argue, is the same question which we posed at the beginning: how to account for the relationship of articulations of a coherent world-view and the practice and knowledge of living a life? In this volume we therefore focus specifically on situations which are characterized by ambiguity, uncertainty, anxiety, creative play and contestation whereby people are engaged in living a life partly (but seldom if ever exclusively) by evoking, claiming or submitting to a sense of higher power. Such situations are not exceptional – they are, in fact, the essential way in which religion is lived as part of human lives in our time, as Lila Abu-Lughod reminds us:

> Yet the dailiness, by breaking coherence and introducing time, trains our gaze on flux and contradiction; and the particulars suggest that others live as we per-

ceive ourselves living – not as automatons programmed according to 'cultural' rules or acting our social roles, but as people going through life wondering what they should do, making mistakes, being opinionated, vacillating, trying to make themselves look good, enduring tragic personal losses, enjoying others, and finding moments of laughter. (Abu-Lughod 1993: 27)

This requires us to choose a different starting point. A religious life is inseparable from the wider course of life which involves different pursuits and interests, different emotions and experiences, varying periods and degrees of engagement, and complex motivations (see, e.g. Stafford 2008). This calls for an approach that is sensitive to the phenomenological unity of being and acting in the world in its complex ways.

Uses and Pursuits

The contributions of this volume develop a perspective on religion that focuses on everyday practice. Such everyday practice is complex in its nature, ambivalent, and at times contradictory. It is embedded in traditions, relations of power and social dynamics, but it is not determined by them. The task of an anthropology of religious practice is therefore precisely to see how people navigate and make sense of that complexity, and what the significance of religious beliefs and practices in a given setting can be.

Focussing on the everyday, we do not aim to make a distinction between experts and laymen, or between institutional and non-institutional forms of religion. In contrast to Nancy Ammerman who argues that 'everyday implies the activity that happens outside organized religious events and institutions' (Ammerman 2007: 5), we argue that everyday practice is not a matter of a social setting or a group of people, but a modality of action.

With the notion of the everyday, we lean on Michel de Certeau's work. In *The Practice of Everyday Life* and other works, de Certeau established the study of everyday life as a valid academic subject in its own right. As his collaborator from the second volume of *The Practice of Everyday Life* Luce Giard writes, de Certeau was interested in 'ways of doing (walking the streets, shopping, cooking, decorating one's home or one's car, talking to one's neighbours)' (2003: 2). His goal was to make 'everyday practices, "ways of operating" or doing things, no longer appear as merely the obscure background of social activity' (de Certeau 1984: xi). By focusing on the 'ways of doing' de Certeau gives previously overdue attention to 'the irreducibility of practice that is a thorn in the side of the crafting of hegemonic knowledge' (Napolitano and Pratten 2007: 5). De Certeau did not agree with the hierarchy of high culture versus popular culture, a dichotomy in which popular culture is always since a second best. But he was highly attentive to the power relations under which everyday practices take place, therefore turning his glance to the way in which people who act under circumstances they have limited influence on make do with them, arrange themselves within them and divert them without challenging them.

This point has found its perhaps most compelling expression in de Certeau's distinction of 'strategies' and 'tactics', the first being characterized by the abstract vantage point of power and a modality of action involved in outlining systems and totalizing discourses, while the latter is characterized by quick moves, manipulations and diversions that make use of the system without seriously trying to challenge it. Such tactical uses, de Certeau argues, are indeterministic but not autonomous: they can divert a system but they cannot avoid it. It is this peculiar relationship of 'strategies' and 'tactics' that in our view makes de Certeau's approach to the everyday a highly fruitful tool for accounting for religious practice, albeit with some modifications.

The most significant modification has to do with the notion of 'uses'. Looking at the practice of consumption, de Certeau asks: 'The thousands of people who buy a health magazine, the customers of the supermarket, the practitioners of urban space, the consumers of newspaper stories and legends – what do they make of what they "absorb", receive, and pay for? What do they do with it?' (1984: 31)

This is, essentially, the question which we can also ask about all those complicated things people commonly call 'religion' – but with the modification that these things are not just out there to be used; they would have never existed without a use. A church is truly a church only when it is an active place of worship. A holy book is truly a holy book only when it is read, interpreted, referred to for guidance, for authority, for divination, for protection. This use is grounded in communities, traditions, hierarchies, but it is also at the same time constitutive of them on a daily basis as the source of countless small adjustments, shifts and pragmatic considerations that, in long run, make up a religion in its historical continuity and geographic spread.

This means that common knowledge and everyday practices are not just a way to manipulate grand schemes, but are constitutive of them on every step. Here it may be necessary to critically revise de Certeau's approach to the relationship of the powerful and the weak. De Certeau's analysis, valorization and, at times, celebration of everyday practice is based on an explicit political concern: 'We are concerned with battles or games between the strong and the weak, and with the "actions" which remain possible for the latter' (de Certeau 1984: 34; see also Napolitano and Pratten 2007). But who, in the case of religious practice, are the strong and the weak? The distinction of powerful clergy and weak laymen was always questionable, and it has become even more so in the current times of lay movements successfully promoting an anti-syncretistic, strict and unforgiving sense of religion and of religious establishments involved in tactical moves towards political powers and public opinion. Thus the 'strategies' of the vantage point of power and spatial planning which de Certeau describes appear as only partly external to the condition of daily 'tactics'. Everyday practice may subvert and divert grand strategies, as de Certeau argues, but it may also be aimed at achieving an even greater rigour. The question, then, is what makes specific articulations so compelling? Why do some search for rigour while some search for reconciliation, and some simply try not to be bothered?

Here Michael Jackson's approach of highlighting the existential primacy of lived knowledge is helpful to amend de Certeau's notion of the everyday. Jackson convincingly argues that we need to be attentive to the practical knowledge of living a life, and to its existential significance rather than its ideological justifications: 'The meaning of practical knowledge lies in what is accomplished through it, not in what conceptual order may be said to underlie or precede it' (Jackson 1996: 34). This, in turn, implies that different practical concerns are likely to inform different articulations of a conceptual order: 'People tend to assent to notions of absolute authority and objective knowledge in situations of personal crisis. On occasion, therefore, such beliefs are instrumentally necessary and existentially true because they help people regain effective control over their lives' (13).

In his recent study on Muslim prayer in Indonesia, Gregory Simon (2009) shows that while the people he worked with would often articulate very clear and specific ideals of proper Muslim subjectivity, their own lives often looked very different. This difference, Simon argues, should not be understood either as people falling short of their religious discourse, or the discourse containing impossible demands. Instead, the Muslim prayer's

> key position as an Islamic practice allows it to serve as a site of crystallization for the tensions that pervade moral selfhood in everyday life. The ritual offers the possibility of experiencing their resolution – or being faced with their stubborn endurance. It may push people toward at least momentary transcendence, but the elusiveness of this promised transcendence may also be a source of anxiety and frustration. (Simon 2009: 265)

Such moments can help us understand how and with what kinds of intentions people may engage with religious notions and practices. Religious grand schemes can be so powerful because believers locate them outside their lifeworld to grant them the purity and certainty which life can never have. This allows them to be evoked to navigate the complexities of life: the horizons, the social relations, the promises, the pressures, the necessities, the desires, the fashions and the discussions that together make up in a given moment what is important, what is possible, what can and what needs to be done and thought. But this does not mean that this actually 'works' in the instrumental sense, nor does it mean that the grand schemes and powers evoked remain truly external, out there in heaven. Robert Orsi (2005) argues that we should understand religious practice and lives as relational, as people develop intimate and emotional relationships with

God, saints, etc., much the way they do with family and friends, and with the same complex and strong emotions like hope, love and consolation, but also pain, fear and betrayal. These are necessarily open and indeterminate relationships that cannot be deducted from discursive rationalizations. They are also highly ambivalent. The things that offer people moments of dignity, hope and recognition are often the same things that also produce greater suffering, further marginalization and repeated denial (Orsi 2005; McGuire 2008: 53). We do not see this as an inconsistency that needs to be solved in favour of the one or other version of people's lives and words. Ambivalence and inconsistency are more helpful for anthropologists when they are taken seriously, rather than just solved (Ewing 1990; Berlin 1990).

Arguing for the openness, indeterminacy and ambiguity of religious practice does not mean choice in a liberal sense. People in most cases have little choice – on the contrary they cope with circumstances over which they have little or no power. This becomes obvious when we look at the issue of consumption that is crucial for the last two empirical chapters of this volume. While consumption under conditions of contemporary capitalism is essentially framed in terms of choice, and also religious trajectories tend to gain the flavour of consumerist choices, in practice being a consumer means facing a powerful framework of compelling pursuits that makes some choices much more likely than others. Both disciplinary (e.g. Appadurai 1996: 66–85) and anti-disciplinary (e.g. de Certeau 1984) approaches to consumption share this insight: to consume is to make do with powerful paradigms of life one faces day by day. As Daniel Miller points out, the practice of 'making do' does contain a transformative power. The object of consumption is transformed by the personal relationships it enters (Miller 1993). The agency of the consumer, however, does not lie in the moment of choice, but in the emotional work of living with what one ends up consuming (Miller 2008).

Therefore we do not follow the line of research that emphasizes individuality, fluidity and choice as characteristic moments of modern religion – or more specifically, religion in modern Europe and Northern America (Ammerman 2007; Hunt 2005; Davie 2000; Hervieu-Léger 1999). While we do argue that there is always some room for playfulness and bricolage, we also want to point out that in most parts of the world – also in many parts of Europe and North America – the spaces of action are limited, and religious experience continues to be characterized by a precarious balance of hope and tragic suffering (Orsi 2005; Smilde 2007; Ortner 1989). Playfulness is the child of this precarious balance.

With this approach, we join a wider current of attempts to find grounds to study the human condition beyond the duality of psychology and society, subject and object, body and mind that is implicit in traditions of anthropology that highlight structures, symbols, meaning and discursive rationality (Jackson 1996; Ingold 2000; Tomlinson and Engelke 2006).

While emphasising the phenomenological unity of knowledge, practice and experience, we do not aim to open a separate empirical field in the study of religion. In fact, the contributors of this volume all take up established topics in the anthropology of religion: divination, ritual, prayer, cult of saints, authority, community, pilgrimage, festive culture, syncretism, congregations, afterworld, etc. But they approach these topics from the specific point of view of everyday practice, an approach which, we hope, will offer a better understanding of what is actually involved in consulting a diviner, performing a ritual, praying to God, venerating a saint, evoking authority, living together, undertaking a pilgrimage, celebrating a festival, combining ideas and expecting a life after death.

Outline of Chapters

The individual chapters of this volume develop the different aspects of the general argument on the basis of detailed ethnographic fieldwork in different locations around the world. Christian and Muslim religious practice feature most prominently, a pragmatic choice based primarily on our view that to include different aspects of the general problematic was more important than including as many religious traditions as possible.

The first two chapters by Knut Graw and Liza Debevec develop the core argument of the volume about the need to look at everyday uses and their existential significance. Graw suggests that we can look at divination in Senegal and Gambia as an 'intentional space' in which people are able to articulate their anxieties, concerns and plans for future. From this perspective, the most important question regarding divination is how people use it to make sense of their often confusing and troubled experiences and expectations. Debevec looks at Muslims in urban Burkina Faso who claim that they are waiting for the right time to start performing the five daily prayers on a regular basis. Their explanations are based on vernacular notions of piety that allow them to accommodate different pressures, urges and aims without having to openly challenge any of them.

The two chapters by Alison Marshall and Giovanna Bacchiddu take up the issue of community-making through everyday sociality. Marshall examines the 'doing' of religion in relation to community-making in a situation where various religious and political discourses came together in the life of a Chinese migrant community in Manitoba, showing how the ambiguity of complex relationships and identities was essential for the Chinese migrants' social and family lives. Bacchiddu highlights the way a unique version of religiosity indirectly pervades social interactions and regularly builds and regenerates the community on the Island of Apiao in southern Chile. While the inhabitants of Apiao insists on being good Catholics, being a good Catholic in Apiao has little to do with adherence to the official Church's doctrine.

The two chapters that follow, by Séverine Rey and Evgenia Mesaritou, turn the focus to the issue of acting under conditions of hierarchy, authority and power. Rey interrogates the apparition of three saints in Lesvos, Greece from a gender perspective. She shows how the theological notion of 'popular piety' was used by the Greek Orthodox Church in a tactical and ambiguous way that allowed it to claim its competence towards laywomen who initiated the apparition. Mesaritou illustrates the role of the spatial context at a pilgrimage site in Italy where the organizers and visitors have quite diverging visions of the proper meaning of the place. Doing so, she thus turns our attention from the tactics of establishing authority to the question of the possible agency of those who are at the weaker end of the relationship.

The last two empirical chapters, by Jennifer Peterson and Samuli Schielke, take up the issue of complexity that appears as the essential condition of everyday uses. Peterson explores a trend of grassroots Egyptian dance music inspired by Muslim saints-day festivals. She explores the ways that the producers and fans of this dance trend navigate notions of both street-smart coolness and spiritual virtue, seeking to strike a balance between the piously moral and the jadedly tough. Schielke explores the intertwinement of capitalist consumption and religious revival in Egypt after the downfall of Arab socialism, showing how economic and religious promises come closely together as a source of both hope and anxiety in people's lives. As such, they are in turn informed and transformed by everyday existential concerns and uses, often in unexpected ways.

In the afterword, Robert Orsi relates these themes to the challenge posed by the persistence of everyday religiosities to modernist visions of world, arguing that if we want to understand the political power of the so-called fundamentalist movements across the world, we must first take seriously the persistent enchantment of the world beyond the binaries that so often characterize academic thinking about religion. For better or worse, the lived reality of gods and great powers is a fundamental moment of the human condition also in the modern era.

Note

Thanks are due to the participants of the 'What makes popular piety popular?' panel at the EASA conference in 2008 and the contributors to this volume, in particular to Robert Orsi for his engagement and good advise, as well as to the editor of the EASA series James Carries and the anonymous reviewers who have offered us very helpful critique and suggestions. We are furthermore indebted to Doreen Teumer and Saboura Beutel for doing a great job in formatting and organizing the manuscript, as well as to the staff of Berghahn Books for their very competent and helpful support in the course of the publication process. Liza Debevec would like to thank her employer, the Institute of Anthropological and Spatial Studies at the Scientific Research Centre of the Slovenian Academy of Sciences and Arts in Ljubljana, Slovenia for providing a great working environment and the Slovene Research Agency for funding her research. Samuli Schielke would like to thank the Collaborative Research Centre 295 (Linguistic and Cultural Contacts) of the DFG at the University of Mainz and the Academy of Finland for funding his research in 2006-7 and 2008, respectively, and the Zentrum Moderner Orient as his employer since 2009 for offering excellent conditions to work on this book.

References

Abu-Lughod, L. 1993. *Writing Women's Worlds. Bedouin Stories.* Berkeley: University of California Press.

Albanese, C. 1996. 'Religion and American Popular Culture: An Introductory Essay'. *Journal of the American Academy of Religion* 64, no. 4: 733–42.

Ammerman, N. 2007. 'Introduction: Observing Modern Religious Lives'. In *Everyday Religion. Observing Modern Religious Lives.* Oxford: Oxford University Press, ed. N. Ammerman, 3–18.

Appadurai, A. 1996. *Modernity at Large: Cultural Dimensions of Globalization.* Minneapolis: University of Minnesota Press.

Asad, T. 1986. *The Idea of an Anthropology of Islam.* Occasional Papers Series. Washington, DC: Center for Contemporary Arab Studies, Georgetown University.

———. 1993. *Genealogies of Religion: Discipline and Reasons of Power in Christianity and Islam.* Baltimore: Johns Hopkins University Press.

Berlin, I. 1990. *The Crooked Timber of Humanity: Chapters in the History of Ideas.* London: John Murray Publishers.

Bowen, J. R. 1993. *Muslims through Discourse.* Princeton, NJ: Princeton University Press.

Bowie, F. 1999. 'The Inculturation Debate in Africa'. *Studies in World Christianity* 5, no. 1: 67–92.

———. 2006. *The Anthropology of Religion: An Introduction.* Oxford: Blackwell.

Cabral, J. de Pina. 1992. 'The Gods of the Gentiles are Demons: The Problem of Pagan Survivals in European Culture'. In *Other Histories,* ed. K. Hastrup, 45–61. London: Routledge.

Davie, G. 2000. *Religion in Modern Europe: A Memory Mutates.* Oxford: Oxford University Press.

de Certeau, M. 1984. *The Practice of Everyday Life.* Vol. 1. Berkeley: University of California Press.

de Certeau, M., L. Giard and P. Mayol. 1998. *The Practice of Everyday Life.* Vol. 2, *Living and Cooking.* Minneapolis: University of Minnesota Press.

Ewing, K. 1990. 'The Illusion of Wholeness: Culture, Self and Experience of Inconsistency'. *Ethos* 18, no. 3: 251–78.

Fawzi, E. 1992. 'Anmat at-tadayyun fi Misr: madkhal li-fahm at-tafkir al-sha'bi hawl ad-din' (Patterns of Religiosity in Egypt: Introduction to the Popular Thought about Religion). In *Ishkaliyat at-takwin al-ijtima'i wa-l-fikriyat al-sha'biya fi Misr* (Problematics of Social Formation and Popular Notions in Egypt), 214–48. Nicosia: Mu'assasat 'Ibal li-al-dirasat wa-al-nashr.

Feuchtwang, S. 2001. *Popular Religion in China: The Imperial Metaphor.* London: Routledge.

Gellner, E. 1981. *Muslim Society.* Cambridge: Cambridge University Press.

Giard, L. 2003. 'Why and When with Michel de Certeau We Paid Attention to Everyday Life'. Paper for CIVIC Centre, *Reclaiming the Right to Performance.* London.

Gifford, P. 1998. *African Christianity: Its Public Role.* London: Hurst & Co.

Gilsenan, M. 1982. *Recognizing Islam.* London: Croom Helm.

Hervieu-Léger, D. 1999. *Le Pèlerin et le converti. La Religion en mouvement.* Paris: Flammarion.

Hirschkind, C. 2006a. 'Cassette Ethics: Public Piety and Popular Media in Egypt'. In *Religion, Media, and the Public Sphere,* ed. B. Meyer and A. Moors, 29–52. Bloomington: Indiana University Press.

———. 2006b. *The Ethical Soundscape: Cassette Sermons and Islamic Counterpublics.* New York: Columbia University Press.

Humphrey, C., and J. Laidlaw. 1994. *The Archetypal Actions of Ritual: A Theory of Ritual Illustrated by the Jani Rite of Worship.* Oxford: Clarendon Press.

Hunt, S. 2005. *Religion and Everyday Life.* London: Routledge.

Ingold, T. 2000. *The Perception of the Environment: Essays on Livelihood, Dwelling and Skill.* London: Routledge.

Jackson, M., ed. 1996. *Things as They Are: New Directions in Phenomenological Anthropology.* Bloomington: Indiana University Press.

———. 2005. *Existential Anthropology: Events, Exigencies and Effects.* Oxford: Berghahn Books.

Laffan, M. F. 2007. 'National Crisis and the Representation of Traditional Sufism in Indonesia: The Periodicals "Salafi" and "Sufi"'. In *Sufism and the 'Modern' in Islam,* ed. M. van Bruinessen and J. Day Howell, 149–71. London and New York: I. B. Tauris.

Le Bon, G. 1895. *Psychologie des foules.* Paris: Félix Alcan.

Mahmood, S. 2005. *Politics of Piety: The Islamic Revival and the Feminist Subject.* Princeton, NJ: Princeton University Press.

McGuire, M. B. 2008. *Lived Religion: Faith and Practice in Everyday Life.* Oxford: Oxford University Press.

Meyer, B. 2006. 'Impossible Representations: Pentecostalism, Vision, and Video Technology in Ghana'. In *Religion, Media, and the Public Sphere,* ed. B. Meyer and A. Moors, 290–312. Bloomington: Indiana University Press.

Miller, D. 1993 [1987]. *Material Culture and Mass Consumption.* Oxford: Blackwell

———. 2008. *The Comfort of Things.* Cambridge: Polity Press.

Napolitano, V., and D. Pratten. 2007. 'Michel de Certeau. Ethnography and the Challenge of Plurality'. *Social Anthropology/Anthropologie sociale* 15, no. 1: 1–12.

Orsi, R. A. 2005. *Between Heaven and Earth: The Religious Worlds People Make and the Scholars Who Study Them.* Princeton: Princeton University Press.

Ortner, S. 1989. *High Religion: A Cultural and Political History of Sherpa Buddhism.* Princeton, NJ: Princeton University Press.

Osella, F., and C. Osella. 2008. 'Introduction: Islamic reformism in South Asia'. *Modern Asian Studies* 42, no. 2/3: 247–57.

Redfield, R. 1960a. *The Little Community.* Chicago: The University of Chicago Press.

———. 1960b. *Peasant Society and Culture.* Chicago: The University of Chicago Press.

Salvatore, A., and D. F. Eickelman, eds. 2004. *Public Islam and the Common Good.* Leiden: Brill.

Schielke, S. 2009. 'Being Good in Ramadan: Ambivalence, Fragmentation, and the Moral Self in the Lives of Young Egyptians'. *Journal of the Royal Anthropological Institute* 15 (Special Issue): 24–40.

Scott, J. 1990. *Domination and the Arts of Resistance: Hidden Transcripts.* London and New Haven, CT: Yale University Press.

Simon, G. M. 2009. 'The Soul Freed of Cares? Islamic Prayer, Subjectivity, and the Contradictions of Moral Selfhood in Minangkabau, Indonesia'. *American Ethnologist* 36, no. 2: 258–75.

Smilde, D. 2007. *Reasons to Believe: Cultural Agency in Latin American Evangelism.* Berkeley: University of California Press.

Stafford, C. 2008. 'What Is Interesting about Chinese Religion'. In *Learning Religion: Anthropological Approaches,* ed. D. Berliner and R. Sarró, 177–89. Oxford: Berghahn.

Stewart, C., and R. Shaw, eds. 1994. *Syncretism/Anti-syncretism: The Politics of Religious Synthesis.* London: Routledge.

Tomlinson, M., and M. Engelke, eds. 2006. *The Limits of Meaning: Case Studies in the Anthropology of Christianity.* Oxford: Berghahn.

van de Port, M. 2005. 'Priests and Stars: Candomblé, Celebrity Discourses and the Authentication of Religious Authority in Bahia's Public Sphere'. *Religião e Sociedade* 25, no. 2: 32–61.

———. 2006. 'Visualizing the Sacred: Video Technology, "Televisual Style", and the Religious Imagination in Bahian Candomblé'. *American Ethnologist* 33, no. 3: 444–61.

1

Divination and Islam

Existential Perspectives in the Study of Ritual and Religious Praxis in Senegal and Gambia

Knut Graw

> The part played by divination cannot be overestimated.
> —J. Spencer Trimingham, *Islam in West Africa*

Introduction

In Senegal and Gambia, as well as in most other African societies, divination forms an important element of religious praxis. Despite of the often private character of divinatory consultation in Senegalese and Gambian society, in most accounts of West African Islamic religious life, the importance of divination and other forms of ritual consultation is acknowledged as a social fact both by the members of these societies as well as by outside observers.[1] In this regard, J. Spencer Trimingham's statement that 'the part played by divination cannot be overestimated' is not exceptional (Trimingham 1959: 119). Similar statements emphasizing the importance of ritual and consultational practices ranging from divination to therapeutic practices can be found in many of the classic studies of the field.[2] Despite of this general acknowledgement of their relevance, however, very few studies have approached these practices as a key to the understanding of the significance of Islamic religious practice in these contexts as such. Instead, most studies tend to focus on issues such as the history of certain religious movements, their organisation and economy, as well as their relation to the colonial and postcolonial state.[3] In most cases, the importance of divination and related ritual or aesthetic practices is, thus, generally acknowledged but does not move to the foreground of the analysis. Attempts to approach religious life through consultational, ritual or aesthetic practices have remained rare. The most remarkable exception in this regard is the extensive study of religious aesthetic practices in the context of the Mouride brotherhood by Allen F. Roberts and Mary Nooter Roberts (2003). This monumental study not only documents the creativity and cultural dynamic of religious visual arts in urban Senegal in an impressive way but represents at the same time an important methodological shift in its attempt to come to an understanding of Islamic religious life in Senegal through the study of artistic and ritual expressions rather than exclusively through the study of historical process, religious doctrine or religious organisation. In this regard, their study represents an important shift away from the institutionalized spheres of religious life towards the everyday of religious life in terms of how religious life is experienced and practiced on a more daily and personal basis.

The present text will follow a similar line. By focusing on the individual and sociocultural significance of divination in the Senegalese and Gambian context, the text sets out to develop an understanding of West African Islamic religious life through the study of a set of practices which despite (or perhaps precisely because of) their seemingly esoteric and private character, may convey a much more direct sense of the individual and sociocultural significance of contemporary religious praxis in Senegal, Gambia, and, possibly, elsewhere, than accounts limiting itself to the sociological or politico-historical dimensions of religious life. Such a more person-centred approach seems all the more important as it allows for a kind of understanding that does not depend upon specialist knowledge, external or internal, of the religious traditions and their historical development as such but which is, instead, reflective of and sensitive towards how specific religious practices are experienced and lived through in practice.

However, in so far as the approach followed in this text entails a certain shift away from the study of the institutional and sociological dimensions of religious praxis towards questions of experience and more implicit fields of meaning, this shift should not be understood as a break. Rather, it will be argued that the understanding of the significance of religious praxis that can be gained through an existential study of seemingly 'popular' dimensions of religious life may actually be crucial to the understanding of the sociological and historical aspects of a specific religious setting by highlighting shared patterns of meaning which are important for the motivations and understandings not just of specific ritual and consultational practices but also for engagements within the religious field more generally. In this regard, the attempt to come to an understanding of (Islamic) religious life through the study of divinatory and related practices rather than religious organization or congregation is meant to be de-delimiting and integrative rather than imposing new delimitations as to which areas should be understood as forming the proper objects of the study of religious praxis. This analytical move is complemented by a similar shift in relation to the topic of divination moving from the study of divination in terms of tradition, intellectual content or cognition towards its study as a hermeneutic and consultational practice. In the last part of the text, the attempt to de-delimit the study of divination by paying particular attention to its more existential dimension is complemented by a more general reflection on the possibility of an existential approach to divination and religious praxis and its relation to phenomenological and existential thought.

Divination and Islam: Integrating Ritual Traditions

In many Islamic societies, especially in the Middle East, the activities of healers and diviners are looked upon with suspicion by the official representatives of religious groups and organizations. Due to this, healers and diviners often have to operate at what appears to be the fringes or outside of what is considered 'orthodox' religious praxis in the respective context. Sometimes healing and divination practices are even banned by the state. In Senegal and Gambia, however, divinatory and therapeutic ritual unfolds in the centre rather than at the margins of Islamic practice. A number of reasons account for this situation. Historically, in most West African societies Islam first spread through scholars who were schooled in the Islamic esoteric sciences and who offered their services to the leading members of local, non-Islamic aristocracies. Due to this early identification of Islamic ritual specialists with esoteric knowledge and services, practices such as divination and the making of protective amulets have been associated with and seen as a proof of the power of Islamic religion for centuries. This strong link between West African Islam and the arts of divination and healing is also reflected in the fact that even diviners and healers without specific knowledge of the Islamic literary corpus and Arabic writing are, as long as they are perceived to operate within an Islamic cultural framework, generally referred to with the same titles that are used to refer to a person renowned for his Islamic education and expertise in the Islamic literary tradition. These titles of respect are, for instance, *mooro* in Mandinka, *serigne* in Wolof, and *thierno* in Pulaar. Reflecting this, the Arabic derived term 'marabout' that is often used by Western scholars as well as by French speaking Senegalese, can equally refer to religious specialists in the scriptural sense as well as to divination and healing specialists. In other words, in Senegal and Gambia being a specialist in divination or healing is practically synonymous to being a religiously learned person and vice versa.[4]

This view of diviners, healers and religious community leaders as being part of the same religious field is not only the result of established modes of perception but also of the active effort of diviners, healers and religious leaders to inscribe themselves into the religious field of which they are perceived to be part of. One of the most important markers in this regard is dress. At least when receiving clients, but also during the rest of the day, all diviners I worked with would usually wear the long-sleeved and ankle-long shirt typical for the male Islamic dress code in Senegal and the Gambia (Mandinka *dendikoo*). No one would wear European-style trousers or shirts. Another important marker of this belonging to the field of Islamic praxis is Arabic literacy. The large majority of the diviners and healers I met had at least some basic notions of the Arabic script and would make use of the Arabic script for writing or at least copying the words and phrases necessary for the drawing of esoteric seals (Mandinka sing. *katimoo,* from the Arabic *khatim*) used in protective and propitiatory amulets referred to as *safee* in Mandinka and *téere* in Wolof.[5] Interestingly, both terms, *safee* and *téere,* make reference to the field of literacy and writing and thus, indirectly, to the Islamic sphere, *safee* meaning something written (from *ka safee,* to write) and *téere* not only meaning amulet but also being the general Wolof term for book. Although not all amulets necessarily contain writing (there are also those made from different vegetal and animal substances), the generalized reference to writing and script in the designation of these objects provides further evidence for the intimate link between what is considered to be part of scriptural Islamic praxis and the divinatory and therapeutical arts that prescribe and make use of these objects. A third, perhaps more general but nevertheless important element adding to the synonymy between diviners and Islamic specialists or leaders is what I would call a kind of shared moral habitus or ethical posture of respectfulness towards others, characterized by the approachability, calmness and impartiality which is often also associated with the figure of the elder (*keeba*) and also required in other offices.

These different elements, together with the fact that historically, in the Senegambia, Islam has been associated with divination and other esoteric practices means that as mooro, serigne, thierno or marabout the figures of diviners, healers, and religious leaders not only overlap but are actually largely interchangeable. As a matter of fact, it is rare that religious leaders or people assuming a certain status due to their religious education, descent or function do not practice divination or the writing of safee at least occasionally. In the same vein, diviners usually perceive of themselves as operating within, not outside the realm of Islam. This is particularly relevant in relation to the study and understanding of divination techniques that are historically not associated with the Islamic esoteric sciences, such as the widespread practice of cowrie shell divination for instance. Also these forms of divination refer systematically to the Islamic charitable practice of *sadaqa* as their most important ritual remedy (Mandinka *sadaa*). Although pre-Islamic in origin, also cowrie shell divination and other forms of divination and therapy not normally associated with Islamic praxis thus work through and within an explicitly Islamic ritual idiom.[6] In this regard, divination is in fact one of the most widespread and resilient institutions of Islamic ritual life in Senegal and Gambia, embedded in and integrating other forms of Islamic ritual such as *sadaa* (donations) and *duwa* (supplicatory prayer), and, thus, resisting categorizations of Islamic religious and ritual practices as pertaining to the realms of either 'popular' or 'official' varieties of Islam.

A Setting

Several people were waiting in the courtyard of the house of the *khalifa*, the religious head and also de facto political head of the village, to be received for consultation. The visitors were seated on the edge of a large and solid earthen platform made from sun-dried clay bricks covered by a layer of cement and equipped with a light roof made from wooden poles and palm leaves, offering protection against the sun and making the waiting more bearable. The shadow of a large Mango tree in the courtyard of the house provided additional shade. The surface of the platform had been smoothened by the continuous use of people resting, meeting or, as on this day, waiting to be received by the *khalifa* Ibrahima Souane, the oldest living representative of a large and long lineage of Islamic religious specialists, based in the province of Yacine in the southern Senegalese region of the Casamance but with roots and links reaching as far as Mali and Mauritania. Some of the visitors had come from nearby villages, others from more far away, following Cheikh Ibrahima Souane's reputation as a diviner and ritual specialist which extended far beyond the region. Many of the visitors had already arrived the day before and stayed overnight. Those not living further away than half-a-day's walk had also paid their first visit to Cheikh Ibrahima the day before, then returned home and come back in the morning. Now they were waiting to be received a second time in order to obtain the results of a divination procedure referred to in Mandinka as *listikaaroo,* a form of dream divination involving the interpretation of what a diviner sees during his sleep following specific prayers, soliciting information on the nature of and the right ritual remedies to his clients' predicaments, reaching from illness and marital conflicts to unemployment and migration.[7] Amadou, for instance, a young and athletically built football player wearing sneakers, tracksuit trousers and a shirt of his favourite European club, had come from Dakar. A journey of at least 10 hours by Sept Places, the famous mostly Peugeot station wagons, the fastest over-land transport option in Senegal, providing, as the name indicates, space for seven passengers at a time. Travelling by the cheaper Car Rapide, the same journey often takes more than a day, involving overnight stays at the border with the Gambia which has to be passed through in order to reach this southernmost region of Senegal. He had come to see the marabout because of certain difficulties he had with his trainer in Dakar, and for acquiring ritual protection against a series of sport injuries he had been suffering from and which, if continuing, could bring his aspirations to a sudden end.

Listikaaroo was often favoured by the more prestigious marabouts who, besides their divination and healing activities, also had a more public religious role to play. They gave preference to this practice over cowrie divination, divination by the use of roots, or other forms of divination that form part of the panoply of forms of divination practiced in this part of West Africa because of the distinctive Islamic credits of *listikaaroo*. The preference for *listikaaroo,* or *istikhara* as it is referred to in Arabic, reflects the general awareness of many practitioners of the fact that this technique, at least as a private practice of praying for guidance and advice, has remained largely exempted from the criticism towards divination practices that has been expressed in many texts and teachings that circulate in many contexts as parts of the curriculum of scriptural Islamic knowledge. By virtue of its legitimacy in the traditions of the Islamic textual scholarship, *listikaaroo* is theologically lifted out of the wider realm of divination of which, at least in the Senegalese context, it has always been part of.

Another form of divination often favoured by practitioners who could draw upon formal religious learning and literacy in Arabic was *khatt ar-raml,* literally, sand writing, that is, the art of Islamic geomancy. Referred to as *ramalu* in Mandinka, it represents a highly complex and more formalized divinatory practice involving both writing and arithmetic procedure. Again, the relative proximity towards and direct association with an explicitly Islamic realm of religious praxis may play an important role in the wide distribution of this particular form of divination in the Senegalese and Gambian context. At the same time, however, regardless of the techniques they preferred themselves, the practitioners usually refused to assume any kind of hierarchy between the different forms of divination and considered them to be different but equally valuable paths of knowledge *(londoo)*. Furthermore, the mutual appreciation of different forms of divination among practitioners was not limited to the discursive level but expressed itself also in the fact that, when consulting other diviners, they often preferred to consult with practitioners using a different technique than their own.

Despite its wide distribution and obvious sociocultural importance, for the outside observer, the significance of divination as part of the larger realm of religious praxis is not easy to grasp. Both the panoply of different techniques as well as their esoteric character may play an important role here, making it an area that cannot be overlooked but which is difficult to observe and to study in any real depth. In this regard, it is perhaps not surprising that many of the classic studies dealing with Islamic life in Senegal have paid little attention to divination or healing, focusing instead largely on questions concerning the social, political and economic organization of Islamic practice, especially in relation to the large Sufi orders which shape religious life in Senegal in important ways (see Cruise O'Brien 1971; Copans 1980; Coulon 1981; Villalón 1995; Seesemann 2011). In comparison, esoteric and private practices such as divination and healing have received relatively little attention, and this remains the case also in the present, with, as mentioned above, the important exception of the monumental study of Sufic practices in urban Senegal by Allen Roberts and Mary Nooter Roberts (2003). Individual divinatory consultations have only rarely been documented.[8]

This relative absence of ethnographic accounts of divination and healing practices in the context of Senegalese and Gambian Islam may have many reasons, reaching from the esoteric and private character of these consultations and resulting difficulties of access to a possible preference for the social over the individual dimensions of life that characterizes the social sciences more generally. Whatever the precise reasons may be, for people in Senegal and other West African countries it is common to consult divination specialists either on a regular basis or at certain crucial moments in life. Divinatory consultations are frequent, for instance, in situations of illness, especially when biomedical help is either not available due to its high financial costs or has failed. Other problems which are frequently approached through divinatory consultation include decisions concerning marriage and divorce, fertility problems, work opportunities, migration, etc. In general, the concern lies in the question of how one's personal situation will develop in the future and what can be done to assure a positive development of one's personal affairs. In this regard, Senegambian divination seems to differ from central and southern African divinatory traditions that have been described as aiming primarily at exploring the hidden cause of past events. But how precisely does divination operate in the Senegambian context? How does it work and what is its precise relation to the larger realm of religious praxis?

The Unfolding and Personal Significance of Divinatory Consultation

Reflecting its purpose of shedding light on and offering ritual remedies to, first of all, individual predicaments, a divinatory consultation starts with the pronunciation of the 'intention' (*nganiyo*) by the client, that is, the silent pronunciation of the client's reason or motivation for the consultation. Pronounced silently and inaudible to the diviner who is supposed not to have prior knowledge of the exact reason of his client's visit, it is the task of the diviner to locate the client's 'intention' through his divinatory abilities. For the client, with the silent articulation of his or her most intimate and urgent personal concern, the divinatory encounter opens up a cultural space that allows the subject to realize and confront the issues which are at the core of his or her concern or affliction (see Graw 2006). Common questions posed are, for instance: Is the person that I have in mind the right marriage partner for me? Will my marriage recover from its present strains? Will my child soon recover from his illness? Will I be able to pass the final exams? Will I find an employment in the near future? Will I get the chance to travel to Europe like so many others? Such questions have a particular currency in the Senegambian context where the financial and general economic situation of many people is chronically unpredictable, where traditional agricultural modes of subsistence seem to fail to provide sufficient income, where regularly paid jobs are unavailable for most, and where the only hope for the young and yearning seems to lie abroad, in Europe or North America. Offering a space to address and deal with these individual concerns and predicaments, the art of divination forms one of the most persevering institutions of traditional ritual practice in Senegal and Gambia. While other forms of ritual expression and action such as initiation rites, spirit possession and healing cults often appear to be under threat due to ideological power struggles as well as often harsh and socioculturally uprooting economic conditions, not just in Senegal but also in many postcolonial contexts, divination is thriving.[9]

After the consulter's initial silent articulation of his or her reason for seeking out divinatory consultation, it is the task of the diviner to identify this reason through divinatory procedure, to spell out his findings and to indicate the right ritual measures apt to solve or counter the situation at hand. The diviner does this through a complex reading of the divinatory patterns appearing in the shells or geomantic signs. His capacity to do so is based both on apprenticeship and experience as well as inspiration and intuition.[10] In the attempt to gain insight and to spell out the possible developments of the client's future, divination is in itself chronopoetic, that is, time-making, shaping and re-shaping the subject's consciousness of the future with every consultation. The crucial point here is to understand that the immediate experience of the working of the divinatory encounter does not depend on later factual developments. Although the actual development of the person's affairs will shape the experience of the divinatory consultation in retrospect, the immediate experience and time-making quality of divination depends primarily on the degree to which the diviner is actually able to address the concerns of the person and to offer ritual solutions to the issues at hand. The significance and potential power of this time-making quality of Senegambian divination comes into view if one considers the sense of desperation and depression a person is confronted with in situations of persisting illness, infertility, long-term unemployment and similar predicaments. What characterizes all of these situations is that for the person concerned the promise of the future has seemingly ceased to exist. As an answer to such situations, divination is able to offer new perspectives that can be further pursued. Seen from the perspective of the consulter, as well as from a more general, existential perspective, the power of the divinatory encounter seems to lie precisely in the producing of a prospect that enables the subject to develop new hope and new confidence by responding to the specific situations of crisis, doubt or affliction that brought the person to the respective consultation. In such a perspective, it becomes clear that divination is not just an expression of a specific religious tradition, cosmology or cognition. Instead, divination comes into view as a cultural technology of hope and prospect, reshaping and recreating the temporal horizon of the individual subject. Such a more existential understanding of divination differs, thus, markedly from perspectives focusing on the historical, symbolic, cognitive or metaphysical-religious dimensions of the divinatory encounter. It emphasizes the fact that divination is, first of all, a consultation, that is, an inquiry geared towards individually and socially situated problems and difficulties, not just a cultural text or cognitive exercise.

Towards an Existential Understanding of Divination and Ritual Praxis

In colonial accounts and descriptions divination and other ritual practices in Africa and elsewhere have often been labelled as irrational, as being part of a universe of 'magic' and 'fetishism', markers of 'primitive mentalities'. While the colonial lexicon has arguably lost much of its power over the way these practices are perceived and represented, echoes of it are still tangible in, for instance, the exoticizing representations of advertisements using non-Western cultural forms and practices as tourist attractions, or in the way they are displayed and promoted in the art trade and other areas. Within the field of anthropology, the study of divination has generally been marked by the attempt to counter these disqualifications and to emphasize the internal coherence and rationality of these practices, their historical and symbolic depth and complexity, as well as their often crucial social importance in dealing with social conflicts and afflictions threatening the social tissue of local communities. An anthropological understanding of divination as a cultural field of hope and prospect shows that divination is neither exotic nor part of a primordial cultural past but a complex and highly topical cultural praxis of understanding and empowerment. Such a perspective on (Islamic) divinatory praxis highlights, in other words, its existential significance, not its otherness.

Due to divination's embeddedness in Islamic ritual, this more existential understanding of divination arguably also bears a potential for a more encompassing understanding of the existential significance of other aspects of Islam in Senegal, Gambia and, possibly, elsewhere. In bringing our attention back to what is immanently and immediately experienced rather than what is entailed by the theological and metaphysical frameworks in which these practices are set and operate, the understanding of divination as a cultural technology of hope may also be relevant to the understanding of ritual and religious praxis more generally.

Concerning the implications of such an understanding of divination in Senegal and Gambia for the wider comprehension of what is relevant and significant about Islamic religious praxis in this context, it is important to note that the charitable practice of *sadaqa* which, as mentioned above, forms perhaps the single most important ritual measure to counter and resolve the situations divination is concerned with, is not the only explicitly Islamic dimension of divinatory ritual. Another important practice linked to divinatory praxis is, for instance, that of supplicatory prayer (*duwa*). This prayer is performed by the client before the actual distribution of the objects, as well as, at least ideally, by those receiving them, rephrasing the initial concern in form of prayer for resolution and thus taking up and finalizing the ritual process which started with the initial silent pronunciation of the person's concern at the beginning of the consultation. While representing, thus, an integral and highly important part of divinatory ritual, the practice of *duwa* also plays a highly significant role in religious festivities and ceremonies, when parting on a journey, as response to a gift, or for the general importance that is attributed to the (non-divinatory) consultation of marabouts. While divination can and should be perceived as a distinct cultural practice of great cultural elaboration, one should, thus, not overlook its intrinsic relation to other (Islamic) practices. Through practices such as *sadaqa* and *duwa*, but also through much more spectacular events of Islamic religious life such as the famous *magal* of Touba, the annual pilgrimage to the capital of the Senegalese Mouride brotherhood in which the receiving of *duwa* plays a central role, Senegambian Islamic praxis contributes to the same cultural space of hope and prospect that is aimed at and generated in the divinatory encounter. In this regard, the study of divination as part of West African Islamic praxis also shows that the highly politicized debates, both within and outside the Islamic world, concerning the role of religion in Muslim societies (and the nature of religion more generally), tend to overlook that for most people, religion is first of all a fundamental cultural attempt of meaningful and dignified being-in-the-world. It is also a cultural way of being that allows the subject (and society as a whole) to deal actively with the predicaments of a postcolonial globalizing world, providing important means of empowerment and participation in a world that for many is increasingly marked by economic and political exclusion.

This larger significance, transcending, so to speak, the transcendental and reaching right into the thickness of the everyday life of religious praxis, becomes particularly clear in a conversation I had with a young taxi driver in his twenties during a ride from the Lebou village and suburb of Yoff towards the city of Dakar. Triggered by a radio program of religious chants our conversation had turned to the magal, the annual pilgrimage to Touba, the flourishing capital of the Senegalese Mouride brotherhood. I asked him if he had been there and he answered that he went there every year. And often not only during the magal but also at other times, whenever he felt like it. For him, he said, visiting Touba was very important.

'Why do you go there?', I asked him.

'Pour avancer!'

In order to advance.

Again, such a seemingly profane dimension of what religion actually means to people may easily escape our understanding. In a certain way, such a perspective on religion could easily be perceived as overly functionalist and reductionist, ignoring the many complex layers of meaning intrinsic to the spiritual, performative and social dimensions of such complex events as pilgrimages or other religious celebrations. From an existential perspective, however, to recognize and grasp the immediate personal significance of pilgrimage as an important means towards gradual self-realization and advancement is not reductionist but an expression of the effort of paying attention to what is actually expressed. Looked at in such a way, the reason given by the young taxi driver for why he would go to Touba every year is not a reduction but a condensation of the meaning of this particular religious activity which, rather than being idiosyncratic, in fact spells out the significance this event has, not just for the individual pilgrim but also more generally for the hundreds of thousand people flocking to Touba during the magal each year.

Anthropology and Existence

Despite their undeniably important place in philosophical thought, in anthropology, explicitly existential perspectives or calls for existential or existentialist approaches have remained surprisingly rare. The most continuous efforts in this direction have been undertaken by the anthropologist Michael Jackson who, in a series of books, has argued continuously for the value, and indeed, necessity of an existential perspective in the field of anthropology (Jackson 1998; 2005; 2007; 2009). For the rest, and unlike in other disciplines such as, for instance, psychiatry or psychotherapy, attempts to consciously work within and engage with phenomenological and existential approaches in anthropological theory have remained scarce, both during the high time of (French) existentialism during the 1960s and in recent times. Even if we include the phenomenological tradition in this review, a tradition which especially in its transformation in the work of Heidegger has been crucial for the development of existentialist thought, the picture is not very different. Not unlike the situation of existential thought in anthropology, phenomenology has been described as not more than 'a vague presence lapping at the edges of anthropology' (Katz and Csordas 2003: 277). Due to this, where such attempts are made they always seem to have to carry the burden of the pioneers who cannot rely on cleared paths or regular posts of supply but who have to bring all the necessary gear with them in order to reach their destination. Similarly, anthropologists engaging with phenomenological or existential thought seem to have to carry their phenomenological gear into the field of anthropology, carrying and translating the notions they need into new areas.[11]

Of course, one may ask what may have been and what are the reasons that account for this situation? Why is it that a discipline which calls itself a science of man refers so rarely to a tradition of thought which centres precisely on the question of human life, how it is experienced, lived through, practiced, lost, challenged and remade? One critical point in what is likely to be a rather long and complex story of intellectual traditions, influences, exchanges and refusals, may have been a certain sociological bias in early British anthropology which has tended to prioritize the social dimension of life over individual and personal experience. In a similar vein, structuralist anthropology largely dismissed individual experiences and concerns in its search for the underlying structures of cultural symbolism and, ultimately, human consciousness. On the other side, it may be argued that even without explicitly dealing with existential thought, good ethnography achieves precisely what existential thought aims at, and that is to develop an understanding of what human life is like by describing in detail how people actually live and experience their lives, and how they conceive of their lives and the world(s) they live in, both individually as well as part of a larger societal context. In this regard, one could argue, good ethnography has always been existential ethnography.

At the same time, however, it cannot be overlooked that large parts of the critique of the anthropological project during the last decades have been directed against tendencies of othering, reification, objectification and scientization which can hardly be called existentially sensitive. While anthropology has changed over the last two or three decades towards an increasingly open, self-reflective and holistic enterprise, the call for everyday perspectives in the study of religious life and other sociocultural formations may still be crucial. In this regard, it is important to remember that the call for everyday perspectives is not new as such but can be traced back as far as Karl Marx's early writings on alienation and political economy (Waldenfels 1985 [1978]). In these writings Marx frequently refers to 'the actual processes of life' (die wirklichen Lebensprozesse) in opposition to mere representations and ideas (Vorstellungen). In a similar vein, Husserl's emphasis on the 'lifeworld' (Lebenswelt) as well as his famous call 'back to the things themselves' (zurück zu den Sachen selbst) were both attempts to counter tendencies within philosophy and beyond to describe the world exclusively in natural scientific or psychological terms and not in the way the world is actually experienced and lived through. Although coming from and moving in very different directions, in both instances, these calls for life-near approaches to human reality were thus critical attempts. They were not just alternative ways of proceeding in a seemingly neutral scientific inquiry but attempts to counter tendencies that were perceived as socially and economically (in Marx's case) or epistemologically (in Husserl's case) objectifying and, ultimately, dehumanizing. Something similar is implied in the call for an existentially sensitive perspective in relation to the study of West African Islamic life as well as religious praxis more generally.

Despite the fact that the practices people engage in are embedded in a variety of theological, social and political contexts, all of which have distinct historical and theological properties, what often matters most are the practices themselves. Furthermore and more often than not, the practices which seem to matter most are often those which are highly personal and thus seem to remain at the margins of public religious life. In this regard, the practice of divination described in this text is only one of many examples. The list could easily be extended to other practices such as ancestral rites in many postcolonial contexts, Marian devotion at unrecognized sites, visionary experiences, religious festivals or the religious practices of minorities which are often perceived as alien or excessive by the majority. In other words, the practices that seem to matter most are often those which seem to resist institutionalization or to which institutionalization is denied. Approaches focusing too exclusively on religious institutions, their history and their role in society, not to mention cognitive and other attempts to study religion 'scientifically', reaching from the neurosciences to biology and clinical psychology, may thus easily overlook what is most relevant for understanding the personal and cultural significance of religious praxis in its respective context, and this almost regardless of the amount of information gathered. In other words, what religious life is about often runs the danger of getting lost in abstraction. It is in this regard that existential perspectives may still offer an important remedy.

Notes

1. The present text incorporates parts of and continues a much shorter and earlier text which has appeared as Graw, K. (2005a) 'Culture of Hope in West Africa', *ISIM Review* 16: 28–29.

2. See, for instance, Christian Coulon's emphasis on the importance of ritual services provided by religious leaders in the Mouride brotherhood (Coulon 1981: 108–11) or Villalón, who remarks that 'marabouts are central to the personal domain' (1995: 122).

3. Cruise O'Brien 1971 and 2003, Coulon 1981, Triaud and Robinson 2000, Samson 2005, Seesemann 2011.

4. Despite the tenuous socio-legal position of healers and diviners in many Middle Eastern societies, the identification of religious learning and ritual capacities in the field of healing and divination is widespread in these contexts as well.

5. For descriptions of these practices in different sub-Saharan contexts, see El-Tom 1985 and 1987, and Hamès 2007.

6. For a more comprehensive study of Senegambian cowrie divination, see Graw 2005b and 2009a.

7. Note that in most Middle Eastern contexts this praxis is not considered as a form of divination but as a kind of prayer to be pronounced by oneself rather than by someone else. As most practitioners in the Senegalese and Gambian context do not consider divinatory practices as contradictory to the exigencies of their Islamic praxis, no effort is made to maintain a strict distinction between *listikaaroo* and other divinatory practices. The treatment of *listikaaroo* as divination in this text is, thus, ethnographical, reflecting local practice, and does not imply a general statement as to the theological status of this practice in other contexts.

8. For examples of anthropological accounts of individual consultations, see Graw 2006 and 2009b. For a linguistic study of an individual ethnomedical encounter, see Perrino 2002.

9. For a study of the culture of spirit possession threatened by Islamic religious hegemony, see for instance Masquelier 2001. For the transformations of traditional ritual institutions in popular culture and religious life in a non-Islamic environment, see De Boeck and Plissart 2004.

10. The large majority of diviners in Senegal are men. Among the many diviners I worked or had contact with, there was only one woman. This situation is largely confirmed even by research focusing in particular on the role of female diviners and marabouts (Gemmeke 2008 and 2009). For a more detailed account of the reading of the divinatory signs, see Graw 2005b, 2006, and 2009a. For reflections on the dialogic dimension of the divinatory encounter, see Graw 2009b.

11. The pioneering dimension of phenomenological/existential anthropology becomes also evident from the text on the back flap of James F. Weiner's study *Tree Leaf Talk* which is subtitled 'A Heideggerian Anthropology'. Highlighting the importance of Weiner's engagement with Heidegger in his explorations of Melanesian ritual and social life, the endorsement refers to his study as 'the first book to explore the relationship between Martin Heidegger's work and anthropology' (Weiner 2001). While there may be earlier references to Heidegger's work in anthropology, the very fact that an anthropological study can be characterized in such a way more than 70 years after the first publication of *Sein und Zeit* is indeed telling.

References

Copans, J. 1980. *Les Marabouts de l'arachide: La confrérie mouride et les paysans du Sénégal*. Paris: Le Sycomore.

Coulon, C. 1981. *Le marabout et le prince: Islam et pouvoir au Sénégal*. Paris: Pedone.

Cruise O'Brien, D. B. 1971. *The Mourides of Senegal. The Political and Economic Organization of an Islamic Brotherhood*. Oxford: Oxford University Press.

———. 2003. *Symbolic Confrontations: Muslim Imagining the State in Africa.* London: Hurst.

De Boeck, F., and M.-F. Plissart. 2004. *Kinshasa: Tales of the Invisible City.* Ghent: Ludion.

El-Tom, A. O. 1985. 'Drinking the Koran: The Meaning of Koranic Verses in Berti Erasure'. *Africa* 55, no. 49: 414–31.

———. 1987. 'Berti Quranic Amulets'. *Journal of Religion in Africa* 17, no. 3: 224–44.

Gemmeke, A. B. 2008. *Marabout Women in Dakar: Creating Trust in a Rural Urban Space.* Zürich: Lit.

———. 2009. 'Marabout Women in Dakar: Creating Authority in Islamic Knowledge'. *Africa* 79, no. 1: 128-147.

Graw, K. 2005a. 'Culture of Hope in West Africa'. *ISIM Review* 16: 28–29.

———. 2005b. 'The Logic of Shells: Knowledge and Lifeworld-Poiesis in Senegambian Cowrie Divination'. *Mande Studies* 7: 21–48.

———. 2006. 'Locating Nganiyo: Divination as Intentional Space'. *Journal of Religion in Africa* 36, no. 1: 78–119.

———. 2009a. 'Beyond Expertise: Reflections on Specialist Agency and the Autonomy of the Divinatory Ritual Process'. *Africa* 79, no. 1: 92–109.

———. 2009b. 'Divination as Hermeneutic Encounter. Reflections on Understanding, Dialogue, and the Intersubjective Foundation of Divinatory Consultation'. In *The Vision Thing: Studying Divine Intervention,* ed. W. A. Christian Jr. and G. Klaniczay, 459–77. Budapest: Collegium Budapest (Collegium Budapest Workshop Series No 18).

Hamès, C., ed. 2007. *Coran et talismans: Textes et pratiques magiques en milieu musulman.* Paris: Karthala.

Jackson, M. 1998. *Minima Etnographica: Intersubjectivity and the Anthropological Project.* Chicago: University of Chicago Press.

———. 2005. *Existential Anthropology: Events, Exigencies and Effects.* New York and Oxford: Berghahn.

———. 2007. *Excursion.* Durham, NC: Duke University Press.

———. 2009. *The Palm at the End of the Mind: Relatedness, Religiosity, and the Real.* Durham, NC: Duke University Press.

Katz, J., and T. J. Csordas. 2003. 'Phenomenological Ethnography in Sociology and Anthropology'. *Ethnography* 4, no. 3: 275–88.

Masquelier, A. 2001. *Prayer has Spoiled Everything: Possession, Power, and Identity in an Islamic Town of Niger.* Durham, NC, and London: Duke University Press.

Perrino, S. M. 2002. 'Intimate Hierarchies and Qur'anic Saliva (Tëfli): Textuality in a Senegalese Ethnomedical Encounter'. *Journal of Linguistic Anthropology* 12, no. 2: 225–59.

Roberts, A. F., and M. Nooter Roberts. 2003. *A Saint in the City: Sufi Arts of Urban Senegal.* Los Angeles: UCLA Fowler Museum of Cultural History.

Samson, F. 2005. *Les marabouts de l'islam politique: le Dahiratoul Moustarchidina wal Moustarchidaty, un mouvement néo-confrériques sénégalais.* Paris: Karthala.

Seesemann, R. 2011. *The Divine Flood. Ibrahim Niasse and the Roots of a Twentieth-Century Sufi Revival.* Oxford and New York: Oxford University Press.

Triaud, J.-L., and D. Robinson, eds. 2000. *La Tijâniyya: Une confrérie musulmane à la conquête de l'Afrique*. Paris: Karthala.

Trimingham, J. S. 1959. *Islam in West Africa*. Oxford: Oxford University Press.

Villalón, L. A. 1995. *Islamic Society and State Power in Senegal: Disciples and Citizens in Fatick*. Cambridge: Cambridge University Press.

Waldenfels, B. 1985 [1978]. 'Im Labyrinth des Alltags'. In B. Waldenfels, *In den Netzen der Lebenswelt*, 153–78. Frankfurt am Main: Suhrkamp.

Weiner, J. F. 2001. *Tree Leaf Talk: A Heideggerian Anthropology*. Oxford: Berg.

2

Postponing Piety in Urban Burkina Faso

Discussing Ideas on When to Start Acting as a Pious Muslim

Liza Debevec

Among the Muslim population of the West African state of Burkina Faso, there is a commonly accepted notion that all persons calling themselves Muslims should regularly perform the five daily prayers. In Bobo Dioulasso, the second largest town of Burkina Faso, a country where religious conversion is not uncommon (Langewiesche 2003) and where there is no distinctive Islamic dress code, the question '*I bi seli wa?*' (Jula for 'Do you pray?') is often used to distinguish a Muslim from a non-Muslim.[1] However, many of my Muslim informants and friends, as well as members of my host family do not pray regularly. Furthermore many do not fast during the month of Ramadan, some also drink alcohol and eat pork, and many engage in behaviour, which when observed in other people, they might condemn as improper or un-Muslim. This is, of course, in no way unusual, as people seldom actually live up in full to their religious and moral maxims. But when praying is elevated from a matter of being a good Muslim to a matter of being a Muslim at all, non-prayer requires explanation.

Many among those of my informants who do not pray regularly suggested that what they are doing is postponing prayer and pious behaviour to a later, more appropriate stage of their life. When asked about what stage in life would be more appropriate, these people provided a variety of answers, all of which are centred around an implicit cultural understanding of the complexity of life, which can interfere with one's ability to act as a pious Muslim. Because of this culturally accepted understanding, people can postpone the act of prayer and pious behaviour to a time when this is deemed both necessary and appropriate and thus also easier. Yet some people do not necessarily start praying at a later time, but simply keep postponing the practice, which could be interpreted to mean that they were never serious about praying in the first place. Thus while the idea of postponing piety is widely spread among the Burkinabé, the reasons for not praying in the present may vary substantially from one person to another.

In this chapter I explore stories of people who, each for their own reasons, are involved in the act of postponing religious practice while living in a Muslim community where religious practice is held in high esteem. Michael Jackson's seminal introduction to *Things As They Are* (Jackson 1996) provides a fruitful approach to understanding the lives of these people. Jackson argues that 'phenomenology calls into question ... the long-standing division in Western discourse between the knowledge of philosophers or scientists and the opinions of ordinary mortals' (1996: 7). He suggests that it is our task 'to revalidate the everyday life of ordinary people, to tell their stories in their own words, to recover their names' (36). Through the introduction of concepts such as 'lived experience' and the 'quotidian world' (Jackson 1989: 2), and 'the practice of everyday life' (de Certeau 1988), anthropologists have turned their attention to the complexity of everyday practices. As Lila Abu-Lughod points out, 'struggle, negotiation, and strategising ... lie at the heart of social life' (1993: 13), and it is exactly such struggles, negotiations and strategies that I wish to explore in my collection of individuals' narratives about their lives as Muslims in urban Burkina Faso. Their acts of postponing piety are part of such struggles, negotiations and strategising in an attempt to get by in the best way possible, to survive each day that they find themselves wondering about what life/God has in store for them that day.

Being a Moderate Muslim in Urban Burkina Faso

The city of Bobo Dioulasso, where I have been conducting research since 2000, is a predominantly Muslim city of about half a million inhabitants, situated in the southwest of Burkina Faso.[2] The majority of Burkinabé Muslims refer to themselves as moderate Muslims; if pressed for a definition of their branch of Islam, they name the Malikite tradition of ritual and law as the one to which they belong.[3] These self declared moderate Muslims are often rather critical of the reformist Muslims, to whom they refer with the generic term *Wahhabi*, regardless of whether these people are Wahhabites, or members of other Islamic reformist groups that can also be found in Burkina Faso today.

This moderate, tolerant Islam and its coexistence with other religions in the region (Christianity and traditional African religions) is not just a cliché created and promoted by the secular government; it is something that can be observed in everyday life in Burkina Faso. In Bobo Dioulasso, a roast-pork vendor stall is often less than a block away from a neighbourhood mosque, Christians attend Muslim celebrations and vice versa, and there are sacred places of ritual importance for members of Muslims, Christians and animists alike (Werthmann 2008). Religiously mixed marriages are a tolerated, though not preferred option. Some parents give their children both Muslim and Christian names, an act that was explained to me as a way of allowing for a child to make a choice about religion when adulthood is reached.

While moderate Muslims pride themselves about their tolerance, they have, at the same time, a very clear definition of what a good Muslim is, which they like to refer to when discussing Islam. Though my research was never about determining who a true Muslim was, I was nevertheless constantly offered definitions by laypeople, or pointed into the direction of some more knowledgeable person, usually an imam, a Qur'an teacher or another, usually older person with religious knowledge, who would be able to provide me with the 'correct answer' to what people thought my question was, when I asked to discuss Islam with them. While there is a general recognition that men of religious learning will be the ones able to give a 'correct' account of Islam, the same people who would refer to those men of learning also have their own accounts and definitions. But these accounts can be rather different from what the men of religious learning are expected to tell, and yet for many of my friends and informants, both can be true, albeit in a different sense. There exists a variety of notions, expressed in different contexts and associated with different social positions of the person expressing these notions, of what constitutes 'true' piety for urban Burkinabé Muslims.

It would be an easy way out to designate one – the discourse of the men of religious learning – as the official, 'proper' version of Islam, and the other – the more pragmatic attempts of people to live a religious life – as its 'popular' counterpart. Such a dichotomous view is made attractive by the way men and women in Burkina Faso themselves belittle their own knowledge and emphasize that only imams, muezzins and other people who have detailed knowledge of the Qur'an can be valid interlocutors when it comes to a discussion about Islam. But as suggested in our introduction to this volume, there is not much use in such distinction, since if there is such a thing as religion proper, it involves all of these moments (see Schielke and Debevec, this volume). The demand that Muslims must pray regularly, and the discussion about how to do it properly, is part of everyday religious life just as much as the claim to postponing piety until a more appropriate moment is. Rather than designating the different moments of speaking about religious practice to specific groups and categories, it is more helpful to understand them as different modalities of speech and practice, different in their contents and consequences, but united by the practice of living a life.

My intention in this chapter is to engage with the experience of being a Muslim in contemporary urban Burkina Faso in an environment that is changing through the process of globalisation in ways that both liberate and put constraints on individuals who are already struggling to find their identity as members of a community – whether that is their extended family, the Muslim community of Bobo Dioulasso, Burkina Faso or the Islamic Umma.

From Satanic Temptations to Lifestyle Choices: The Reasons Not to Pray Regularly

While it is not for the anthropologist to engage in theological discussion about the correct way of praying or about 'true' Islam, it is important to outline the ideal of a 'good' Muslim that my friends and interlocutors refer to and possibly strive to achieve in the future. They were unanimous in their belief that a true Muslim is one who accepts that Allah is the one and only god and Mohammed is his last prophet, prays regularly, fasts during the month of Ramadan, does not eat pork or drink alcohol, pays alms (*zakat*) to the needy and, if she or he has the means to do so, will also perform the pilgrimage to Mecca. The imams and other locally respected Muslim elders whom I interviewed suggested that a child, either male or female, should start praying at the age of seven and if by the age of sixteen she or he has not taken to regular prayer, the father has the right to chase the child from the family compound.

The people who are postponing prayer in their adult age have all learned to pray as children, many attended Qur'anic classes for several years, and some have prayed for a certain time during their lives, but in the present, they say that they do not pray but that they will pray later. In the following section, I take up some of their narratives to take a closer look at the reasons and common explanations they offer for not praying in the present.

Bintou Ouattara, my main informant, an unmarried 38-year-old woman (and a mother of two daughters out of wedlock), gives the following explanation:[4]

> There are people who are so used to praying that when they are asleep, when the time for prayer comes, even if they are in deep sleep, it is like someone taps them on their shoulder and tells them, 'get up, it is time to pray'. … Myself, there were times when I prayed, and it was like that. Early in the morning when the muezzin would call to prayer, it would enter my ears and I would get up, as long as I would not pray, I could not go back to sleep. Even if I would find myself somewhere else, I would be in a rush to pray, even if I were in a foreign town, I would want to enter a strange compound to pray on time.
>
> … But there are also moments, Satan there, it totally detours you [*ça te de-route*], you are there, people are praying, you are looking at them and it does not incite you to pray. What we just discussed, this woman Ami, we used to go to her house and at the time of prayer, we'd get up and pray and she would just sit and watch, never joined us in prayer.

... There comes a time, in the early morning, you hear the call to prayer, but it is like something is pushing you, it's like you've been bitten by a bug, which is telling you 'stay in bed, don't get up'. So you don't get up. And then there are times, you pray, you ask God, like, I'm not married, and I want a husband, you speak, you speak, in your prayer, you ask and speak, but there you are, and not even a decent boyfriend, let alone a husband. So I say to myself, I have prayed, God is not listening to me. And the prayer not being easy and all, you find all this even more discouraging, you are discouraged. In my case, what I find discouraging is that the prayer is already very difficult and you realize that God is not accepting my prayers. So why do it? You should get a rest. Because in my compound, as you yourself know, it is very crowded. ... [T]he water for the prayer should be totally clean, there should be no bits of food and oil or soap in the water, the calabash you use to take the water should not be greasy, yet in our compound, the kids take this dirty calabash and use the water for the prayer, and I look at them and think, how can that count ... .

[Here another informant, Mina, intervenes: 'It is God's decision to accept or reject these prayers.']

... Well, I think... , well, there are times I say to myself, if God decides to give me a husband, and I have a house of my own, I know how to perform the prayers. Because you are on your own, you have all your things, you are organized, it's your house. ... If I had the means to do this, I would get a place of my own, I have my room, no one sees you, it is my wish to have my own place, with a shower and I do my thing, I sit and do the ablutions and I have a clean place and I pray and there I am, no one has to see me. When you have the money, you have your own place and it is clean, you do your prayers correctly and you know that God will accept them since everything is clean. But where I live, in the extended family compound, you know, nothing belongs to you, you don't even have a chair to sit on, you have to squat at all times and you see the water is dirty, it is strange, it doesn't even give you the courage to pray. Me, in any case, I wish to have a place of my own. I am not saying my husband should be a millionaire, but that he has the means to put me up. I know how to worship God, and I will pray until my death, to have my sins forgiven, as I know that presently I have sins, I acknowledge that I have sinned. There, that's it.

This monologue, explaining various and somewhat diverging reasons for not praying at the moment – Satan detours her; she is disappointed with God; and in the compound where she lives it is difficult to find the cleanliness and privacy to pray – was part of a group discussion with Bintou and her two friends Mina and Haoua.[5] Like Bintou, Mina and Haoua are both without a husband, one abandoned by her spouse and the other widowed. Both pray regularly but say that Bintou had a valid argument, and agree that the fact that Bintou does not pray is not an active choice on her part, but something that was the work of the devil, who does everything to prevent you from praying. They all genuinely believe that Bintou will start praying eventually, although they also say that they cannot know when and how this will happen, as it is all the will of God.

During this discussion, Mina also spoke of her own period of not praying, when she was first married with her now late husband, who was a pious and practicing Muslim. He tried to incite her to pray, telling her he would not eat the food she prepared, as she was not praying, but she stubbornly refused to pray. She said that Haoua used to come over and her husband would say: 'See your sister, how she prays, why don't you do like her?' but Mina refused to do so. Sometimes she would pray and then abandon it again. Then a moment came and she started praying regularly, but she said that it was about the same time her husband died. She now prays regularly, but says, 'I pray God that I continue to pray and not be pushed on the stray road by the devil.'

Bintou's example is not unique, and several imams have mentioned examples of people being tempted by the devil not to pray and to act in un-Islamic ways. According to imam Issiaka Sanou, the imam of the oldest mosque in Bobo Dioulasso, bad people exist in all things, thus also among Muslims, and bad people are those who don't pray, who drink, who lie, cheat etc. However, someone who does not pray but generally acts in a pious way by respecting their elders and being kind to the fellow human beings is not automatically 'banned from going to Heaven'. According to imam Issiaka, and to several other imams, it is quite possible that God will send an individual who did not pray but mostly acted in a good way to Heaven rather than someone who prayed regularly but acted in un-Islamic ways by lying and cheating.

Hamidou, an unmarried man in his early thirties, of mixed Dafing/Marka/Fulbe origin from a village in the north of Burkina who has been living in Bobo since his teenage years, with a short period in between spent in Ivory Coast, also does not pray regularly. Like Bintou he suggests that it is the harsh living conditions in the city that prevent him from engaging in regular prayer. He prides himself of his youth, when, he says, he used to pray '100 per cent, even the fasting I did, but well now, as everything is mixed up [*a be kera nyagamin*], my father is in the village, I am alone here, the situation is difficult, with the poverty, the religion is difficult'.

To my question if he believed that religion was more difficult for those who were poor than those who were wealthy, he replied:

> Ha, I think that if you are … you know here religion, if you have some money, Liza, it's ok. If you have money, you are at ease, you are calm and you can do your prayers calmly, you know. But when you are poor, there are times when the prayer time comes up, you've totally forgotten about the good God.

Another reason Hamidou gives for his current non-prayer is his lifestyle of a tourist guide:

> If one is struggling [in French, '*on se cherche*'] it is very difficult even to dedicate yourself to prayer. For example, you are with your tourists and it is the time of prayer, and you could tell them you need to pray, they will not prevent you from doing so, but you're always catching up and so you are forced to let the prayer time go by and you do your job. And then when you get home, you

have five prayers you need to catch up with and so if you were to do all that, it's really complicated, so you kind of have to get rid of this, it's too hard to do all that.

Moussa, a young man who like Hamidou works as an independent tour guide says that he is a believer, but he feels that his current lifestyle does not allow him to pray regularly, since he, as he puts it himself, engages in un-Islamic behaviour. He does, however, pray to God in a non-ritual way, sometimes reciting the Fatihah (first chapter of the Qur'an), or simply asking God to protect or help him in his daily activities. Unlike Bintou, Moussa does not suggest that his non-prayer would be an unconscious act prompted by an outside force beyond his control. He agrees with Hamidou that it is hard to pray when your living conditions are precarious and you have too much to worry about, but he does not see that as the main impediment for praying regularly. He wishes to engage in youthful behaviour, go to clubs, have many girlfriends, drink beer. But he sees such behaviour as being part of the young age and thinks that he will adopt a more pious behaviour with age.

Also Baba, a 34-year-old blacksmith, who in his early twenties worked as a smuggler on the border with Ghana and Côte d'Ivoire, speaks of postponing piety as a conscious decision, based on his belief that it is more sinful to pray and act in un-Islamic ways than not to pray at all. In his case, he cites drinking alcohol, eating pork, being unmarried and lying about the price of the sculptures he sells as some of the things that prevent him from praying. He does, however, fast and pray five times a day during Ramadan: 'I am believer, I believe in God, so that is the least I can do.' Baba was one of the people who initially refused to discuss religious matters with me, saying that he did not know much about Islam because he is not an imam. Once he understood my interest, he was happy to discuss his experience and also made strong statements about 'good' and 'bad Muslims'. He claimed that engaging in un-Islamic behaviour and not praying in one's youth was essential, as one needed to give into temptation in order to not be interested anymore in old age. He cited examples of his uncles and grandfathers, who all 'did bad things in their youth and now they pray and do not want anything to do with their past actions'. He said that most of the older population has no problem tolerating the impious behaviour of the younger generation. When asked when he thinks he will start praying, Baba replies:

Later, I will pray later, when I have the means. I'm waiting until I have enough money not to have to ask from others. A good Muslim has to be able to help others . ... A poor person can pray regularly, but they have to be really courageous, they have to have a really strong mind. What I have remarked is that most young people who pray regularly come from well-off families, that is what I have noticed.

While postponing regular praying for a later time in one's life is not encouraged by those who pray regularly, it is nevertheless widely accepted that those who do not pray now are likely to pray and enter the 'right path' [*sira nyuman* or *le bon chemin*] later in life. Thus a woman whose husband does not pray will not automatically condemn her spouse for not praying, but may refer to this being a result of a discouragement and pray that a day will come when her husband will become a pious Muslim. Fati, a 42-year-old pious woman whose husband was unemployed for twenty years after graduating from university with a law degree, always referred to him as '*découragé*' and never stopped praying that he would get a job. What may seem as lack of initiative on his part to an outsider is, in the eyes of the man's family, a result of outside forces, of unfortunate life circumstances, which left him discouraged. While he was not working and not praying, his mother went to Mecca and upon return brought him an outfit that is usually worn by return pilgrims. His wife commented that the mother had not stopped believing that he would pray someday. When a year later he finally got a job and ended up even signing a contract and began receiving a regular salary, his wife was immensely pleased and suggested that this may be a direct result of their prayers. While he has never indicated that he may start praying now (he is, in fact, one of the rare informants who openly criticized what he referred to as 'the hypocrisy of the Muslim community', expressed doubt in the meaning of religion and never suggested that his 'not praying' was a temporary thing), since getting a job he has occasionally mentioned prayer time in conversation with me, in a joking manner, but making clear that the time in his life had come when he really was expected to start praying.

The Ages of Prayer

Anthropological literature on Muslims in West Africa contains some references to the practice of postponing piety or putting off the act of ritual prayer, but it usually limits itself to suggestion that this is linked to a transition from youth to adulthood, and is therefore something that changes with one's age. Marie Nathalie LeBlanc writes that in Côte d'Ivoire, and among West African Muslims in general pious behaviour is usually reserved for the elderly (2006: 174). Benjamin Soares, writing about the Halpulaaren in Mali and Senegal (and in France), notes that 'before reaching adulthood, it is not uncommon for many young men not to perform their ritual daily prayers' (2004: 920). Somewhat differently, though still in the same line, Adeline Masquelier writes about young Nigerien Muslims who 'are less insecure about their status as Muslims than their parents ... were a decade or so ago' and also do not feel the need to display their piety in visible ways (2007: 244). Also in regard to Burkina Faso it can be said that people go through various degrees of piety and religious performance which roughly correspond to the different age groups they belong to at a given time: childhood and youth, married age, and old age. This is not simply a matter of people starting to pray at a certain age, however. Age is often a shorthand explanation for the changing concerns and priorities in one's life, and in order to understand why some ages are more likely ages for prayer, it is necessarily to look at these changing concerns.

Childhood/Youth

Muslim children from the age of seven onwards are considered to be mature enough to start praying regularly. That is also the age many families send their children to Qur'an summer school, either with the local imam or *marabout* (*karamogo*), or, as is the case with wealthier urban families, to a one of the more up-market summer programmes of Islamic education. Most imams suggested that it was acceptable for parents to physically punish their children if they did not pray, but this seems to rarely be the case. While parents may encourage their children to perform their prayers by asking them whether they have prayed that day, they do not force them to get up in the morning for the first morning prayer, nor have I seen them punish children for not praying during the rest of the day. Parents who pray regularly may call upon their children to join them in prayer. During the month of Ramadan when the prayer *Maghrib* (evening prayer) is attended at the mosque by all – even those who do not normally pray at a mosque – children may follow their relatives and pray there. Young girls often struggle to find a veil or an outfit that covers their body and may be told off by their family for wishing to attend the prayer in an inappropriate outfit. During the rest of the year I have rarely seen children praying. Despite the official discourse prescribing that children pray from an early age, most of them don't do it as a regular daily practice. However, as Hamidou said, some young adults remember their parents' influence on their prayer practice and regret not having the same structure and prayer-inducing environment in their adult age.

In my host compound, young unmarried women in their twenties were always told off for not praying regularly, and upon hearing such remarks they often got up, however grudgingly, and performed a prayer. The young (and adult) men who did not pray at all were neither reprimanded about their lack of prayer nor was it ever mentioned in public. In conversation with the two men in the family who don't pray I discovered that their late father, a primary school principal, was less strict about their prayer ('*mon père n'était pas très porté par la question religieuse*', said one of the brothers) than the mother, and so if the mother pressed them to pray, the father may have told her to leave them alone. These two men prayed as young boys but stopped when they started attending secondary school (*le lycée*) around the age of 15. This is an age at which boys often stop praying. After that they only attended the prayer during Ramadan and on *Tabaski* (Feast of Sacrifice) for a couple more years, until stopping completely.

There are, of course, also exceptions – young people who act piously, regularly perform religious acts and are truly dedicated to religion. While such behaviour is praised by people, I have also often heard people say that such a person will not have long life, since he or she is striving to be close to God, thus God will take him or her to be beside him. Pious behaviour among young people is also often viewed with suspicion by those who do not pray, suggesting that these young people are secretly engaged in all kinds of illicit behaviour.

Married Age

Many of my informants suggested that it was with marriage that one would start acting as a pious Muslim, pray regularly and stop being tempted to engage in un-Islamic activities. When asked why they don't pray, they would simply retort: 'I'll pray when I get married.' While there is no statistical data available on this issue, I have observed that among my informants, married (or widowed) people pray more regularly than those unmarried. The interviews with unmarried informants showed that all those who do not pray at the moment intend to do so (or claim that they will) when they get married. Marriage is a central rite of passage from youth to adulthood (Brand 2001; Soares 2004), but as the age at which men and women get married in West Africa has risen significantly over the last couple of decades because of the rising cost of the marriage, the age of adulthood has risen accordingly. Once married, women have a special reason to start praying and acting piously, especially after they have had their first child, since there is widespread belief that a mother's behaviour determines the future success of a child (Debevec 2007).

Old Age

Old age is commonly seen as the time when there are no more excuses for acting in impious ways. One's this-worldly needs are considered to be fewer, as one is getting closer to death and so this is the final chance to make amends with God and try to secure one's way to Heaven. This is also the age when many Burkinabé Muslims get to do the pilgrimage to Mecca. A person who completed the hajj returns with a clean slate, all the sins washed away, and from that point on, it is therefore important to act in a pious manner and not do anything sinful to spoil one's chances for Paradise. It thus seems that in old age it is imperative for one to pray and act piously, since there little time left to make up for whatever sins against God one has committed thus far. Women and men attend all the five daily prayers at the mosque; they often participate in study groups that meet in the evenings; and they attend all the funerals, name-giving ceremonies, weddings and other ceremonies that may include prayers and blessings. While many old people go to these events because there is free food, their presence is also a blessing for those celebrating, especially if the old person has been to Mecca. As one of my informants said, old age is the appropriate time to act in a pious way, since one has no other work to do than to pray and attend ceremonies.

Apart from age, one's social standing allows for temporal variation in one's piety. On the one hand, wealth and a respected social status are associated with the expectation of consistent prayer. On the other hand, poverty is used as an explanation by people who claim to be postponing their religious behaviour. Bintou, Hamidou, Moussa and Baba all see poverty as a contributing factor for postponing piety, though they agree that there are poor people who pray regularly. They believe those people are particularly courageous and have a lot of will power to endure the hardship of life and maintain their piety at the same time.

My findings in Burkina Faso certainly testify to the existence of an understanding about appropriate ages for various forms of religious engagement of an individual; however, the reasons people have for postponing piety go beyond the dichotomy of a carefree youth versus a more (if not completely) sober old age. While many young people put off regular prayer for a later time, that does not mean that they would not have prayed before, nor does it guarantee that they really will pray at a later time in their life. Their reasons to pray and to postpone prayer are complex and multifold, often inconsistent, and what McGuire refers to as 'an ever-changing, multifaceted, often messy – even contradictory – amalgam of beliefs and practices that are not necessarily those religious institutions consider important' (2008:4). As such they do not necessarily allow for a clear-cut simple analysis but instead compel us to find ways to account for their complexity.

Conclusion: The Uses of Postponing Piety

The idea that one's extent of piety is dependent on age and social position is widely accepted in Burkina Faso. While this contradicts the notion that Muslims should be pious at all times, no one – neither the ordinary Muslims nor the religious leaders – really expects that of all their family or friends. Stopping short of suggesting that they believe there is a time in one's life when it is wrong to be pious, people present the act of postponing piety as one of common sense. The actual reasons and motivations are more specific, however, and often difficult to verbalize. Some choose to speak of the devil tempting the person, of discouragement, etc. Others speak of their life situation as unsuitable for prayer. Fewer express a more explicit dissatisfaction with religious practice.

The common acceptance of postponing prayer for a later time could be seen to contradict the widely accepted idea that performing the five daily prayers is the most clear sign of being a Muslim. Positing one against the other would lead to the conclusion that practice equals belief. This could lead us to the conclusion that Muslims who do not pray are not believers. That, however, is something the narratives presented in this chapter clearly testify against. All my informants who engage in the act of postponing piety see themselves as believers and any suggestion on my side that their lack of prayer could indicate their doubt in the existence of God was quickly and categorically dismissed as ridiculous.

In Burkina Faso there is no room for being atheist or not belonging to a religion. An impious Muslim is still a Muslim, and postponing piety does not draw piety itself in question. On the contrary, what all these people postponing their prayers have in common is a way of idealising the prayer ritual and setting very high standards for what it means to be a proper Muslim. Their act of postponing piety comes along with a clearly pronounced respect for the purity of Islam, expressed, for example, in Baba's claim that it would be blasphemous to indulge in alcohol, pork or adulterous behaviour and to pray at the same time. In a way, by claiming this, he is actually presenting himself as potentially more pious and more God-fearing than his fellow Muslims who pray but still sin (occasionally, or regularly).

This does not mean that while postponing one's piety one could ignore religious and communal obligations altogether. In Mande societies that Bobo Dioulasso is a part of, appearances do matter a lot (Brand 2001). As people who postpone prayer do not engage in the most visible aspect of Muslimhood, they are compelled to compensate by being involved in other visible forms of Muslimhood. They all invest in the social capital by attending Muslim life cycle ceremonies, and making sure that they participate with the small amount of money they have in order to keep the reciprocity chain going.

I would like to suggest that the act of postponing prayer and pious behaviour among many urban Burkinabé is a sign of individuals' struggle with the constraints of a complex life under conditions of an economically harsh environment, which is not made any easier by the very strict and detailed prescriptions of a proper life as a Muslim. People juggle and accommodate a variety of pressures, goals and needs, and they try to get by in life in the best possible way. Religion can be both a solace to them and a burden, which is why there must be space for different interpretations and practices at different times in life. Postponing piety can be understood as a combination of tactical moves, a way of making do in de Certeau's sense (1988) that can help people accomplish a variety of things, among which an important one is getting a grip on both personal and social conflicts which arise from the contradictory expectations that social life imposes on them.

Unlike the interlocutors of Gregory Simon in his study on prayer in Indonesia who express a sense of shame and guilt for not regularly engaging in ritual prayer (2009), my interlocutors go on with their regular life without any sense of guilt. Following Michael Jackson's suggestion that we need to look not so much at how concepts explain the world but at what people try to accomplish through them (Jackson 1996: 34), postponing piety does seem be a successful solution to the potential conflict of pious ideals and a complex life. Postponing piety is thus more than an excuse. It is a way to solve potentially unsolvable conflicts that could result from attempts at a perfectionist pious life by postponing them to a time when the conflict no longer arises because one's life situation has changed.

The conflict which people try to postpone could also be understood as conflict between the real and the ideal world of the people of Bobo Dioulasso. The real world is the actual one people experience every day, what Edmund Leach called 'real society', and the ideal world is the one that exists in people's minds, the so-called 'conceptual model of society' (1993 [1954]: 4). In an ideal world all Muslims would start praying in adulthood, but in that same ideal world all adults would have the financial means to get married and support their families. The world however is far from ideal and people struggle in their lives; as Jackson puts it, they are 'working within the limits placed on [them] by birth, role and duty' (2005: xxxi). As anthropologists (of religion) we should pay attention to the multiplicity of people's stories and the emerging possibilities (Orsi 2005: 204) and account for the complexity of the religious experience we encounter in the field rather than try to make it fit into pre-existing boxes. As Meredith McGuire puts it rather bluntly: 'by emphasizing individuals' practices in everyday life, we may avoid some conceptual muddle' (2008: 16).

Notes

1. See LeBlanc for a similar question in Northern Côte d'Ivoire (1999: 489).
2. For a detailed history of Islam in the area, see Audouin and Deniel 1978; Cissé 2003; Otayek 1996; Traoré 1984.
3. Many Sunni Muslims in Bobo Dioulasso will claim they are not Sunni, but Malékite (or malikite), because they wish to distinguish themselves from Wahhabis, who refer to their own movement as '*mouvement sunnite*' (see Traoré 1984: 86–87). For most Burkinabe who are not familiar with term Sunna as the shorthand for the practices and sayings of the prophet Muhammad, the terms Sunni and Sunnite are considered as designating the orthodox branch of Islam, often referred to as '*les intègristes*'. The historian of Islam in Bobo, Bakary Traoré, suggests that oral accounts of religiously uneducated informants often do not help clear the confusion about belonging to one or other religious branch (1984: 87).

4. This is part of a group interview with Bintou and two of her friends, who unlike her, both pray regularly.
5. All informants' names have been changed.

References

Abu-Lughod, L. 1993. *Writing Women's World's: Bedouin Stories.* Berkeley:
University of California Press.
Audouin, J., and R. Deniel. 1978. *L'islam en Haute-Volta à l'epoque coloniale.*
Paris: L'Harmattan.
Brand, S. 2001. *Mediating Means and Fate: A Socio-political Analysis of Fertility
and Demographic Change in Bamako, Mali.* Leiden: Brill.
Cissé, I. 2003. 'L'islam au Burkina pendant la période coloniale'. In *Burkina Faso:
Cent ans d'histoire 1985-1995,* ed. Y. G. Madiéga and O. Nao, 935–56, Tome I.
Paris: Karthala.
Debevec, L. 2007. 'Religious Practices: Ablution, Purification, Prayer, Fasting
and Piety: West Africa'. In *Encyclopedia of Women and Islamic Cultures,* ed.
S. Joseph, 280–281, Vol. 5. Brill: Leiden.
de Certeau, M. 1988. *The Practice of Everyday Life,* trans. S. Randall. Berkeley:
University of California Press.
Jackson, M. 1989. *Paths toward a Clearing: Radical Empiricism and Ethnographic
Inquiry.* Bloomington: Indiana University Press.
——. 1996. 'Introduction: Phenomenology, Radical Empiricism and Anthropo-
logical Critique'. In *Things as They Are: New Directions in Phenomenological
Anthropology,* ed. M. Jackson, 1–50. Bloomington: Indiana University Press.
——. 2005. *Existential Anthropology: Events, Exigencies and Effects.* Oxford:
Berghahn Books.
Langewiesche, K. 2003. *Mobilité religieuse: Changements religieux au Burkina
Faso.* Münster: Lit Verlag.
Leach, E. 1993 [1954]. *Political Systems of Highland Burma.* London: Athlone
Press.
LeBlanc, M. N. 1999. 'The Production of Islamic Identities through Knowledge
Claims in Bouaké, Côte d'Ivoire'. *African Affairs* 98, no. 393: 485–508.
——. 2006. 'Proclaiming Individual Piety: Pilgrims and Religious Renewal in
Cote d'Ivoire'. In *Claiming Individuality. The Cultural Politics of Distinction,*
ed. V. Amit, 173–200. London: Pluto Press.
Masquelier, A. 2007. 'Negotiating Futures: Islam, Youth, and the State in Niger'.
In *Islam and Muslim Politics in Africa,* ed. B. Soares and R. Otayek, 243-62.
New York: Palgrave Macmillan.
McGuire, M. B. 2008. *Lived Religion: Faith and Practice in Everyday Life.* Ox-
ford: Oxford University Press.
Orsi, R. 2005. *Between Heaven and Earth: The Religious World People Make
and the Scholars Who Study Them.* Princeton and Oxford: Princeton Univer-
sity Press.
Otayek, R. 1996. 'L'islam et la révolution au Burkina Faso: mobilisation politique
et reconstruction identitaire'. *Social Compass* 43, no. 2: 233–47.

Simon, G. M. 2009. 'The Soul Freed of Cares? Islamic Prayer, Subjectivity, and the Contradictions of Moral Selfhood in Minangkabau, Indonesia'. *American Ethnologist* 36, no. 2: 258–75.

Soares, B. F. 2004. 'An African Muslim Saint and his Followers in France'. *Journal of Ethnic and Migration Studies* 30, no. 5: 913–27.

Traoré, B. 1984. 'Le processus d'islamisation à Bobo-Dioulasso jusqu'à la fin du XIXe siècle', unpublished MA thesis, Université de Ouagadougou.

Werthmann, K. 2008. 'Islam on Both Sides: Religion and Locality in Western Burkina Faso'. In *Dimensions of Locality. Muslim Saints, their Place and Space*, ed. G. Stauth and S. Schielke, 125–47. Bielefeld: Transcript Verlag.

3

Everyday Religion, Ambiguity and Homosocial Relationships in Manitoba, Canada from 1911 to 1949

Alison R. Marshall

In this chapter I explore the possible reasons for the emergence of everyday ambiguous and relational behaviours among a mostly male Chinese settlement in the province of Manitoba, Canada from 1911 to 1949 when the last Chinese dynasty had ended and the Chinese Nationalist Party (Zhongguo Guomindang) became the de facto government for Chinese living within and outside China.[1] There were very few Chinese women and children in early settlements because of racist immigration laws that were in place beginning in 1885, when all Chinese immigrants, upon entry to Canada were required to pay a $50 head tax. In 1900, the Chinese Immigration Act doubled the amount to $100, and by 1903, the head tax stood at $500. Although the Chinese Immigration Act did not prohibit the entry of women and children to this nation per se, even wealthier Chinese families could only afford to send one family member here. That family member was usually a father or son. Chinese immigration was almost stopped from 1923 to 1947 when a new version of the act excluded all immigrants except merchants, students, and diplomats and their staff.[2]

In the absence of women, Sun Yat-sen (1866–1925), a revolutionary credited with ending the last Chinese dynasty in 1911, became a powerful, galvanizing figure who visited Winnipeg, Manitoba (and other Canadian cities) in 1911. Dr. Sun was also the first and provisional president of the new Chinese republic for almost four months in 1912, and after that was the figurehead of the Chinese Nationalist Party (Zhongguo Guomindang or KMT). Leaders of the KMT recognized his widespread appeal to overseas Chinese men who like Sun came from southern China and now lived outside of it and used propaganda to inculcate loyalty and respect for Dr.

Sun (and China). These initial top-down efforts turned into a grassroots movement whereby Sun attained god-like status. To those men who had heard Sun speak in Manitoba, he remained a symbolic ruler until he died in 1925, and after that lived on as a god.

As Chinese immigrants settled into Canadian prairie society, got involved in the KMT and Christian organizations and strove to become modern, everyday religion developed that combined Nationalist, Confucian and Christian beliefs and practices. Meredith McGuire has suggested that in order to recognize the everyday practices that characterize lived religion outside of the realm of traditional religiosity, 'a good starting point might be a better appreciation of the many and complex ways ... religions are the products of considerable human creativity, cultural improvisation, and construction from diverse elements, only some of which were inherited from the same tradition' (2008: 185). Everyday religion makes room for things that ordinarily are classed as social not religious activities, such as banquets and other food events. But the term also includes the 'boundary resources' provided by ethnic associations that help define the community as a group, connect it to others, and serve practical and therapeutic needs (Carnes and Yang 2004: 13–15).

Because this everyday religion developed on the Christian frontier of Canadian society and had Confucianism as its foundation, I use the term Frontier Confucianism to describe its general characteristics. Frontier Confucianism, a term first used by Esta Ungar (2010) to capture the kind of Confucianism that arose in sixteenth-century Vietnam, emphasized two modalities or ways or doing religion in the Chinese cultural sphere – all male or homosocial relationships and Confucian or classical education. These modalities accentuated imperial metaphors and authority in order to unite local Chinese settlements with the KMT centre (in Canada and China) (Feuchtwang 1991). Frontier Confucianism also downplayed other traditional liturgical (rituals performed by Chinese specialists), cultivational (i.e. meditational) and immediate practical (i.e. divination) modes (Chau 2009) because ritual functionaries and temples were seldom available.

De Certeau's notion of the everyday (1984) provides a useful framework and starting point for understanding the complex range of factors that influence actions in Chinese settlements just being conceived. Following de Certeau, this chapter highlights the agency of relationality in transforming religious behaviour, individual male bonds, and new immigrant hierarchies. According to him, agency is achieved through alienated minority group tactics and the larger dominant society's strategies. Where de Certeau's interpretation differs from the one presented here is in its dualistic structural assessment of power relationships. Such neat dualistic categories of doing are entirely absent in this chapter because the particular modalities of everyday religion and Frontier Confucianism are rooted in ambiguity. Sometimes people are in positions that enable them to use strategies, for instance as Chinese Nationalist Party leaders who punished disloyal party members by photographing them with dog tags and then sent the photographs to the local press and central party headquarters in China.[3] At other times these same party leaders held concurrent positions as laundry workers and labourers in cafes that required tactics. In these positions, they had no authority and stood outside of the boundaries of the larger dominant society. Frontier Confucianism and a set of strategies and tactics emerged as intercultural bridges and relationships formed among, across and through Chinese and non-Chinese communities. The boundaries between secular life and religion, Christianity and Confucianism, and China and Canada were blurred.

Ambiguity and Efficacy

Ambiguity and efficacy are key aspects of the discussion and help us understand Chinese religiosity both in China and in overseas Chinese communities. The term 'religion' (Latin: *religio*; Chinese: *zongjiao*) is not native to China. It was imported there from Japan in the late 1800s. Although there is no equivalent term for religion in Chinese, this does not mean that Chinese people do not behave religiously. In daily life and during festivals they create and maintain a bond between themselves and divine beings who hold the highest and revered positions. But the way that the bond is established is different and more ambiguous than the way the bond is established in Abrahamic religious traditions. Gods do not have all the power and nothing is absolutely right or wrong, or good or bad. Religion and religiosity are determined by traditions. Behaviours that function in religious ways to Chinese people (for instance relationships) seem less religious to others.

Julia Ching emphasized ambiguity as an essential facet of Chinese religion that enabled flexible links to form between the past and the present through different types of ritualized actions that regulated friendships, religious activities, work and civic responsibility, the family and customs. These links acknowledged the positions and hierarchies of deities, spirits and deceased ancestors (Ching 2001: 213–23). They also maintained the social traditions and everyday behaviours during festivals that had important religious dimensions. Deities and other divine beings such as ancestors required people to behave sincerely towards them, following established traditions for offerings and prayers and other forms of worship. Performing offerings and other rites sincerely ensured that a deity or divine agent responded appropriately and that the practical need of the performer was met.

The sincere performance of rituals and maintenance of traditions is called efficacy (*ling*) which is at the core of Chinese religion. It has been referred to as a magical power created by both worshippers and deities that materializes because of human efforts and out of human needs (Chau 2006). Power between gods and people is negotiated and determined by five relationships that structure Chinese society and religious acts and begin with the ruler: 1) subject and ruler; 2) father and son/daughter; 3) husband and wife; 4) son and son/siblings; 5) friend and friend.[4]

Relationships not only had religious dimensions; they also constructed gender roles and provided rules for social conduct as well as political, civic and economic responsibilities and opportunities. They changed in the modern period that began in 1900 to accommodate homosociality (male friendships and the predominance of the male bond) and the ambiguity of life on the Canadian frontier away from large Chinese communities, Chinatowns and family. By 1912, KMT offices came to function as pseudo-religious institutions where men could congregate and 'worship' their new god Dr. Sun (after 1925), remember early settlers and peruse the library's traditional texts and those written by Sun Yat-sen that imparted appropriate Confucian and nationalistic values. Relationships in Manitoba, Canada and other areas of settlement were no longer defined just by blood. Friendships, which were the lowest ranked of the traditional five relationships, took on important modern religious dimensions, connected men to the KMT, and gave them agency (Marshall 2011).

The foreignness of the term religion allowed Chinese living at home and in overseas communities a certain degree of creativity and agency in their interpretation. Depending on the circumstances, Chinese could honestly say that they were Christians, Buddhists, Confucians or had no religion. Chinese also came to associate the term 'religion' with normative Christian behaviour. Many men living in Manitoba, Canada became nominal Christians or self-identified as Christian on tax rolls and in other public ways. Thus the unfamiliarity with and ambiguity of the term 'religion' enabled men to acculturate, experiment and try novel socially appropriate ways of behaving in new worlds. As Seligman, Weller, Puett and Simon point out, '[i]n dealing with ambiguities, ritual engages boundaries: boundaries are crossed, violated, blurred, and then, in an oscillating way, reaffirmed, re-established and strengthened' (2008: 44). Ambiguity (and the actions that became ritualized in response to it) was at once part of traditional religious practice in China and a modern immigrant innovation. Chinese men had ambiguous gendered, social, economic and religious subjectivities that required them to play different roles, and to belong to overlapping groups. As Chinese religious behaviours were altered for life in Canada without women, relationality, and Confucian and nationalist texts and their associated ideas came to have added importance and to redefine efficacious modes of ritual action. Efficacy was at the heart of Chinese religion. Everything else could change as long as the reason things were done was for efficacious reasons.

The flexible understanding of efficacy meant that it could be easily reworked to suit the needs of life in Manitoba, as men joined the KMT and Christian groups and became modern western Confucian elites. After 1911 these men appeared in an almost uniform manner. They cut their queues (the Manchurian hairstyles forced upon them during the Qing dynasty) and wore short Western hair styles. In daily life, they dispensed with Chinese long tunics and baggy pants, and wore a Western uniform often comprised of the favoured three-piece suit, tie, fedora, cashmere coat (in winter) and polished shoes. In these ways, the ambiguity of their outer appearance matched that of their new subjectivities. It also displayed their willingness to adapt and fit in.

The first Manitoban Canadian settlers arrived in the late 1870s. At this time men resided with other men in what were termed 'bachelor' societies outside of traditional family structures, doing the jobs no one else wanted. Although they were often referred to as 'bachelors', many of the men had wives and children in China. Others maintained a family in China and a small number married second Ukrainian wives (usually) in Canada and started families with them. While the men were free to exist as both bachelors and married (often polygamous) men, their first Chinese wives from whom they were often separated for a lifetime by an entire continent and ocean were expected to be chaste, loyal and frugal with remittances that were sent home for investment.

At first the men worked in wash houses and by the late 1800s they did so in cafes. It was the rare man who had ever cleaned clothes or made a meal prior to his arrival to Canada, as these activities were domestic work traditionally performed by women in China. In China up until 1911, normative understandings of gender were socially, not sexually, constructed. From a young age, generally speaking, men and boys were taught that their everyday lives were located in the outer quarters tilling fields, being merchants, or studying for the state examinations in order to become an official. Women and girls generally and by contrast were responsible for domestic arts such as cooking, cleaning, sewing and child care. Although clearer gender and social boundaries existed in China, there was a near complete absence of them in overseas Chinese communities. In Manitoba there were very few women until after 1947, and the Chinese population was spread out beyond Chinatown. Therefore neither kin nor ordinary gender dichotomies existed. Under these circumstances, homosocial relationships took on necessary religious dimensions, connecting men to each other, to Sun Yat-sen, to China and to the Canadian landscape.

Economic identity was as ambiguous as gender for the group of Chinese settlers living in Manitoba from 1911 to 1949 where they existed like peasants working from early morning until late in the evening for very little money. What money they did earn was used to feed, clothe and sustain themselves here in Canada, and often their parents, or wives and children in China. To their Chinese families the men were seen as gentry because of the remittances they had sent to wives to be invested in local building projects. The men were also perceived as gentry because their Canadian wages had also provided enough to repay immigration debts (i.e. the $500 Head Tax) and to make donations to Canadian KMT branches. Chinese men who did not purchase Chinese Nationalist bonds to fund party efforts in China could be punished or publicly humiliated. The Manitoba KMT's executive committee made exceptions for poorer men. The need to meet demands of those in both their home and host countries complicated identity and behaviour.

As Chinese settlers became accustomed to a multi-faceted ambiguous existence in Manitoba, new efficacies and rituals developed to help them cope. For men, it may have been socially appropriate or efficacious to worship traditional Chinese gods such as Guanyin, Mazu (Buddhist goddesses associated with salvation) or Guangong (a god associated with Chinese brotherhoods and Daoism) in the late 1890s. But by 1911 Sun Yat-sen, the "Father of Modern China", had begun his eventual transformation into a god and the earliest settlers were becoming new ancestors to be acknowledged in a special annual grave custom called Decoration Day. Decoration Day, which is discussed later in this chapter in more detail, was performed around father's day for fictive kin (those not related by blood) (Yang 1994) and the earliest settlers. It was different than other traditional grave customs such as Qingming or Chongyang performed in the spring or autumn, and it was the predominant grave custom until wives and children were able to immigrate to Canada after 1947 when the Chinese Immigration Act was repealed. Throughout Canada, from 1921 to 1927, Chinese Nationalists increasingly encouraged members to distance themselves from traditional Buddhist and Daoist practices and public identities, and Christian conversion (Marshall, forthcoming). This chapter presents a case-study of Frontier Confucianism in Manitoba between 1911 and 1949 that may have broader applications for Chinese nationalists resident beyond Canadian Chinatowns in the same period.

Frontier Confucianism as Everyday Religion

There has been debate over whether Confucianism is a religion or a philosophy. Some scholars have avoided the term religion altogether and have instead pointed to its religious dimensions, which I have also done here. In Manitoba, and elsewhere throughout Canada, nevertheless, Confucianism was a historical category of religious self-identity in the 1911 and 1921 Canadian census surveys alongside the dominant nominal Christian one. While just fifteen per cent of settlers in Manitoba self-identified as Confucian in 1911, by 1921, there were over fifty per cent of them. Chinese settlers may have grown up learning that Confucianism was an autocratic system of values associated with imperialism that they should have rejected when they voiced their support for the KMT and Sun Yat-sen. Some aspects of Confucianism such as the imperial rites, sacrifices, and notions of the mandate of heaven (that a ruler was given a mandate to rule by the divine and that bad omens signalled his demise and a change in the understanding of his efficacy as a ruler) were eschewed by nationalistic bachelors in favour of those that associated with a more modern republic and nation. But others remained and were developed in both large and small Chinese Canadian communities. In Victoria, British Columbia, the Chinese Benevolent Association had an offering hall called the Palace of Sages (Lie Sheng Gong) on its top floor that by 1889 included an altar for Confucius. Ancestral veneration continued (and continues) before Lee, Wong, Yee and other family association altars throughout Canadian Chinatowns. From 1916 until it became an official holiday in China, communities were encouraged by the Freemasons and Chinese Benevolent Association to close KMT and other offices and celebrate Confucius's birthday with teas and banquets; but this day only became known as Teacher's Day in China in 1931. I propose that it was the influence of the KMT and the importance of being a modern Western Confucian elite that perpetuated these religious behaviours and created this new form of self-identification on the census survey.

It would be easy to attribute native understandings of Frontier Confucianism to the later efforts of Chiang Kai-shek. Chiang founded the New Life Movement that was designed to further Sun Yat-sen's goal of a new modern China. But years before its creation in 1934, there was already a fully-formed version of Confucianism here in Manitoba and throughout frontier Chinese communities in Canada. Like its eventual counterpart in China, it was efficacious as a socially not spiritually constructed religiosity that highlighted the value of virtues such as benevolence, loyalty and sincerity in creating and maintaining connections, relationships and economic contributions (Nedostup 2007).

Frontier Confucianism as an identity and set of everyday religious behaviours was constructed by the earliest migrants to this province as a way to straddle the boundaries of home and host nations and to succeed. As I define the term here, it encouraged the sentiment that the veneration of Chinese deities with incense, spirit money, the use of mediums, and other personal-cultivational, liturgical-ritual or immediate-practical modalities that from a modernist perspective had come to appear as 'superstitious' were a blight on the image of the modern educated gentleman. In the early period of settlement, it was acceptable to revere sages such as Confucius in Victoria's Chinatown, and for women and labourers to use prayer beads or practice other Buddhist or Daoist personal or immediate modalities beyond it in small town Canada. But by the 1920s, there was a strong feeling among Chinese nationalists resident in Canada that this kind of weak ambiguity sullied an otherwise pure modernist self-image. Private rituals and customs belonging to these modalities could be only be tolerated in the farthest back regions of life – if indoors, then out of view in a bedroom, and if outdoors, then in a secluded area of the backyard or garage. People could offer lit incense, meals, whiskey and flowers in public at grave sites during Decoration Day or Qingming and Chongyang but these non-normative behaviours had to be offset by relationality and scriptural/doctrinal modalities vested with the authority and power of nationalism (Chau 2009). The leadership thereby encouraged KMT members to forge relationships with those within and beyond the Chinese community. Better educated Chinese nationalists turned to Confucian classical texts to understand virtues such as loyalty, humaneness and righteousness. Everyone memorized the nationalist anthem and became familiar with the Will of Sun Yat-sen that explained the social significance of the three principles of livelihood, nationalism and democracy. They were to also venerate Confucius as a teacher, and when their children came to the country they were urged to transmit the same knowledge and virtues to them. One research participant explained: 'There was a Chinese school. It was organized by the Chinese community and it was held in the KMT building. … We used to have to go for two hours after school every day and two hours on Saturday mornings.' After Saturday morning Mandarin classes at the KMT most of the children would then go to Bible study classes at the local church. Familiarity with the words and lyrics of the nationalist anthem, the Will of Sun Yat-sen, and the study of classical texts taught overseas Chinese how to behave religiously by guiding social relationships, ensuring harmony and directing men's attention to the KMT, Sun Yat-sen and China (Stafford 2007).

Men who eventually joined the KMT were first attracted to it by Sun Yat-sen. Many old timers tell how their parents 'worshipped him like a god,' 'had the twelve-pointed star in their hearts,' and gave generously when the KMT asked for donations. Manitoba Overseas KMT offices were sent all sorts of propaganda to distribute. This propaganda was in addition to the signed calligraphy with his three principles (democracy, livelihood and nationalism), couplets with Nationalist sayings, oil paintings, photographs and reams of cheaply printed posters of him that adorned office walls and filled its drawers. Over time a myth developed (and was perhaps circulated) that Sun Yat-sen had been so interested in the men of the Manitoba KMT that he had visited the branch three times (when in fact he had only been there once in 1911). Robert Orsi has written about the power of media such as rosaries that makes the Virgin Mary present in everyday lives. More than reminders of Mary, Orsi noted that this media showed the daily interactions on Earth with someone residing in Heaven (2005: chapter 3). Sun's mementos began as top-down efforts to reinforce the idea that he was the de facto leader and had actualized a nation's dream for a modern and Western Chinese republic. Eventually, however this media came to have its own agency at the grassroots level. Men bequeathed the bonds, certificates, dollars, copies of Sun's Will and other media to others, transforming Sun into Frontier Confucianism's god who could help followers now living far away from China. Sun also became the vector through which homosocial relationships, group involvements and new efficacies intersected and found meaning.

During his life Sun Yat-sen used charisma and Christian rhetoric to 'divinize himself' (Puett 2004: 19) and provide special access to his vision for a new nation. Although he was a trained medical doctor, he was neither an intellectual nor a classically trained scholar. Still, Sun drew on what he knew about traditional thought and culture (and Christianity) to write speeches conveying his belief in ideas such as the mechanics of the master-retainer relationship in Chinese history that ensured respectful and benevolent superiors the loyalty and trust of those in inferior relationships. Thus, if Sun was loyal and sincere and tried to provide the men with a new nation, they would believe in and support him. With Dr. Sun as their leader, if only briefly for a few months after his visit in 1911, overseas Chinese men continued to feel like they were part of China. As expected, most tried to generously contribute to the growing movement there while diligently and quietly working in Canada. Laundry and later restaurant work was difficult and tedious but life became better during the many events that were hosted and organized throughout the year. Following his death in 1925, Sun continued to be remembered and revered through the same picture, the invocation of his Will, and toasts given in his honour at all events.

Sun Yat-sen and the KMT fortified the Manitoba men, providing an identity that was both modern, Chinese and Confucian, and at the same time Western. But most of all the KMT facilitated the creation of hybrid Confucian relationships and bridges both vertically with others who were living the same kinds of immigrant lives and horizontally with Sun Yat-sen, and new ancestors through the annual grave custom of Decoration Day (Marshall 2009). Started by the KMT and Manitoba Chinese Benevolent Association around 1914 (and in other regions of Canada around the same time) it was a way to recognize the first laundrymen and cafe owners who died and were buried in Manitoba graves. When a settler died, the KMT elders usually arranged for a Methodist or Presbyterian minister to perform a service. Then KMT (and others within the Freemasons and Chinese Benevolent Society) in addition to Christian groups would follow the body in an all male procession that marked KMT and Chinese territory from Chinatown to the cemetery. Once the body had been lowered into the ground and Christian prayers had been said, everyone would return to Chinatown to share a meal. Each year, in late spring and around Father's Day when the snow had melted, Chinese settlers would be led back in a procession from Chinatown to the graves where Chinese men had been buried. They would tell stories about them, offer sticks of incense, and bow. Then they would all gather for a large banquet to mark the occasion. Decoration Day, through the annual performance of ritual actions, reified (and continues to reify) Chinese settlers as ancestors and bound (and continues to bind) the community through the commensality of food. The solidarity of the community needed to be continually affirmed through ritual modes of action such as the Decoration Day because even though men were connected by a common Chinese identity and reverence for Sun Yat-sen, this bond was sometimes fractured by competing clan or family allegiances. The Lee and Wong families were particularly influential in Manitoba, and for decades dominated KMT governance structures here.

Ritual actions expressed by the everyday religious behaviours of Frontier Confucianism established novel structures and frameworks that knit men into neighbourhoods, communities, villages, towns and cities. It also gave them positions and status within frontier native communities and pantheons. What resulted were mostly welcoming communities. Here, relationships created through ambiguity, and the positioning of appropriate everyday behaviours on front-stage or back-stage[5] as needed meant that if one worked hard, avoided opium dens, and did not drink or gamble, then one could dramatically elevate one's social status in a relatively short period of time and succeed in Canada.

New Forms of Hierarchy and Social Relations

The new forms of hierarchy that developed in Manitoba produced the structures for relationality and the foundations for the building of bridges and connections among Chinese and non-Chinese communities. The first Chinese groups to appear in this province were the Chinese Freemasons and the Tongmen hui (Chinese United League) who opened branches around 1910. They shared offices in the heart of Winnipeg's Chinatown (Quo 1977: chapters 2–3). Membership in both the Chinese Freemasons and Chinese United League overlapped, and the two joined together in April 1911 to invite Sun Yat-sen to Winnipeg while he was visiting Canada. It also grew dramatically once Dr. Sun's efforts to overthrow the last Chinese dynasty succeeded in late 1911 and the KMT established two Manitoba offices (one in its largest city of Winnipeg and another in Brandon) a year later. While the Freemasons and Chinese Benevolent Associations still existed in Manitoba after 1912, the KMT was the lead organization at least in this province. Over the next fourteen years, Sun's 1911 tour that brought him here, and elsewhere in Canada and the United States, had a remarkable impact on overseas Chinese communities, connecting him to local leaders and members he had met and now knew by name. Dr. Sun (or KMT bureaucrats and leaders acting as him) maintained those relationships, sending personally addressed letters and telegrams that conveyed the sentiment that Sun sympathized with the men who had mortgaged their clubhouses to donate to the revolution and later the KMT.

Sun Yat-sen was at the top of a political hierarchy, assisted by a network of local, provincial, national and international KMT leaders. All of those within the KMT governance structure and bureaucracy provided a connection to China as well as to non-Chinese communities. Because these migrants were denied full legal rights in Canada, KMT Chinese leaders were perceived to be members of the de facto government in Manitoba. These individuals were expected to take care of the social welfare of the region's new settlers. Events that were hosted in this province drew on the popularity of Dr. Sun who acted like a magnet pulling men west from Saskatchewan and east from northern Ontario towards Winnipeg's Chinatown to various celebrations throughout the year.

New rituals developed to solidify the position of Sun Yat-sen at the top of the hierarchy as the Father of China, and after 1925 the modern nation's god. These rituals distinguished Sun Yat-sen as leader and others as his followers who bowed once the toasts were given in his name, and after his death in 1925 once his Will describing the importance of the three principles had been read. His supremacy in that organization was also enforced by the consistent placement of his portrait on a table with fresh flowers at every KMT event. Provincial members who were Overseas KMT chairs and secretaries would be in charge of the reading of the Will, and the toasts. They would also sit in the centre of the group, along with national Chinese and non-Chinese leaders and dignitaries who were invited for the event. Below Sun Yat-sen, and the national and provincial leaders, but still holding an honoured place within the organization, were the loyal KMT members who donated the food for every event. This was a valuable contribution because the women who had been in charge of making the food for festivals and other events in China were scant in Manitoba. The final KMT ritual act that took place at picnics and banquets was the singing of the Nationalist anthem. While new ritual actions such as toasts, the placement of Sun's photograph and the reading of the Will assigned and maintained roles and seniority within hierarchies, the musical performance of the Nationalist anthem united and bound KMT members together.

As a result of these new ritual actions, people came to have status and positions within a hierarchy and to feel they were part of a group with shared values. Events functioned to carefully nurture a sense of belonging and to instil shared nationalistic values that became religious. They also trained the settlers to be loyal to China and the KMT. For most men who had been fortunate to bring over families or who married here community came before family. Those who were loyal members and leaders of the KMT, CBA, Chinese Freemasons and clan associations were expected to spend what little leisure time they had to help new settlers.

Building the loyalty of newcomers followed set patterns. Newcomers arrived by train and always found a KMT elder waiting to take them out for a meal. The elder then arranged for them to live in the KMT dormitory until they found places to work and live in Winnipeg or in small villages, towns or cities beyond its perimeter. Once they lived elsewhere, the KMT office remained at the core of their lives, and they returned to Chinatown for meetings, political events, banquets, and even on their days off work to play a game of fantan, paigow or majiang. If they had children here, they sent them to the office for Saturday morning Mandarin lessons. If a member had financial, immigration, legal or medical problems, KMT leaders or their lawyer on retainer could help. New settlers became bound and indebted to the KMT for this assistance and support. For those who were not loyal and were perceived to betray either China or the KMT, party membership could be revoked; immigration, visa and passport documents could become difficult to obtain; and life could become very lonely. Aside from helping members get settled and obtain immigration and other documents, local leaders assisted members as they navigated many obstacles in Western society and built intercultural bridges. KMT leaders used banquets, picnics and other events to fundraise and to bring Chinese and non-Chinese communities together and to create under-standing, especially during the period from 1937 to 1945 during the second Sino-Japanese war.

Frontier life transformed Chinese relationality in remarkable ways. Relationships between men and within governance structures were ranked, no longer voluntary, and had become the heart of Frontier Confucianism. In China, a man would have had a specific place within the social, political and economic networks defined by education and family. In Canadian post-colonial settlements beyond Chinatowns, the men were inventing their own hierarchies and social mobility was relatively easy, especially for successful business owners. If one got involved in brotherhoods such as the KMT, the Chinese Benevolent Association (CBA) or the Freemasons, or in any Christian organization (before 1921), one could easily succeed. The key to doing well was through homosocial relationships and connections. These relationships were friendships that were the least important of the traditional five relationships in their homeland.

The spheres of influence and connection in China were understood as defined by four of these five relationships that linked the family to the state. As Norman Kutcher observes, friendship, the fifth relationship, was ' ... different. [Friendship] was neither a family bond nor a state bond. ... One was obliged to serve one's family ... and obliged to serve a virtuous ruler, but there was no requirement that one make friends. Finally, friendship was the one bond that could be non-hierarchical ...' (Kutcher 2000: 1615). Family life did not exist for most early Manitoban settlers, making friendship the fundamental relationship. And because of inchoate social and political hierarchies, relationships were not voluntary, and they were not equal. Prosperity depended on the social capital that grew out of these relationships forged with mostly Chinese men who became acquaintances on the ocean liners that took them to Canadian ports, during detainment in Victoria, Canada's prison-like immigration cells, and later on the journeys they shared along the horse trail, railway and highway and also in the dormitories they shared while they looked for work. Others got to know each other at KMT offices, through roles as chairman or vice-chairmen in its overseas governance structures, at political meetings and during missionary and church activities. Men loaned each other money, opened businesses together and became fictive kin. The period between 1912 and 1949 when the KMT arose in Manitoba (and throughout Canada) contained powerful moments in Manitoba's community formation, but they could not have been possible without the bridges that had materialized among the men, missions and other Christian organizations. It was these relationships with non-Chinese ministers, missionaries and businessmen that settlers drew on to establish themselves in the emerging Chinese Canadian society.

Christian Relations on the Frontier

Although relational and doctrinal/scriptural modalities cultivated solidarity and Chinese religiosity among KMT members and the Chinese community in general, they also provided the means for bridge-building with non-Chinese communities. KMT members drew on relationships with non-Chinese ministers, Methodist and Presbyterian missionaries and businessmen to establish themselves in society. Over time, KMT, Chinese Benevolent Society and Freemason members were additionally members of Christian organizations. They had ambiguous and overlapping memberships and identities.

The earliest Winnipeg Chinese missionary work coincides with the arrival in November 1877 of Charley Yam, Fung Quong and an unnamed woman by stage coach from the United States. Baptist, Methodist and Presbyterian men and women from that time forward began to visit laundries and cafes and invite the mostly male labourers to Chinese Sunday school services and Saturday evening Bible classes. Missionaries also ran the soup kitchens in Winnipeg (Wickberg 1984: 13). The year 1894 saw Reverend Bethel Argue establish the Bethel Methodist Mission that provided legal, medical, financial as well religious, family and social counselling to non-English speaking Winnipeggers. By the early 1900s small numbers of Winnipeg Chinese were converting to Christianity, being baptized in the city and participating in Church-run English classes. Methodist and other missionary groups were at the forefront of discussions about how to deal with the burgeoning 'Asiatic' population not only in Manitoba but in other parts of Canada. A 1908 report mused: 'The Orientals are here, and a time will come when they will be here in larger numbers. How shall we deal with them? Shall we regard and treat them as barbarians, a menace to society, to be mobbed, boycotted, driven out of the country?' (United Church Archives 1908, Foreign Work)

The comments here show a remarkable degree of empathy for the newcomers and an acceptance of the idea that new immigrants, though uncivilized, are strangers who need to be understood. Over time racist statements that Chinese and other new immigrants were barbarian elements would disappear as the understanding between the deeply imbricated groups grew.

In 1911, John Maclean (1851–1928), a Methodist minister known for his work with First Nations people in Alberta, Saskatchewan and Ontario, took over the operation of the mission then located at 719 Pacific Avenue. This mission provided Sunday afternoon Chinese services and Saturday evening Bible classes with small student-to-teacher ratios, visited Chinese settlers at their place of business, and visited those who were sick. Seven years later, Bethel Mission was renamed the John Maclean Mission to reflect Maclean's leadership in that organization (*Winnipeg Evening Tribune*, 2 December 1939: 26; *Manitoba Free Press*, 7 March 1928). By 1933, the Maclean Chinese Mission had 500 Chinese men from all over the province who were active members under its care (United Church Archives 1933). Only a handful of them had actually converted, however, as a notation from an October 1907 report conveyed: 'Lenny Hap, [Chung], [Chan] and Hong Yee. They are deep sorry their sins and was repent confess Jesus Christ is their Lord and Saviours. They said we believe the gospel is perfectly [better] than Confucius work. One of them will receive the Baptism' (United Church Archives 1907–1908). Missionaries and pastors eventually accepted that Chinese were indifferent to conversion. The acceptance and support shown by missionaries towards new immigrants helped Chinese settlers adapt native customs for life in Canada and learn Western Christian ones too. Chinese and non-Chinese Christians formed strong bonds. A heart-warming example of the friendships that developed may be found in the story of an elderly Chinese man who had been living in a nursing home for years and was escorted back to China by his Christian nurse.

Beginning in 1913, Winnipeg also had its own branch of the Chinese YMCA in a home where the living and dining rooms as well as the upstairs bedrooms were rented out to Chinese bachelors for six or seven dollars a month, and there was a communal kitchen in which everyone took turns preparing meals. Men who belonged to this group had their own soccer team and played in a league against other overlapping members in the KMT and CBA (Wickberg 1984: 14–16). On one level, the games were just for fun and displayed the random individual groupings of Chinese settlers, all of whom were KMT members. But on another level, those who played on the YMCA team and lived in the Christian dwelling (not in a KMT dormitory) were the least Chinese and lowest ranked in society, as they had likely experienced more of a pull towards Christianity than the nominal Christian KMT members on the other two teams. In contrast, the KMT and the CBA were the superior and elite organizations and their players were the most powerful and successful in the community. Iconic ideas of Chinese migrant manhood developed in and through participation in sports. But it was not a manhood associated with ruggedness or a muscular physique. It was one that bolstered the values of the modern Western Confucian elite, as men learned the rules of each game, sportsmanship, team work and self-restraint on the field.

The importance of the Chinese YMCA in the community was eclipsed when in 1917 the boards of Presbyterian and Methodist missions arranged for a new missionary to work in Winnipeg. Chinese missionary Ma Seung (1870–1951) came to Winnipeg in 1917 and established the Chinese Christian Association. Residing in Winnipeg from 1917 to 1934 Ma Seung ministered to Chinese in all of Manitoba, Edmonton and Calgary, Alberta (1924-1926), the Kootenays in British Columbia (1927), and to the east side of Saskatchewan and Lake Superior in Ontario. Ma Seung made tours of rural and urban Chinese communities outside of Winnipeg, visited two Sunday afternoon Chinese church classes each week, organized gym classes and one of Canada's first Chinese boy scout troupes. As well, he organized evening Bible classes and Sunday schools, as well as banquets, picnics, teas and socials. Membership rosters for the Chinese Young Man's Christian Association and the KMT show that men from Lee, Wong, Lim and other clans were members and the local leaders of these Christian groups as well as the political organization such as the KMT. By 1921, the work had become much more difficult and Chinese nationalists were increasingly resistant to baptisms or public identification as Christians. By 1927, Ma Seung began to encounter extreme Chinese Nationalist resistance in many Canadian communities, including British Columbia, Alberta, Manitoba and Ontario. Seven years later, frustrated by his failed efforts to minister and convert, he retired to China (Marshall Forthcoming).

The everyday religious dimensions of Frontier Confucian were hybrid, Chinese and between 1911 and 1921 publicly Christian. Between 1911 to 1949 there were many public events organized and sponsored by overlapping members of Chinese and Christian groups. These included numerous annual teas, picnics, banquets and socials. There were private events that both groups worked together to host and in which both participated. These included birthday parties, marriage, funeral and graduation ceremonies, Decoration Day and grave customs. The cooperation required to organize, host and participate in the events cemented social relations and interfaith bridges for understanding. Almost all men's lives were more animated by KMT related ritual actions such as the bowing before the portrait of Sun Yat-sen, singing of the Nationalist anthem, and for educated men diligently reading Confucian and other texts. There was a decade in which Chinese nationalists and Christian missionaries worked together. But from 1921 to 1949 Confucian and nationalist identity became normative in Canadian Chinese bachelor society. Chinese men may have still associated with Christian groups but far fewer men took part in baptisms, communion, church services, prayers and the reading of Christian scripture as the dominant moments of religious life.[6]

Conclusion

Responding to the strangeness of their new lives in Manitoba, Canada, Chinese settlers relied on their native traditions and organizations to cope. To some extent being defined just as Chinese in Manitoba where the population was too small and there were very few women or children was not enough. But it was not just the local reality that created the need for Chinese to look beyond their own customs and groups for support. Chinese men also joined Western Christian groups because of the unique geopolitical situation of post-1911 life. They lived in a world where imperial China was over and a new modern China had been born. This China and Sun Yat-sen, the man credited with being its leader, yearned for Western democracy and associated values. By 1911 Sun Yat-sen and others had already started to form partnerships with Christian missionaries and Western dignitaries.

Ambiguous identities and relationships provided for the needs of Chinese men who lived between China and Canada. To non-Chinese immigrants who came to rural and urban parts of Manitoba, picnics, socials, teas and Sunday school lessons were the focal points of social and family lives. Churches provided moral guidance and religious functionaries to help families when newcomers made the transition from their homeland to Canada. Most new Chinese immigrants, however, were not Christians and never were baptized. They also came to Canada largely without families. Nominal Christian identities and group involvements sustained their public lives. These ambiguous identities helped them to become welcomed and accepted by the larger dominant Christian society. But they also needed the nationalistic, Confucian and more traditionally Chinese behaviours and identities that characterized their private ones.

Public and private lives and identities were just as intertwined as group involvements. Confucian scriptures and doctrines guided polite forms of behaviour, were used in Canadian nationalist speeches, and helped maintain relationships and social harmony. Without these traditional modes, Chinese men would not have been able to accept or become accepted by the Christian strangers who shared their communities. Moreover, because Chinese religion was ambiguous and had everyday as well as divine aspects and agents, it was easily adjusted for life in a foreign world and culture. The men could say that they were Christian and did not believe in God. They could also say they were Confucians and/or Nationalists. Relationships and ambiguity gave them agency.

Notes

The research in this chapter was funded by the Social Sciences and Humanities Research Council of Canada, Brandon University and the Rural Development Institute. I am grateful to Sarah Ramsden who worked on the project as a research assistant for two years.

1. In 1949, the KMT, then led by Chiang Kai-Shek (1887–1975), lost the civil war against the Chinese Communist Party (CCP) and fled to Taiwan where it is the ruling party today.
2. Chinese Immigration Act, 1923, S.C. 1923, c. 33, s. 5.
3. Canadian New Nationalist Press (Jianada Xinminguo Bao). 29 May 1940. KMT Archives, Taiwan.
4. The five relationships are defined in the *Doctrine of the Mean* (Zhongyong), a text ascribed to Confucius's (551–479 BCE) grandson Zisi.
5. Here I employ the terms front-stage and back-stage to refer to the public and private motivations for social behaviour in everyday life (see Goffman 1959).
6. A small fraction of early Chinese Manitobans were defined not by politics or religion but instead by theatre and involvement in the Chinese Dramatic Society. I explore this group in later works on the religious dimensions of friendship and Chinese Canadian manhood.

References

Canadian New Nationalist Press (Jianada Xinminguo Bao). 29 May 1940. KMT Archives, Taiwan.

Carnes, T., and F. Yang, eds. 2004. *Asian American Religions: The Making and Remaking of Borders and Boundaries.* New York: New York University Press.

Chau, A. Y. 2006. *Miraculous Response: Doing Popular Religion in Contemporary China.* Stanford, CA: Stanford University Press.

——. 2009. 'Modalities of Doing Religion (Zuo Zongjiao de Moshi)'. *Journal of Wenzhou University (Wenzhou Daxue Xuebao) Social Sciences (Shehui Xue)* 22, no. 5: 18–27.

Chinese Immigration Act, 1923, S.C. 1923, c. 33, s. 5.

Ching, J. 2001. 'The Ambiguous Character of Chinese Religion(s)'. *Studies in Interreligious Dialogue* 11, no. 2: 213–223.

de Certeau, M. 1984. *The Practice of Everyday Life.* Berkeley: University of California Press.

Feuchtwang, S. 1991. *Popular Religion in China: The Imperial Metaphor.* London and New York: Routledge.

Goffman, E. 1959. *The Presentation of Self in Everyday Life.* New York: Doubleday.

Kutcher, N. 2000. 'The Fifth Relationship: Dangerous Friendships in the Confucian Context'. *The American Historical Review* 105, no. 5: 1615–29.

Marshall, A. R. 2009. 'Everyday Religion and Identity in a Western Manitoban Chinese Community: Christianity, the KMT, Foodways and Related Events'. *The Journal of the American Academy of Religion* 77, no. 3: 573–608.

———. 2011. *The Way of the Bachelor: The History and Religion of Chinese Settlers in Western Manitoba.* Vancouver: University of British Columbia Press.

Marshall, A.R. Forthcoming. *Confucianism and the Making of Chinese-Canadian Identity.* Vancouver: University of British Columbia Press.

McGuire, M. B. 2008. *Lived Religion: Faith and Practice in Everyday Life.* New York: Oxford.

Nedostup, R. 2007. 'Civic Faith and Hybrid Ritual in Nationalist China'. In *Converting Cultures: Religion, Ideology, and Transformations of Modernity,* ed. D. Washburn and A.K. Reinhart, 27–56. Leiden: Brill.

Orsi, R. A. 2005. *Between Heaven and Earth: The Religious Worlds People Make and the Scholars Who Study Them.* Princeton, NJ: Princeton University Press.

Puett, M. J. 2004. *To Become a God: Cosmology, Sacrifice, and Self-Divinization in Early China.* Cambridge, MA: Harvard-Yenching Institute Monograph Series.

Quo, F. Q. 1977. 'Chinese Immigrants in the Prairies', Preliminary Report Submitted to the Minister of the Secretary of State, Simon Fraser University.

Seligman, A. B. et al. 2008. *Ritual and its Consequences: An Essay on the Limits of Sincerity.* New York: Oxford University Press.

Stafford, C. 2007. 'What Is Interesting about Chinese Religion'. In *Learning Religion: Anthropological Approaches,* ed. R. Sarro and D. Berliner, 177–90. Oxford: Berghahn Books.

Ungar, E. 2010. 'Aspects of "Frontier Confucianism": Place, Being and Text', AAR Annual Meeting, Atlanta, American Academy of Religion, 30 October – 1 November 2010.

United Church Archives-Winnipeg. 1908. Foreign Work. The Eighty-Fourth Annual Report of the Missionary Society of the Methodist Church, Toronto: Methodist Mission Rooms. 'Asiatics in Canada', 36–39.

———. 1908–1941. All People's Mission Papers, Box A, File 2; 1907–1908 Reports – Undated October Report Notes.

———. 1933. All People's Mission Papers, Box B, File 1; Calendar: The Missions.

Wickberg, E. 1984. *Edgar Wickberg Fonds.* Chinese in Canada Series. University of British Columbia Archives.

Yang. M. M. 1994. *Gifts, Favors, and Banquets: The Art of Social Relationships in China.* Ithaca, NY: Cornell University Press.

4

'Doing Things Properly'

Religious Aspects in Everyday Sociality in Apiao, Chiloé

Giovanna Bacchiddu

> Robbed of its grounding in the supernatural, religion is everyday life.
> —David Schneider, *A Critique of the Study of Kinship*

The above statement by David Schneider seems to perfectly capture the spirit of this book, and it quite appropriately sums up the approach to religion that is experienced in Apiao, the small island in southern Chile to which this chapter is devoted.

In her important review of the complex relationship between anthropological enquiry and Christianity, Fenella Cannell writes that the questions that anthropologists ought to be asking themselves are, 'what, in any situation is Christianity, and how can one possibly discern its lineaments from that of the social context in which it lives' (2006: 13).

Many scholars of communities which happen to be Christian accept that Christianity is present in their anthropological investigations as a background canvas, on which different peoples paint unique stories of lived experiences, oriented by distinctive and nuanced appropriations of the matrix of world religion. In some cases, no attempt is made to expose Christianity's form and consequences in specific communities, or, in other cases, only obviously Christian practices are considered: cults, pilgrimages and so on. If, for once, we put aside such attractive and easy-to-pin-down aspects, we have to face the task of precisely locating religion in everyday life. This could represent an interesting challenge and could force us to deal with the invisibility and visibility of religion. In this chapter I will focus on aspects of Christianity that are interspersed in Apiao social life, being in turn a reflection of an Apiao cosmology.

Apiao is a small island of the archipelago of Chiloé, where approximately 700 inhabitants live in households scattered around the landscape. Its indigenous inhabitants, descendants of the Huilliches, a southern branch of the Mapuches group, live by a subsistence economy centred on agriculture and small animal farming, combined with fishing and shell and seaweed collecting. Apiao island is tucked between other small islands and the continent, and is reachable, weather permitting, by a three- to five-hour boat trip. Local boats transport passengers and goods twice a week to the nearest commercial and administrative centre, the small town of Achao, which hosts a small hospital, a school, a bank and a post office together with the local government offices. Chiloé is predominantly Catholic; some of its characteristic wooden churches, with their tiled roofs and exterior, have been recently declared humanity cultural heritage by UNESCO, contributing to the reinforcement of an historically grounded identity of the region as inherently Catholic. Nevertheless, a very small Protestant minority represents a recent possibility of choice in religious matters, after centuries of undisputed Catholic hegemony (see Bacchiddu 2009).

The average Apiao inhabitant would enthusiastically declare to be, and to have always been, a good Catholic. Apiao's encounter with Christianity began with the arrival of the Franciscan and Jesuit religious staff following the Spanish colonization in the sixteenth and seventeenth centuries. Chiloé inhabitants have historically been consistently portrayed as humble, compliant and submissive, making the task of the Spanish colonial missionaries an easy and rewarding one (Urbina 1983). Sources report that they embraced Catholicism and co-operated with the routine established by the priests, who organized a system of seasonal visits to the islands, called 'circular missions'. Given the extension of the territory, its geographical remoteness and the bad weather that plagues the region for most of the year, they involved and trained local individuals, naming them official representatives of the Holy Church, founding the institution of the *fiscales*. The missionaries visited the islands only once or twice a year, leaving most responsibilities to the *fiscales*.

Three centuries later, little has changed in insular Chile. Apiao, like other remote islands, receives the visit of religious staff once or twice per year. These religious officials come from Chiloé towns, continental Chile, or abroad; they call themselves missionaries and are animated by proselytising zeal. The *fiscales,* who voluntarily choose to perform this role within their community and are not remunerated, try to mediate between the Church they represent and the social group they belong to.

The attitude of Apiao people towards their geographical remoteness takes two different expressions. On the one hand, they have a well-developed internal system of strong alliances that provide for most needs; and not all, but much of what is needed is produced locally. And yet the increasing presence of modernity in urban centres such as Achao, their main reference town, causes growing and widespread complaint about the lack of electricity that prevents them from benefiting from electrical appliances, making them feel neglected by the Chilean state. While Apiao people feel they have grounds for complaining, they also recognize that the flip side of their isolation is the possibility of enjoying a relative independence and a certain autonomy in both the organization of their work and the expression of their religious credo. This invariably means that the islanders are often ill-at-ease with visiting outsiders who, unacquainted with the local customs, might misunderstand or not appreciate local practices.

This chapter has two objectives: the first one seeks to illustrate what it means to be religious in Apiao by focusing on the various ways in which the domain of religion permeates everyday life on the island. The second theme of my contribution will situate Apiao ways of 'doing religion' vis-à-vis the normative doctrine of the local Catholic Church. This will be done specifically by looking at the events surrounding the visit of a lay missionary from Santiago. What such an episode highlights is the contrast between the orthodoxy, represented by the Church official, and the local ways to practice and experience Christianity. The missionary epitomizes the Catholic orthodoxy, the official Chilean Church with its institutions, teachings, officials, and its capacity to impose its point of view as the true one. As such, the articulation between what I here call 'orthodoxy' and local religious expressions, judged as imperfect by religious officials in charge, is a relation of power.

What Does It Mean to Be Religious in Apiao?

Religion is pervasive and all-encompassing for Apiao inhabitants, and to think of religion as a separate sphere or a discrete domain would not only be erroneous but also quite difficult. Focusing exclusively on 'religion' is in fact applying a label that, as Stewart and Shaw point out, corresponds to a culturally constructed Western category that may not be significant in other cultural contexts (1994: 10). This general point has been made by several authors (including Stewart and Shaw 1994; Wagner 1974; and Jackson 1996), and Gow, talking of Amazonia, refined it further by stating that 'to abstract the social logics of indigenous Amazonian societies from their cosmologies does not make much sense' (2006: 212). Reconciling the cosmological beliefs and the social views of a people is crucial when attempting to approach and explore their worldview. Keeping this in mind, it becomes easier to see how the social and the cosmological are reflections of one another.

Since the category 'religion' is not entirely adequate to describe the complex interaction of cosmological beliefs, social imperatives and attitudes towards the supernatural, miraculous entities that constitute the Apiao world, perhaps the easiest way to tackle this issue is to ask what it means to be a 'proper' person in Apiao. I will argue that the two concepts – being a proper person, and being a good Catholic – correspond.[1]

It would be problematic to expect Apiao inhabitants to talk about their religious beliefs, to explain them or to discuss their faith. People are not necessarily articulate when discussions on topics such as world-views are prompted. This proves once more the point made by Stewart and Shaw (1994: 10), when they underline the fluidity and contingency of boundaries when dealing with 'religion'. Religion in Apiao just surfaces in everyday activities and practices. Paraphrasing Joanna Overing, we can say, '[B]link, and you miss a religious expression in Apiao'. In Apiao, like among the Piaroa, 'most ritual activities are carried out casually as part of everyday activity. The most normal looking procedures in daily life could deeply signify' (2003: 301).

To better explain what it means to be religious for an Apiao individual, I will illustrate this concept with some ethnographic descriptions, inserting them in a general context of the way life is experienced. I will do this through considering everyday life, where sociality is expressed in daily interaction and constant exchange.

Following de Certeau's call to study the practice of everyday life (1984), several anthropologists have recently turned their attention to the basics of everyday life, realising that daily routines hide a wealth of aspects that are crucial to understanding the values held by a group of people (see, e.g. Overing 2003, and the various contributions in Overing and Passes 2000). Looking at everyday life in Apiao, and at its values, one immediately notices the strong focus on the individual's autonomy. Every child grows up aspiring to become like the adults that surround him or her: people who are able to take care of themselves, their household and family fields, as well as any task related to everyday life. A proper adult is one who is able to cook, chop wood, carry heavy loads, plough the fields, fish and collect seashells, irrespective of gender. Children impatiently wait for the time their parents will trust them enough to give them tasks to perform, because that is their chance to prove their capacity for responsibility and their skills.

A proper adult is one who knows the crucial importance of 'how to do things properly' whenever dealing not only with his or her own family, but also with people who do not belong to their household. The expression, 'hacer las cosas como corresponde', is often heard in connection with events involving two or more households, where several people are involved, and people can prove their social and moral skills in front of the community. On such occasions, adults are expected to act according to an unwritten code of conduct that revolves around the imperative of reciprocity and is regularly expressed in the fundamental social rule of hospitality.

Once individuals are able to take care of their own belongings, the immediate concern is that of earning respect in the community. A 'proper' person welcomes guests when they visit, pays them the respect of offering food and drink in the appropriate manner, attending them in all their needs or requests. Similarly, an adult that knows how to behave appropriately knows what to do whenever visiting a fellow islander, introducing himself and thanking people with the proper formulas, accepting food and drink offers without checking the quantity or the quality of it,[2] uttering requests in a polite manner, and always returning whatever favour, words, or items were once offered and given. These practical acts are never divorced from a wider cosmological landscape: they embody and enact the values that regulate not only relations between humans, but also relations between humans and supernatural entities.

Religion as a Matter of Daily Existence

In his eulogy of phenomenology Michael Jackson wrote that 'use, not logic, conditions belief' (1996: 12). The principles that inform the practical world are continuously tested and confirmed as valid. Then they are transposed into a wider level, with a cosmic resonance.

Although Apiao people insist they are Catholics, and good ones, expecting the standard form and practice of Catholicism in Apiao would end in disappointment. They experience their religious affiliation as a set of beliefs and practices that are inextricably tied to their unique moral universe. The values that have no particular relevance in the local context are left out, irrespective of their position in the conventional Christian doctrine. For example, there is no concern about attending mass or taking the communion. There is no emphasis on the cult of the Virgin Mary, or the significance associated with her in the mainstream Catholic Church. There is no discourse, or opinion, of heaven, hell, or salvation. There is no interest in dogma, and people ascribe no particular importance to most religious rites of passage, such as first communion, confirmation, marriage vows, or god-parenthood. All these are statuses officialized by the Church with a religious ceremony, generally celebrated by the bishop, but are de facto an opportunity to form or strengthen alliances with fellow islanders; this is their main significance for Apiao people. The only two partial exceptions to this seem to be baptism and funeral rites. Unlike the rituals just mentioned, however, both these rites are celebrated on the island by the *fiscales*, allowing the community a certain independence from the official Church. Baptism is considered extremely important, and it is believed to confer social status to a person.[3] If a young child dies without being baptized, this is regarded as a serious fault, and a dangerous predicament. In such cases, the *fiscal* performs a quick ceremony of posthumous baptism before proceeding with the mortuary rituals.

Funerals are long and complex rituals, only parts of which are celebrated in church and the cemetery. Most of the mortuary rituals take place in the household of the deceased. Despite the fact that these rituals revolve around Catholic religious rites, their raison d'être is twofold: on the one hand they respond to a need to respect and honour the dead, granting them the appropriate religious procedure; on the other hand the family of the deceased has the moral and social duty to host and attend the community, gathered around the bereaved during the nine-day long celebrations. These rituals concern the living as much as, or possibly more than, the dead, and they are firmly grounded in the social imperative of reciprocity, of paying back one's debts.

The *Fiscales* Pray All by Themselves in the Church

One Sunday afternoon, soon after my arrival on the island, I noticed that the door of the imposing wooden church was open, and I went inside. The church was usually kept closed, to be opened only for special events. That time, two men were standing on the altar, singing and praying, doing some readings from the liturgy, and reciting some litanies towards an imaginary audience since they were the only people in the building, besides me. One of them even preached a sermon, starting with the words '*Queridos hermanos*' (Dear brethren), which at the time I found quite amusing. That was my first encounter with the *fiscales*, the voluntary and unpaid position that requires time, patience and good will. When I asked them the reason for the total absence of churchgoers, they said that people hardly go to church at all in wintertime. 'Perhaps in summer someone stops by, on Sundays. But whenever there is a pilgrimage in the nearby island of Caguach things are different: that is an ancient tradition!'

This apparently trivial episode serves as a good introduction to the way Apiao people experience their devotion to Catholicism.

Why would people disregard the local religious celebration, leaving the *fiscales* to pray and preach all by themselves, and instead flock in hundreds to take part in a pilgrimage to a nearby island? Together with the Caguach pilgrimage that takes place twice a year, Apiao people are particularly devoted to the image of a miraculous saint, San Antonio, that resides in Caguach but is regularly brought to Apiao to celebrate novenas (nine-day ritual prayer meetings) in fulfilment of a promise. These celebrations, always performed in private households, attract large numbers of participants, in spite of the often dire weather conditions.

The reason for the discrepancy between church attendance and participation in celebrations honouring a saint lies with the rule of reciprocity that characterizes the Apiao way of experiencing the world in all its aspects. While people have a strong sense of respect towards God as a powerful, transcendental entity, they place little value in attending church because they have not committed, as individuals, to fulfil a promise or attend to a pact. In this sense, their presence is not 'due'.

Strongly egalitarian, they view the world as a constellation of social relations to actively entertain. These relationships are always experienced as strongly reciprocal, even when the other party is God or a miraculous saint. Whether the other is a powerful supernatural entity, a neighbour, or a family member, people give – always expecting in return the same amount that was originally offered, or something equivalent. They also know that when they make a promise, that act is a commitment that must be honoured. In this sense, religious observance is strongly entwined with other social practices and replicates them, while shifting the interlocutor. The powerful other is addressed, engaged in a dialogue, asked for something and offered something in return (see Bacchiddu 2011). In other words, God and the saints are 'socialized', brought into an active social relation and experienced as interlocutors.

To borrow an expression from Meyer (1994), Apiao people 'vernacularized' Catholicism, making it their own according to the values that inform their everyday life. These values are part of the practical reality of life as experienced in Apiao: reciprocal exchange, attending to commitments, paying back what is due. The social imperatives that regulate social life are transposed onto a supernatural plan involving meaningful relationships with God and the saints – what social scientists would identify as the religious realm.

Tracing the Boundaries

While some specific feasts and celebrations are the obvious loci for what anyone would define and recognize as religious expressions (going to church, attending mass, going on a pilgrimage), most activities that comprise the everyday in Apiao are religious in nature. And despite their mundane appearance, most actions that tie community members to one another in a web of alliances have a strong resonance in a context that is profoundly religious.

The co-existence of religion as an everyday practice and a normative doctrine apparently does not seem to concern Apiao people themselves, who simply experience life the way they deem appropriate, following the imperatives of their moral world. When on their own island, they do not feel under the scrutiny of official Church powers, nor do they feel any obligation to perform in specific ways according to Catholic orthodoxy. Apiao religious attitudes and affiliation, however, do come into question whenever the locals are confronted with outsiders, who are generally not familiar with the local ways and have different ideas on how life and religion should be experienced.

One manifest example of such a confrontation on the island is the presence of two evangelical missionaries who reside there and regularly attempt to convert the Catholic majority to evangelical Protestantism. In such situations, Apiao people make a point of reiterating their self-perception that they are proper Catholics, because 'one is born into Catholicism and that is a status that cannot change': any post-baptism conversion would be fake and pointless. A discourse of descent and inheritance, never voiced for issues of kinship, is brought forth whenever the enthusiastic approach of the evangelical missionaries forces the locals to define who they are in religious terms (Bacchiddu 2009). In the confrontation with the evangelicals, two different religious affiliations, two religious traditions and two entirely different sets of values clash with one another. In such circumstances, Apiao people manage to reject the values introduced by the evangelicals on the basis that they are alien to them and do not correspond to their idea of 'doing things properly'. In doing so, they adamantly proclaim to be Catholics, and good ones at that.

Are Apiao People Good Catholics?

Resistance to the novel religious horizons made visible by the evangelicals reinforced the islanders' sense of community and confirmed the importance of their traditional social and religious values which, I argue, overlap. After all, they perceive their Catholic roots as coinciding with their history: that, by itself, is the strongest statement of affiliation to a religious faith. Evangelical Protestantism was introduced in Apiao only recently (approximately in the mid 1990s), and, although it appeared attractive at first, it was relatively easy to trace the boundaries between themselves and 'the others'. Defining themselves, and defending their values vis-à-vis the Protestants was, overall, a relatively easy task.

It might prove less simple when attacks on long-held values come from the same Catholic Church to which Apiao people adamantly proclaim they belong. As previously stated, Apiao geographical remoteness and relative isolation has favoured the development of a unique form of local Catholicism, mostly practiced without the intervention or mediation of the official Church. A priest visits the island only once a year, and so does the bishop. Occasionally the bishopric demands that specialized staff be sent to remote areas largely neglected by the Church. In summer, small groups of voluntary Church staff (laypersons) travel to the island, visiting each household during a one-week stay. During my fieldwork, one missionary from Santiago was sent to organize and lead celebrations on the occasion of Holy Week, as Easter Sunday approached. During such encounters inevitably the Apiao religious autarchic approach meets ecclesiastical notions of orthodoxy, thus causing an assessment and a questioning from the established Catholic Church counterpart.

What is the appropriate way to be religious? Are there good and bad ways to be Catholic? And who decides what is good and what is bad? If, on the one hand, the religious officials are believed and even expected to know what is appropriate by virtue of their access to privileges denied to marginal peasants, on the other hand they might have their own fixed expectations of the way the islanders should practice their faith. Such encounters might reveal precisely the complex interaction between attempts to articulate an orthodox doctrine that is expected to become the guideline for Christian lives, and the ways in which Christians actually experience their religion as part of their lives – a core object of investigation in this volume. While religious officials insist on their understanding of proper practice in religious contexts, Apiao people dissent from such a rigorous view, in that their approach to religion is not necessarily tied to the Church's strict interpretation of religious practice. It does, however, adhere to a local code of moral conduct that, as we have seen, is summarized in the often-heard expression *hacer las cosas como corresponde:* 'to do things properly'.

The Catholic Missionary

On the occasion of Easter 2002, a Catholic missionary, a man, came from Santiago to stay for Holy Week. Apiao people are accustomed to the presence of missionaries, whom they host regularly. A few months before, the island had received the visit of a small group of Catholic missionaries from Santiago. They had stayed on the island for a week, visited each household and brought Holy Communion to elderly people. Their presence was appreciated by the locals, who remarked that they were *buena gente,* good people. To be *buena gente* does not require much effort: by being kind, open, positive and not judgmental of the peasant community, such city people earned Apiao's acceptance during their short stay.

Unlike them, the missionary man adopted a different attitude. Meeting the *fiscal* on his arrival, he immediately enquired about the 'organized activities' that were to take place in the local church for Easter Week; the man shyly replied that nobody had organized anything so far. It was autumn: the season for harvesting and threshing wheat, and for making apple cider, *chicha.* Every household is bursting with activity in autumn, and the *fiscal,* as much as any other Apiao inhabitant, had a busy schedule at home.

Only a small number of people went to church on the Wednesday or Thursday; however, on Good Friday the church was crowded. Good Friday is a crucial date in the calendar, and people respect several obligations and prohibitions traditionally associated with this holy day. They would not work, yoke their animals, or start to weave a blanket; they would chop wood but sign themselves first, asking for forgiveness. In the past people would not cook or comb their hair. No one would miss a visit to the church on Good Friday, unless extremely ill or too old.[4]

The church was crowded with people of all ages and both sexes, yet the missionary was clearly upset. He preached his sermon aggressively, complaining about the lack of church attendance in the previous days, and for the local ingratitude. He accused them of keeping a filthy church, arguing that the lack of cleanliness obviously reflected the hygiene of each household. 'Well', he added, 'it must be admitted that you are left alone a lot, because of the lack of ministers in your dioceses. However, I don't see any willingness to get better and that is very sad.' He patronisingly remarked that he knew the area well and was familiar with island inhabitants, to demonstrate that the locals could not fool him, and he warned that he would report the situation to the Chiloé bishop, who had sent him personally to the island. He then announced that he was going to proceed with the celebration and urged everybody to listen carefully to try to understand what was being said, and not to make any noise.

The missionary gravely insulted and seriously offended Apiao people in at least two ways: first, by using an aggressive and authoritarian tone that implied he was of a superior standing, and that they were inferior. Second, he attacked them with a list of serious abuses, stating that they lacked the hygiene standards of proper people, and implied that they were incapable of understanding and attending to religious matters. Furthermore, the threat to report their perceived transgressions to the bishop, the highest local religious authority, particularly hurt the islanders, who felt they had managed to earn the prelate's respect and esteem. Finally, they were insulted by one of the worst accusations that can ever be uttered on the island: to be inhospitable and ungrateful. The missionary's words were strong and demeaning, and they had been proffered in an aggressive and condescending tone. The contained reaction of those present in the church was impressive: beside a few women whispering to each other, there was a respectful silence.[5]

After his angry outburst, the missionary continued the Good Friday celebration, urging some people to hold candles, firmly instructing them to stand in front of the altar. In Apiao there is a strong etiquette concerning manners, and ways of addressing people. This is always expressed in fixed ritual formulas that have the purpose of gracing one's interlocutor and predisposing the communication to a favourable outcome. The sense of respect contained in these stylistic communication devices is profound and strongly guarded. In such a context, the imperative tone of the missionary and his accusatory manner were a striking example of a violent breach of the local etiquette, and a humiliating power play enactment.

The unanimous complaint that followed the episode – besides obvious remarks on the man's rudeness and inappropriate commentary – was that someone from 'outside' (*de afuera*) should not come to Apiao to order people around. According to a group of people with whom I conversed about the events:

They come here, think they understand everything and speak loud. This is not the city: we have our custom here, and that is not to be changed. They come here once per year and cannot just change the way things are. They must keep in mind that they are visitors, they are guests. They are meant to be much better than any one of us, but they are much worse than us. They are nothing. They cannot tell us what to do here, in our own land. We were given our religion from our ancestors, and we don't need someone that comes here once a year to change our ways.

The words of my Apiao friends highlight their strong sense of identity as people that know the proper way to practice their religious beliefs, given to them by their ancestors. The missionary was expected to be an especially virtuous and pious man, but he had fallen short of expectations, showing himself to be useless, and, in fact, a nuisance. Awareness of being good religious people, despite the missionary's opinion, is strong in Apiao discourse; local values are deemed valid and reaffirmed. The silent reaction to the man's accusation in the church was not coming from a humiliated crowd: it was rather a polite expression of disagreement, and a statement of assertion of their identity.

Predictably, hardly anyone attended the Holy Saturday celebration. I was on the church esplanade with some other young people when the missionary appeared and brusquely urged us to quickly get into the building because we were late for the celebration. The missionary's comment on 'being late' was perhaps appropriate to the Santiago parish scene, but nonsensical in a place where people have no fixed timetable, no watch on which to keep an eye, and have free choice as to what they do at any given time of the day. The freedom enjoyed in Apiao was suddenly obvious, that evening, where the relaxed pose of the locals, lying on their sides on the green grass, contrasted strongly with the tense expression of the missionary, standing nervously above them, preoccupied with strictly and successfully adhering to his carefully arranged schedule. The man's imperious attitude was striking, and he tended to use the imperative whenever addressing someone, something which in Apiao hardly ever happens, and is indeed considered to be extremely rude.

Apiao people, when in charge of something, would do all they possibly could to downplay their temporary difference in status, blending their requests with an assortment of apologies, pleas and humble wishes to those present, always keeping a modest demeanour. Asking for something implies an elaborate ritual that follows a specific code of decorum (see Bacchiddu 2010). That code was painfully ignored by the missionary, who in a short space of time had managed to break the boundaries to which the community carefully adheres in everyday life.

Once in church, we had to endure the Holy Saturday celebration, staged by the missionary as a replica of a city parish service. The few individuals who attended were ordered to follow instructions: light a candle at a specific moment, walk outside to light a symbolic fire, sing a song, walk back into church, exchange candles with their neighbour as a token of friendship, and finally hold the neighbour's hand while reciting the Holy Father. Tailored for the city's pilgrims, the whole ceremony was totally out of context in Apiao. When urged to hold the neighbour's hand, people gave each other the right hand, as when shaking one's hand, rather than holding hands to form a circle. Why would people hold hands, if not for briefly shaking someone's right hand to politely greet them, Apiao people wondered?

The following day, Easter Sunday, the church was crowded, although many, feeling resentful, had refused to take part. It was yet another celebration with rituals that made little sense to the locals. When the missionary authoritatively proclaimed the instruction for people to hug their neighbours, loud laughter came from a group of youths assembled next to the entrance of the church. Later on, when a whistle announced the start of the football match in the church esplanade, the whole group left hurriedly.

The missionary's presence was still the subject of irate conversations months later. The common complaint was that a host should never speak the way the missionary had, and no one must be allowed to act as owner (*hacerse dueño*), especially the visitors to the island.

Conclusion: Religious Imperfection: An Ethnic Problem?

The presence of the town missionary and the issues provoked by his expectations and attitude are far from unusual, nor specific to Apiao. The very notion of orthodoxy clashing with vernacular ways of being Christian is an historical phenomenon well recognized and recorded for the last several centuries, from the Spanish conquest onward (see, e.g. Harris 2006). Invariably, those who practice religion in a way that is judged imperfect are peasants of indigenous origin who live in distant communities in marginal territories. And those who approach them by imposing their view of the correct way religion should be practised are white, middle-class, educated townspeople. The fact that the Church feels the need to send missionaries in the present day reveals the widespread opinion that there are still portions of the population that need to be attended and saved from ignorance and pagan residue. Although the Santiago missionary did not directly address his audience in ethnic terms, the presence of a strong divide between 'civilized people' and 'uncivilized people' loomed large in his Easter Week discourses.

The issue of indigeneity in Chile is burdened with extremely negative stereotyping and stigmatization. Apiao has the highest concentration of indigenous surnames in the Chiloé archipelago area, together with one or two other islands. Although the overwhelming presence of Spanish surnames in the area certainly does not indicate the lack of indigenous people, the strong concentration of Huilliche surnames marks Apiao as a particularly disadvantaged territory, a favourite destination for whoever is looking to undertake a civilising mission. The island is generally regarded by the local authorities (governmental officials, medical staff and teaching staff in addition to Church staff) as intensely underdeveloped, backward and in serious need of civilising interventions. Interestingly, this sums up the description of the entire Chiloé area as a land of 'lack', in the comprehensive human geography study by Grenier (1984). Chiloé, Grenier argues, is affected by poverty, unemployment, lack of professionals and technicians, lack of capital, unequal distribution of land, cultural backwardness (*retard culturel*) and systematic migration (Grenier 1984: 16). Grenier blames the lack of economic development, communication, progression and access to modern technology on the handicaps of insularity, marginality and dispersions of inhabitants. This description can make us appreciate even more the weight of the missionary's attitude, and its significance in the reproduction of a hegemonic hierarchy.

The political weight of the population of remote Chiloé islands, and their visibility, is modest; therefore all these issues are somehow beneath the surface, kept out of sight. This is because Chiloé people, unlike their northern neighbours the Mapuches, have never been threatened to be deprived of their ancestral land, or confined to reservations with restricted access to land and its resources. Similarly, their ways of life and activities have never been exposed to risks from the Chilean nation-state. Apiao people are aware that their peculiar geographic position limits their access to technology, and they certainly wish the local government would put more effort into bridging the distance they feel with the more privileged townspeople. They also acknowledge, by contrast, that their relative isolation protects them, granting them the freedom to organize their own work schedule, their religious practice, and independence from outsiders' impositions.

In this chapter I have attempted to illustrate the irreducibility of practices of everyday life to a category such as 'religion': the way people understand and experience life in society transcends and encompasses fixed classifications, making us aware of the fluidity of the boundaries of analytical categories such as 'religion'. The gap perceived by the missionary between the nominal affiliation to religion and the effective behaviour of Apiao people showed him a flawed religiosity, to be corrected and refined with the help of external sources. Conversely, the Church official betrayed the expectations of the locals, in that he appeared not as an inspired spiritual individual but as a judgemental and partial outsider, materialising the deeply-held local concerns of having to be confronted by a guest and being judged for not offering adequate hospitality.

As Cannell (2006: 5) pointed out, there is not 'one' Christianity, and as Stewart and Shaw (1994: 16) remind us, religions are not given entities. Most of the authors I have referred to in this chapter, notably Cannell,

Harris, Stewart and Shaw, see religion as a contested domain, and they highlight the constant presence of ambiguity in boundaries, definitions, inclusion and exclusion from orthodoxy. De Certeau (1984) raises this very concept in his consideration of cultural practices of everyday life. He underlines how beneath the Spanish colonisers' apparent 'success' over the Indian populations of South America lay the crucial ambiguity of the specific use that the Indians made of the Spanish cultural impositions. Apparently submissive and consenting, native Indians were in fact able to subvert the dominant power by making a 'different' use of the imposed social order, thereby deflecting its power. 'The strength of their difference', argues de Certeau, 'lay in procedures of "consumption". To a lesser degree, a similar ambiguity creeps into our societies through the use made by the "common people" of the culture disseminated and imposed by the elites' (1984: 3). What scholars must concentrate on, then, is the particular meaning that lies beneath the unique use that people make of cultural impositions – even if these have been acquired centuries ago. He urges us to pay attention to the 'innumerable and infinitesimal transformations of and within the dominant cultural economy' that users make, 'in order to adapt it to their own interests and their own rules' (1984: 3). Human creativity overcomes and deflects impositions by appropriating and re-appropriating any material, and returning it with unmistakably local markers.

This is what Apiao people do when they 'vernacularize' Christianity, creating a unique version of it through their continuous use of it. The notion and continued experience of reciprocal exchange is cosmologically central to the Apiao lived world. Consequently, the unique Apiao approach to religion is fundamentally and intrinsically relational: Christianity on the island mingles with social obligations, and it effectively coincides with them. The specific focus on certain aspects of Christianity (such as, for example, attending to social and religious obligations according to the value of reciprocity), and the total neglect of others (such as going to church regularly or following strictly the official Church doctrine), allows the islanders to reaffirm those values that resonate as significant and coincide with their understanding of the universe and of the self.

Notes

This chapter is based on ethnographic fieldwork conducted in Apiao in 2000–2002, 2003 and 2007–2008. The research was partially sponsored by a grant from the Regione Autonoma della Sardegna (Assegni di Studio Post-Laureaml), which is gratefully acknowledged. Thanks are also due to the editors for their invitation to be part of this volume, and for their helpful comments on earlier drafts of the chapter, as well as to Peter Gow, Joseph Tendler and the late Steven Rubenstein, for their kind and timely help. Steve promptly provided insightful observations with his characteristic generosity and enthusiasm, and I will always treasure his suggestions and attitude. All mistakes remain my responsibility. All translations from Spanish into English are my own.

1. This is true for the majority of Apiao inhabitants. The Evangelical minority until 2007 corresponded to approximately five per cent of the population, and the converts are seen as voluntarily withdrawing from the social group and forging new rules for themselves (see Bacchiddu 2009).
2. This misbehaviour, locally identified as *reparar*, is much deplored (see Bacchiddu 2007).
3. This is in line with other Amerindian Christianities: see, for example, baptism rituals in the Andes as noted in Canessa 1999 and Harris 2006: 55.
4. The scarce attendance at the church during the year coupled with the attention devoted to special days such as Good Friday, Christmas or the patron saint's *fiesta* seems to be historically recorded throughout Chiloé (Urbina 1983).
5. Compare Overing's description of Piaroa silent anger (1989: 178).

References

Bacchiddu, G. 2007. 'Gente de Isla - Island People. An Ethnography of Apiao, Chiloé, SouthernChile'. PhD dissertation. University of St Andrews.

———. 2009. 'Before We Were All Catholics': Changing Religion in Apiao, Southern Chile'. In *Native Christians: Modes and Effects of Christianity among Indigenous Peoples of the Americas*, ed. R. Wright and A. Vilaça, 53–70. Farnham, UK, and Burlington, VT: Ashgate.

———. 2010. 'Getting Tamed to Silent Rules: Experiencing 'the Other' in Apiao, Southern Chile'. In *Mutuality and Empathy: Self and Other in the Ethnographic Encounter*, ed. A. S. Grønseth and D. L. Davis, 21–34. Wantage: Sean Kingston Publishing.

———. 2011. 'Holding the Saint in One's Arms. Miracles and Exchange in Apiao, Southern Chile'. In *Encounters of Body and Soul in Contemporary Religious Practices. Anthropological Reflections*, ed. A. Fedele and R. Blanes, 23–42. New York and Oxford: Berghahn.

Canessa, A. 1999. 'Making Persons, Marking Difference: Procreation Beliefs in Highland Bolivia'. In *Conceiving Persons: Ethnographies of Procreation, Substance and Personhood*, ed. P. Loizos and P. Heady, 69–87. London: Athlone Press.

Cannell, F. 2006. 'Introduction: The Anthropology of Christianity'. In *The Anthropology of Christianity*, ed. F. Cannell, 1–50. London: Duke University Press.

de Certeau, M. 1984. *The Practice of Everyday Life*. Berkeley: University of California Press.

Gow, P. 2006. 'Forgetting Conversion: The Summer Institute of Linguistics Mission in the Piro Lived World'. In *The Anthropology of Christianity*, ed. F. Cannell, 211–39. London: Duke University Press.

Grenier, P. 1984. *Chiloé et les Chilotes: Marginalité et Dépendance en Patagonie Chilienne: Étude de Géographie Humaine*. Aix-en-Provence: EDISUD.

Harris, O. 2006. 'The Eternal Return of Conversion. Christianity as Contested Domain in Highland Bolivia'. In *The Anthropology of Christianity,* ed. F. Cannell, 51–76. London: Duke University Press.

Jackson, M. 1996. 'Introduction. Phenomenology, Radical Empiricism, and Anthropological Critique'. In *Things as They Are: New Directions in Phenomenological Anthropology,* ed. M. Jackson, 1–50. Bloomington and Indianapolis: Indiana University Press.

Meyer, B. 1994. 'Beyond Syncretism. Translation and Diabolization in the Appropriation of Protestantism in Africa'. In *Syncretism/Anti-Syncretism: The Politics of Religious Synthesis,* ed. C. Stewart and R. Shaw, 45–68. London and New York: Routledge.

Overing, J. 1989. 'The Aesthetics of Production: The Sense of Community among the Cubeo and Piaroa'. *Dialectical Anthropology,* no. 14: 159–75.

———. 2003. Introduction to *Reason and Morality,* ed. J. Overing, 1–28. London and New York: Tavistock Publications.

Overing, J., and A. Passes, eds. 2000. *The Anthropology of Love and Anger: The Aesthetics of Conviviality in Native Amazonia.* London: Routledge.

Schneider, D. M. 1984. *A Critique of the Study of Kinship.* Ann Arbor: University of Michigan Press.

Stewart, C., and R. Shaw, eds. 1994. *Syncretism/Anti-Syncretism: The Politics of Religious Synthesis.* London and New York: Routledge.

Urbina Burgos, R. 1983. *La Periferia Meridional Indiana: Chiloé en el Siglo XVIII.* Valparaiso: Ediciones Universitarias de Valparaiso.

Wagner, R. 1974. 'Are There Social Groups in the New Guinea Highlands?' In *Frontiers of Anthropology: An Introduction to Anthropological Thinking,* ed. M. J. Leaf and B. G. Campbell, 95–120. New York: Van Nostrand.

5

The Ordinary within the Extraordinary

Sainthood-Making and Everyday Religious Practice in Lesvos, Greece

Séverine Rey

The process of sainthood-making is usually analysed in connection with the notion of popular religion. However, different kinds of hierarchies hide behind this notion, as emphasized by Liza Debevec and Samuli Schielke in the introduction: not only the pure doctrine of the specialists as opposed to the syncretistic practices of the ordinary people, but also class relations, political power and, as I wish to add, gender hierarchies. My purpose in the present chapter is to analyse the social dynamics at work in one case of sainthood-making: far from being a pure expression of mass veneration, the phenomenon is characterized by an intertwining of spheres and competing discourses. My case study, in the field of Orthodox Christianity, is the (so-called) apparition of three saints in Lesvos, Greece at the beginning of the 1960s.[1] The process was launched by the dreams and mysterious phenomena recounted by villagers, mostly women and/or refugees from western Anatolia that had settled on the island during the Greco-Turkish war of 1919–1922 (and the population exchange that followed). Sceptical, the local church rejected these forms of piety at first, seeing them either as signs of (female/popular) credulity or of diabolical temptation. Later, Church authorities nevertheless launched an investigation and began the process of official recognition of the new saints.

Examining this phenomenon gives me the opportunity to consider the various interests of the actors involved in the making of sainthood and what was at stake for them, as well as the part played by the 'popular sphere' and gender in religion. I will analyse how the extraordinary (new saints) meets the ordinary (everyday religious practices) and will introduce the various competing discourses about sainthood and the conceptions and practices behind each of them. The faithful considered these saints concrete models to follow and identify with. They established complex and personal relationships with them, gathering new means for their everyday religious practices in the process. For its part, the Church tried to control the phenomenon, at first by rejecting it (as questionable 'women's tales') and then by recognising its authenticity as a narrative expressed by humble men and women, poorly educated but more receptive to the divine messages. Thus the ecclesiastics insisted on the exceptional and commemorative patterns of the saints. Ultimately, this article will interrogate the (alleged) opposition between religious doctrine and everyday practice, and between popular and official religion, from a gender perspective.

History of the Agios Rafaíl Monastery and Its Edification

The Agios Rafaíl monastery (*ágios* means 'saint' in Greek) was built in the 1960s. It is located on the island of Lesvos, in the Aegean Sea, northeast of mainland Greece. The Turkish coast is only a few nautical miles away. It lies in the heights of the village of Thermi, about 15 kilometres away from Mytilene, the island's town. Over the span of a few decades, the monastery became a well-known Christian Orthodox shrine for Greeks and Cypriots as well as for Greeks from abroad. This centre attracts many devotees and pilgrims (and also tourists), especially over the summer. The monastery commemorates three recently 'appeared' saints: Agios Rafaíl, Agios Nikólaos and Agia Iríni. At first, they were venerated through popular practices in the early 1960s; later, the local church, followed by the national church, began to support the new figures, and the Ecumenical Patriarchate of Constantinople officially recognized the saints in 1970. Since their 'apparition', they are believed to have performed various miracles, such as curing disease and infertility.

The story of the saints' 'apparition'[2] deserves brief mention. In the late 1950s, a family living in the village of Thermi decided to build a small chapel in one of its fields of olive trees. In doing this, Vasiliki and her husband Angelos[3] intended to fulfil a vow taken by her mother, who was a native of Asia Minor (western Anatolia, near Lesvos) and, like many others, was forced to flee the country in 1922 during the conflict between Greece and Turkey. She found refuge in Lesvos and made a promise to the Panagía (the All-saint, the Madonna) to build her a chapel if she were able to stay and live in Lesvos with Vasiliki – her newborn baby. She made this promise at the exact place where the chapel was built thirty years later because the Panagía was already informally worshiped at that spot by the locals. The spot was known as a kind of abandoned church, lacking any tangible marker other than a piece of marble at the foot of a large tree. Traditionally, without remembering the reason, people had always gathered there on the Tuesday following Easter to light a candle and worship the Panagía. This woman's promise was thus, in reality, double-sided: in addition to expressing the hope of being able to live in Lesvos, near her homeland, her purpose was also to give the Panagía a real place of worship.

In July 1959, during the construction of the chapel, a grave containing a human skeleton and a brick with an engraved cross dating back to Byzantine times (in this particular case to the thirteenth and fourteenth centuries) were found along with architectural vestiges qualified by the archaeologists as 'paleochristian' (Charitonidis 1968). Other skeletons, ruins and objects were later discovered, among them a fourteenth-century medal representing the Christ *Pandokrátor* (All-Powerful). Extraordinary and mysterious events began to occur: objects were suddenly too heavy to carry until people crossed themselves, a monk-like figure appeared, dreams were reported and miracles performed (curing, faith). In some dreams, the monk gave his name (Rafaíl), said that the bones were his own and, later, gave details of his life and death. In an attempt to convince Church authorities of the veracity of these dreams and to provide physical evidence for the stories, excavations were carried out. Other objects and ruins were discovered, among them some which had been referred to in dreams. Various figures appeared in dreams and narrations: well-known saints such as Panagía and Agia Paraskevi, along with anonymous people, among them the monk Rafaíl and, later, Nikólaos (described as a deacon) and Iríni (a young girl).

For about a year, the case remained informal, but nobody in the area felt unmoved. More and more people ascribed divine character to the events; on the other hand, many remained sceptical. For their part, religious authorities did not seem to be interested in this phenomenon and criticized it as a sign of imagination and credulity, a characteristic that everyone (the Church as well as detractors) attributed mainly to 'simple people and above all women'.[4] It was only later that the local church decided to investigate, sending a priest to interview some of the 'dreamers'. Thanks to this enquiry, the Mitropolítis (bishop) of Mytilene, Iákovos Kleómvrotos, came to the conclusion that, firstly, the dreams matched what was being discovered during the excavation and, secondly, that some miracles could be confirmed as real, like the transformation of an atheist into a believer following the apparitions. He consequently launched the process of recognition of the saints by addressing a report to the Holy Synod.[5] At the same time (in September 1962), without waiting for formal recognition, the decision to build a monastery to commemorate the saints was officially made.

The entire process of recognition was undertaken mainly by the villagers who had experienced the dreams (*onireméni*, 'dreamers') and by various members of different levels of the clergy: together they gathered a collection of dreams and testimonies (later published in Kondoglou 1962) in order to convince the public and to document the 'apparition' of the new saints. The story they managed to reconstruct is the following one: Rafaíl was an archimandrite (head of a cloister) in a monastery located at the same place the chapel was later built. He was among the people killed by the Ottomans on the Tuesday after Easter in 1463. Nikólaos the deacon, Iríni, the daughter of a prominent figure in the nearby village, and other villagers who had gathered for the Easter celebration were also slain. This massacre supposedly occurred in response to a popular uprising against the recent annexation of the island, which was previously under Genoese dominion, to the Ottoman Empire.

Because of the way they died, these saints are considered 'neomartyrs', a title attributed by the Church to those who died fighting for their faith under Ottoman rule. No written archives mention these people or the monastery: in the absence of any information, the only record that can confirm the existence of the cloister is the medal found during the excavations, a patriarchal seal given to major monasteries at that time. As Mitropolítis Iákovos Kleómvrotos wrote, 'today we only know about eighteen of the thirty monasteries in Lesvos that existed back then and naturally, it is not impossible that this one ... would be one of those which are unknown'.[6]

Over the centuries, the collective memory forgot this episode of local history. It is said that among the villagers of Thermi, some claimed to have seen a monk walking around, carrying a censer and disappearing in a flash of light, or sometimes helping people (by showing them directions, for example). Some said that the hills were haunted because shepherds and others told tales of a monk wandering or of hearing bells and songs – which explains why the place was also called 'Kalógeros' (monk).

This phenomenon presents a multitude of research opportunities: through the course of events and the dynamics they caused, it offers a rare occasion for the anthropologist to study a process of collective elaboration of meanings stemming from a possibly anecdotic event (the discovery of a grave). It offers the opportunity to analyse how a belief is constructed: in the present case, one shared by laity and clergymen. It also introduces various ideas of holiness and different uses of sainthood. Here, I only focus on facets of everyday religion that are directly related to the historical process of sainthood-making, but it would be worth examining this field case as it relates to topics such as dreams, pilgrimage, miracles, and so on – each of these themes could offer deep insights on contemporary lived religion. My analysis is based on information from archives, books and discourse referring to the past: in this indirect way, access to actual practices is limited.

The Making of Sainthood:
Popular Veneration Controlled by the Church

The Church's stance on this 'apparition' is fascinating when one analyses the construction of religious duality and the opposition between everyday practice and normative doctrine or popular/official religion. My objective here is to show that the 'popular' character of the phenomenon so crucial for the ecclesiastical authorities was actually a discursive construction and an argument developed above all for internal use. I will also underline the modalities of the development of this case, in particular during the procedure of canonization, in the discourse the authorities employed.

Canonization in Orthodox Christianity is generally based on popular practices (narratives about the life of the holy person, testimonies about the fulfilment of miracles): these practices prove reverence and honour and lead the Church to integrate a new name among the recognized saints. This characteristic of the Orthodox Church differs from the Catholic practice in that canonization is a process which endorses popular veneration in a particular way. Such veneration is actually considered evidence of divine grace affecting an individual. In order to avoid abuse, the Ecumenical Patriarchate issues special encyclical letters in which the Holy Synod 'recognizes' popular convictions about a saint (Bebis 1990). Concretely, the principle is that the Church has to record signs of sainthood, but that God decides on the actual sainthood:

> Canonisation is only a formal act of the Church in response to the judgement of God on its saints. *Various signs express this judgement and the ecclesiastical act has only to note and record them in order to testify to a clear manifestation.* Most often, at the origin, we find the *vox populi,* the popular local veneration. It attracts the attention of church authorities, and if the investigation confirms that it is founded, the Church canonizes the person through its [ecclesiastical] act. This in no way prejudges the decree of God; it specifies the signs that show it and make it known to the terrestrial Church. (Evdokimov 1971: 137–38, emphasis added)

The 'popular' characteristic is an aspect that seems to be essential and central to the process of recognition of new saints. In this case, it is expressly stated by the ecclesiastical authorities. In the 1960s, at the time of the 'apparitions', the bishop Iákovos Kleómvrotos did not want people to believe that he attributed meaning to the dreams. Doubting their significance, he asked for evidence. For him, the exhumation of a tomb and the dreams that followed were not inevitably a divine sign, and he discredited the dreams, which he thought to be related to female imaginings or even caused by the devil. He stressed that, in the end, the dreams should reveal a clear sign: this insistence was at the same time a modality of his own construction of the belief and a way to conform to the prescriptions of the Church. The fact that many people had dreams that complemented each other was not in and of itself significant as long as there was no definite purpose that justified them.

Mitropolítis Iákovos Kleómvrotos took several steps in order to obtain proof. First, he sent a prelate to investigate the main 'dreamers' who spoke of new saints, and secondly, he asked these believers to provide a number of pieces of evidence, either through excavation, or through the verification of certain information contained in the dreams they had. Once convinced of the sanctity of these figures and of the miraculous character of the events, Mitropolítis Iákovos Kleómvrotos addressed the Holy Synod of the Church of Greece with a report totalling several pages (dated 8 December 1960) in which he presented the case and gave an inventory of the major discoveries. One of the arguments he developed was a reminder of the traditions of the Church and of times in ecclesiastical history when similar events were officially recognized. This reference enabled him to conclude that, because of these precedents, he had decided not 'to stop the course, moreover uncontrollable, of the devotion of [his] faithful spiritual children towards the recently appeared saints'.[7] The fact that the bishop judged the phenomenon as 'uncontrollable' reveals the ambiguity of the Church's position and power very meaningfully. With this statement, the bishop recognized the vitality of the new devotion, the unbreakable links between the faithful and ecclesiastical institution and the necessity for the latter to control the development of the situation. From then on, the texts and comments on the 'apparition' describe the *oniremēni* as 'simple', 'humble', 'poor' or 'innocent' (in the case of children) people, terms that echo some passages from the Bible ('Blessed are the poor in spirit … ', 'Blessed are the pure in heart … ').

Questioned about the proclamation of sainthood in general, the current bishop of Mytilene, Mitropolítis Iákovos Frantzís,[8] stressed that it could not be performed immediately and without verification. The Church has various criteria for recognition: possible evidence ('signs') include martyrdom, a particularly well-preserved body (certifying incorruptibility) or exhumed relics that have a pleasant smell. There is also 'the miracle … which means that there are other elements which happen progressively so that the proclamation can be carried out'. Successive testimonies of miracles (dreams containing 'revelations', their correspondence with the discovery of objects or remains at the time of the excavations, cures or recovery of faith) complete the file and are signs that show holiness. Lastly, he added another important element: popular practice. This aspect explains why the accounts and texts written by the Church always quote popular practices or what appear to be legends, or to quote him again, 'the awareness and the memory of the people'.

In our case, Mitropolítis Iákovos Frantzís specified another criterion for dreams:

> Here in Mytilene [in the case of Thermi], we do indeed have dreams: they are dreams that not only one individual had, it is very important, but many people had them, … men, women and children – children are innocent, aren't they? – and people who were not strong believers. Therefore, dreams have a place in our Church, but of course we cannot generalize them … [Having dreams continuously] is not possible.

However, the fact that many people were having dreams became significant at a later point: once the purpose of the dreams was revealed, their scale was also interpreted as a sign of the revelation intended by God. Ecclesiastical argumentation considers this an additional element, but only once evidence is found that validates the dreams (in particular the coincidence between the content of some of them and the excavated 'discoveries'). In other words, a large number of 'dreamers' does not automatically justify a revelation, although in certain cases a large number is regarded as a sign of divine power, which is considered to be the only force that can touch (and, in a way, 'coordinate') so many people at the same time.

To conclude this level of analysis, it can be said that the popular character of veneration is primarily constituted through the discourse of Church representatives. It is the way they qualify a phenomenon that does not arise directly from the institution – or more precisely, that should not seem to arise from it or with its help. This discourse underlines the fact that people belonging to the Church or in close contact with it (some priests, theologians, a famous iconographer) were involved in the process: it does not hide this reality but presents it as a consequence of popular action and of its credibility. Besides this exteriority, the Church refers to a certain way of divine expression which had already arisen in the past: this is a recognized religious motive that emphasizes the popular dimension in order to justify such phenomena. In short, it is above all an argument which serves as a sign of conviction for the Church and which is an acknowledged feature of the discovery of new saints or of holy icons.

The Making of Sainthood:
Expression and Means of Everyday Religion

The initial actors involved in this episode of sainthood-making were mainly (but not only) refugees who had settled in Lesvos: people who had fled Asia Minor (western Anatolia) during the conflict between Greece and Turkey in the 1920s. Some of them fled the massacres, and others left afterward due to the population exchange in 1923, a result of the Treaty of Lausanne, which fixed the borders of the Turkish state. Overall, these people were mostly women. They were moved by the discovery of the first grave and took care of the bones of the unknown deceased as they would have done for a member of their family (and in memory of those they left in Asia Minor). This behaviour indicates precisely how, from the beginning, people established a personal relationship with the saint. They felt emotion for him and with him; they took care of him. Because sainthood-making is not a simple process, they fought and struggled for him and the other bodies who would later be found. This situation illustrates the approach of Robert Orsi perfectly, who defines 'religion as a network of relationships between heaven and earth involving humans of all ages and many different sacred figures together. These relationships have all the complexities – all the hopes, evasions, love, fear, denial, projections, misunderstandings, and so on – of relationships between humans' (2005: 2). I will point out some characteristics of those relationships below.

In Greece, the ritual exhumation of bodies is a traditional practice usually performed by women (normally three or five years after the funeral): it is the first element that connects the discovery with regular religious activities. In our case, these women wanted to pay tribute to the unknown man and treat him like any other deceased member of the community. The only information they had about him was that he was a Christian because they saw that his hands were crossed on his chest and a brick with an engraved Byzantine cross was found in his grave. They cleaned the bones and placed them in a small box, which they planned to bring to the village cemetery in order to hold a memorial service. Later, along with a few men (also refugees), the women testified about the dreams they had had and the information they had obtained through them. Accused of credulity, it is only in a second phase that the dreams were relayed by the ecclesiastical sphere – whose hierarchy is exclusively male. The case is therefore indicative of and structured by the social division of labour between the sexes.

To speak of gender and division of labour is, in my view, to speak of social construction, power and hierarchies (Scott 1986; Delphy 2001). The fact that social roles are usually attributed to women according to their 'nature' (in other words, in line with their potential maternity) has two consequences, both in society and in the social sciences: women are automatically associated with domestic work and with the private – and often secular – sphere (Mathieu 1991; Ortner 1996; Clark 2001). If social reality often forces us to think about these female domestic/private roles, analysis has to go further without confining social actors to pre-established categories. In the case I analyse here, women are indeed associated with domestic work, but I would insist on two special features. Firstly, this association is in no way a simple one and it should be examined carefully; and secondly, it may well be the case that standard categories are not entirely accurate here. In Greece, a well-organized home entails not only satisfying immediate material needs but also respecting the sacred world by observing fasting periods and feasts. The gendered division of labour assigns domestic tasks to women, who play a central role in the family's running smoothly. Regardless of any paid employment, they give birth to and raise children, prepare meals, maintain the memory of the dead, organize activities in connection with the feasts of saints, and are responsible for the practice of fasting. They are continually concerned with the materiality of everyday life and with its sacred dimensions at the same time. They are thus guarantors of both social and moral or religious order, and have the role of 'spiritual guardians' of the home, whose task it is to take care of the spiritual well-being of their family (Dubisch 1983).

The women's relationship with the religious sphere should be analysed from this perspective: they are not simply more pious or, according to some people, more credulous. Rather, they have a role to play as women which involves bearing a set of loads. It is in this context that we must take into account the visits they make to churches and shrines (it is mostly women who go on pilgrimage) and analyse how female roles are expressed, especially in communication with saints (Hirschon 1983; Rey 2001). Because of this gendered division of labour, women have the role of mediators between the family and the divine. They have a special relationship with the saints, to whom they turn in order to find answers to everyday problems and means of action. The vow I mentioned earlier is an example of this: when she settled in the area, Vasiliki's mother asked the Panagía to assist her. Addressing the saints is a way to find answers to various questions. When new saints appear, women gain new interlocutors who are their counterpoint in their work as mediators between 'here below' and 'hereafter', and who furthermore prove themselves very effective.

The attention to women's practices in matters of everyday religion implies questioning women's association with the private and secular spheres (see, e.g. King 2000; Castelli 2001). Jill Dubisch (1991) notes that religion, particularly in Greece, was systematically considered a male-dominated system: after all, men are the only ones with access to the ecclesiastical hierarchy and responsibility for executing formal rituals. She nevertheless argues that there is certainly an androcentrist bias to analysing women's activities as 'domestic', 'peripheral', or 'complementary to' a system structured by men. When women go to church or on a pilgrimage or make their devotions, they are approaching the divine on the margins of the ecclesiastical institution. In no way are they limited to the secular sphere. Furthermore, this observation is true more generally for all the lay actors. When participating beyond the secular space, they bypass the limitations imposed on them: through the holy figures they choose, they address an omnipotent God, the source of life in this world as well as in the afterlife. They then have the opportunity to seek solutions to problems they (or their relatives) have and give them meaning, but they can also, in a way, circumvent ecclesiastical power.

Saints accompany people in their everyday lives, providing support and taking requests, but in this case they also proved themselves to be very active in their own 'revelation' and sometimes even demanding of their human interlocutors or displeased with them. Accounts of dreams are full of situations which describe relationships and modes of communication between saints and the faithful. For example, in one dream, Rafaíl says: 'I am the holy martyr Rafaíl. I want to get out freely, but I do not have this right if the Bishop does not give it to me. How long will I be left unknown? I want my icon and my liturgy' (quoted in Kondoglou 1962: 60). This dream stages the reciprocal needs of the actors (saints and humans) in order to legitimize the discovery. This is fundamental for analysis of how to convince and be convinced.

The process of sainthood-making, initiated by the *onireméni* alone but completed together with the Church, exemplifies the distinction between tactics and strategies as explained by Michel de Certeau (1984). Even if the Church was not the origin of those dreams and stories, it nevertheless had the means to control their development by giving (or denying) them official support. As the 'subject of will and power' (de Certeau 1984: 35–36), the Church introduced a strategy of establishing the criteria for the saints' recognition. The actions of the *onireméni* developed on the basis of this framework and were the very definition of a tactic:

> A calculated action determined by the absence of a proper locus. ... The space of a tactic is the space of the other. ... It operates in isolated actions, blow by blow. It takes advantage of 'opportunities' and depends on them, being without any base where it could stockpile its winnings, build up its own position, and plan raids. ... It is a guileful ruse. (de Certeau 1984: 37)

Whatever the motivations of the faithful (expression of popular piety, a way to appropriate their new space of life, an interest in economic development and tourism), they acted in a field where much was at stake. As soon as the Church committed itself, they met its demands, collected accounts, and found the required proof, pushing their case as well as they could. The identification of saints is one example of this kind of negotiation: some well-known saints, such as the Panagía, appeared in dreams. But these saints were already worshiped in nearby places, a fact which had little impact on the emergence of a new shrine. Those holy figures were progressively represented in the sole role of mediation and of authority, and a new character – Iríni – arose, introduced by the Panagía, who told a woman in a dream: 'I will introduce little Iríni to you tonight. ... [S]he endured martyrdom for me. ... But all of you, for so long, you do not remember her. Is it not a pity that you look down on her?' (quoted in Kondoglou 1962: 89). Unlike Rafaíl and Nikólaos, Iríni does not belong to the holy order. It seems that she is an example of the 'uncontrollability' expressed by the bishop. If the Church had had complete control of the situation, it would certainly have preferred to recognise only Rafaíl and Nikólaos, members of the ecclesiastical order, as neomartyrs. The *onireméni* had to be insistent in order to obtain Iríni's recognition along with the other two saints, demonstrating that she played an important part in the story and in its revealing. A trace of this difference remains: the girl does not appear on the first official icon of the saints. It is only because of her own and the other saints' insistence in dreams (i.e. the insistence of the villagers) that she was added to the icon and the liturgy at a later point.

Trajectories Worthy of Sainthood

One other fact is worth examining: the difference between the Church and the laity in regard to the (extra)ordinary nature of sainthood. An important facet of the Church's discourse is demonstrated by the emphasis on the unusual character of the case. The bishop did not establish a position at the beginning, perhaps in order to see if the story would persist or fade away. When he finally intervened, he mainly insisted on the similarity of this case with some central events in the Church's history,[9] the miraculous nature of some of the discoveries, and the exceptional amount of dreams experienced, which became a source of revelation of mysteries arising from the devil's inspiration. Whatever the bishop's doubts and initial reservations, it is significant to note that after the liberation of the island in 1912, the diocese of Mytilene tried to identify local saints forgotten due to Ottoman rule or not recognized as such. In the mid 1930s, Lesvos' saints' calendar comprised only 5 saints' days. In 1996 there were 35. For a theologian of the diocese, the 'discovery' of the saints of Thermi is an 'acme'[10] of the local hagiography.

Moreover, the extraordinary is expressed by the Church through the figures of the saints themselves: the religious leaders emphasise some features of the saints' lives (mainly their religious status) and, especially, the way they died and the fact that they died as martyrs, 'for the holy faith in Christ and the freedom of the Fatherland'.[11] As I mentioned earlier, the saints of Thermi are recognised as 'neomartyrs', a term used specifically for martyrs from the period of Ottoman rule (the prefix 'neo' is used to differentiate them from those of the early Christian era). The neomartyrs are celebrated by the Church for their sacrifices: they died for their faith and in order to defend it, thus offering others the opportunity to live their faith. As underlined by Jean-Pierre Albert (2001), the martyrs provide a feeling of belonging and produce an ancestral effect. Neomartyrs are usually members of the institution (priests, bishops or monks), and they are a way to collectively represent the role of the Church against Ottoman rule. The Church thus constructs its own role in the freedom and liberation of Greece: to commemorate neomartyrs is to celebrate the leadership of the Church during the occupation and, in particular, its fight against it.

The lay actors of sainthood-making put great emphasis on the lives of the saints: for them, the category of neomartyr seems unimportant. These new saints certainly died as martyrs, but the model they provide is concrete, almost within reach: it is because of their life paths and their actions that they are worthy of sainthood. What is important for the people is not the historical basis but rather the daily basis: they are examples to follow and individuals to identify with. The accounts insist on one such important influence Rafaíl the priest had during his lifetime: he was charismatic, and the faithful were generous to the poor under his influence, housing them or distributing food or clothes. 'The philanthropic work of Agios

Rafaíl was dreamed by many people', writes Vasiliki Ralli in her testimony (1998: 104). Such accounts move the villagers and reinforce their belief in his holiness. Even before many miracles were attributed to the saints, Rafaíl was seen in dreams wearing a white doctor's coat – an interesting picture combining miracle, medicine and contemporary life with a character anchored in history.

As for Iríni, the villagers (especially women) established a form of parental connection with her, strengthening their emotions and their personal relationship with the saints. After one dream, Vasiliki said:

> How I felt pity for this martyred child! Every time I go [to the shrine], I will sit down beside her little grave, and I will cry, as if she were my own child. Imagine, torturing the child in front of her father, in front of her mother who gave birth to her! It seems to me that there is no worse torment for parents! (quoted in Kondoglou 1962: 163)

This 'adoption' reaching across centuries is emblematic of the profound feeling of closeness felt by the villagers for the saints: they appropriated their history and made it their own. They even identified with them: in the accounts, the presence of Iríni, her parents and other people is of course a way of recounting what happened to these figures at the time, but it is mostly a representation of what could have happened to them, the villagers, under the same circumstances. There are clear parallels between their life paths: the saints were killed by the Ottomans and the refugees fled the Turks and saw members of their family perish. Through the saints, the refugees of Asia Minor found a way to transpose their fate and to make their experiences more meaningful. The event legitimated and marked their presence in their new home, and it developed above all a strong sense of companionship (between refugees, but in the larger community of the village and the region) founded on emotion, struggle, shared beliefs and mutual support.

Power Relations and Intertwining Fields

To conclude, I would like to highlight the power relations prevalent in such a case. Here, the Church's emphasis on the 'popular' character of sainthood-making is revealing. No one and nothing is intrinsically 'popular' by nature: everything exists within a social system marked by certain oppositions, or at least by a demarcation, more or less clear and structured by power relations. Here I second Stuart Hall's analysis about 'popular culture', where he indicates that 'the structuring principle of "the popular" … is the tensions and oppositions between what belongs to the central domain of elite or dominant culture, and the culture of the "periphery"' (2006: 483). We cannot talk about popular or subordinate per se without talking about relations between social groups first. But we can and must study the modalities of action and the discourses of each group in a symmetrical way, without assigning to one group the very characteristics that the other group has defined.

During the process of sainthood-making, a transformation occurred: before the inquiry, people who doubted the phenomenon, including Church representatives, emphasized that these dreams, stories and rumours were 'women's tales' (*mithévmata ginaikón*). Even though this expression does not appear in the official documents of the Church, some contemporary sources[12] attribute it to Mitropolítis Iákovos Kleómvrotos himself, who justified his suspicions by emphasising the simplicity of women: 'Keeping in mind on the one hand the exaltation and credulity of simple people, especially women, and on the other the machinations of the devil, master of evil, introducing himself as an angel of light, we were rather circumspect at the beginning'.[13] Once evidence was gathered and the issue reassessed, a transformation occurred in the Church's discourse. Scepticism of female credulity turned into a celebration of the people's humility (both men's and women's) and finished by assigning no specific position to women. An explanation emerges in the Church's discourse: what is at hand are no longer 'women's tales' but 'stories of simple people', testimony supported by humble and barely educated people's very modesty and their receptivity to divine messages: 'Who are the people who deserved to see and to hear these terrible mysteries? Are they distinguished, famous and important people? No. Most are humble beings, with little or no education, without wealth and some even living in black poverty' (Kondoglou 1962: 215).

The expression 'stories of simple people' transforms the discrediting of women's 'mythomania' into a miracle of faith. The transformation leads to a unilaterally religious deciphering, from the human (female) imagination to divine action, which had to be decoded by the Church through examination (evidence) and its authority (knowledge of religious history, interpretation of signs). It is also a way to regain control of the phenomenon (practice and discourse, in brief its meaning). Then, the discourse of the clergy calls women back to the forefront, but with a status change: from fanatics possibly inspired by the devil, they now recall the Myrrh-bearing women discovering the empty tomb of Jesus Christ after the crucifixion. Therefore we come back to a reading in religious (Biblical) terms made by people positioning themselves outside the category. In this way, there is a deep dependency and interconnection between the official Church and 'popular' or 'feminine' religion: the Church interprets this female/popular/humble imagination, but it also needs it.

Emphasizing everyday religious practices allows us to avoid strictly separating ecclesiastical institutions (or doctrine) from popular religion. As I have shown, sainthood-making was a complex process in which lay people, clergymen, and saints took part, each of them with their own specificities. The question is to underline certain means of action that individuals can develop in a proper way. Through sainthood-making, they initiated, developed and lived a full relationship with the saints. Whereas the Church recognized something it had not initiated and which was external to it as 'popular' action, the goal for the actors involved in sainthood-making was not to demonstrate religiosity in compliance with ecclesiastical criteria. Instead, their actions must be analysed as ways of operating that gave significance to their own trajectory and means of dealing with everyday life. Thus, we stand in front of two registers of explanation which make sense only when examined together.

Notes

1. Most of the information presented here was collected during field research in Greece, mainly between 1997 and 1999, carried out with the financial support of the Swiss National Science Foundation and of the Société académique vaudoise. I would like to thank Daniela Cerqui and Nathalie Monnet for their help and comments on earlier drafts of this text, as well as Alisa Burkhard-Shadrin who revised the text. My gratitude goes to Liza Debevec and Samuli Schielke for their support and very stimulating comments during the entire writing process.

2. For more details about this case of sainthood-making and the factors at play, see Rey 2008.

3. Because Vasiliki wrote a book about this story (see Ralli 1998), I did not observe the usual rules of anonymity here.

4. Excerpt from the bishop's report to the Holy Synod of the Church of Greece, in *Pimín* [The Parish Magazine of Mytilene] (1961): 10.

5. The Holy Synod is the highest authority in the church. In Greece, it gathers all the bishops in office under the chairmanship of the Archbishop.

6. In the newspaper *Dimokrátis,* 21 July 1960.

7. *Pimín* (1961): 11.

8. Quotations from the Mitropolítis Iákovos Frantzís are taken from an interview I had with him on 29 May 2002.

9. One of them is the discovery of the holy icon of the Panagía on the island of Tínos. For an analysis of this story and of the shrine, see Dubisch 1995 and Seraïdari 2001.

10. Georgios Sotiriou, 'I topikí agiología is tin Lésvon katá tin teleftaían triakon-tapendaetían' [The Local Hagiography of Lesvos during the Last Thirty-five Years], *Pimín* (1968): 183.

11. *Pimín* (1962): 118.

12. Stratis G. Paraskevaïdis, 'Lesviaká: Delthíon tis Etairías Lesviakón Meletón, Tóm. E' [Lesviaká: Annals of the Society for the Study of Lesvos, Vol. 5], *Lesviakós Kírix,* 25–28 July 1966; Panos N. Anagnostou, *Pétrina Chrónia: zoí ki agónes* [Stone Years: Life and Battles], Mytilene, 2001.

13. Excerpt from the bishop's report to the Holy Synod, *Pimín* (1961): 10.

References

Albert, J.-P. 2001. 'Sens et enjeux du martyre: de la religion à la politique'. In *Saints, sainteté et martyre: la fabrication de l'exemplarité*, ed. P. Centlivres, 17–25. Neuchâtel and Paris: Editions de l'Institut d'ethnologie/Editions de la Maison des sciences de l'homme.

Bebis, G. 1990. 'The Saints of the Orthodox Church'. Greek Orthodox Archdiocese of America. www.goarch.org/en/ourfaith/articles/article8044.asp (retrieved 12 May 2005).

Castelli, E. A., ed. 2001. *Women, Gender, Religion: A Reader, with the assistance of R.C. Rodman*. New York: Palgrave.

Charitonidis, S. 1968. 'Palaiochristianikí topografía tis Lésvou' [Early Christian Topography of Lesvos], *Archaiologikón Dheltíon* [Archaeological Annals] 23: 12–13.

Clark, E. A. 2001. 'Women, Gender, and the Study of Christian History'. *Church History* 70, no. 3: 395–426.

de Certeau, M. 1984 [1980]. *The Practice of Everyday Life.* Vol. 1. Berkeley: University of California Press.

Delphy, C. 2001. *L'ennemi principal.* Vol. 2: *Penser le genre.* Paris: Syllepse.

Dubisch, J. 1983. 'Greek Woman: Sacred or Profane'. *Journal of Modern Greek Studies* 1, no. 1: 185–202.

——. 1991. 'Gender, Kinship, and Religion: "Reconstructing" the Anthropology of Greece'. In *Contested Identities: Gender and Kinship in Modern Greece*, ed. P. Loizos and E. Papataxiarchis, 29–46. Princeton, NJ: Princeton University Press.

——. 1995. *In a Different Place: Pilgrimage, Gender, and Politics at a Greek Island Shrine.* Princeton, NJ: Princeton University Press.

Evdokimov, P. 1971. 'La sainteté dans la tradition de l'Eglise Orthodoxe'. *Contacts: revue française de l'orthodoxie* XXIII, no. 73–74: 119–90.

Hall, S. 2006 [1981]. 'Notes on Deconstructing "the Popular"'. In *Cultural Theory and Popular Culture: A Reader,* ed. J. Storey, 477–87. Harlow, Essex: Pearson Education.

Hirschon, R. 1983. 'Women, the Aged and Religious Activity: Oppositions and Complementarity in an Urban Locality'. *Journal of Modern Greek Studies* 1, no. 1: 113–29.

King, U., ed. 2000 (1995). *Religion and Gender.* Oxford: Blackwell Publishers.

Kondoglou, F. 1962. *Simíon méga: ta thávmata ton Agíon tis Thermís Rafaíl - Nikoláou - Irínis* [A Large Sign: The Miracles of the Saints of Thermi Rafaíl, Nikólaos et Iríni]. Athens: Astir.

Mathieu, N.-C. 1991. *L'anatomie politique: catégorisations et idéologies du sexe.* Paris: Côté-femmes.

Orsi, R. A. 2005. *Between Heaven and Earth: The Religious Worlds People Make and the Scholars Who Study Them.* Princeton, NJ: Princeton University Press.

Ortner, S. B. 1996. *Making Gender: The Politics and Erotics of Culture.* Boston: Beacon Press.

Ralli, V. 1998. *Kariés: o lófos ton Agíon Rafaíl, Nikoláou, Irínis: éna chronikó tis evréseos ton ierón lípsanon ton Agíon* [Karies, Hill of Saints Rafaíl, Nikólaos and Iríni: A Chronicle of the Discovery of the Holy Relics of the Saints]. Athens: Akritas.

Rey, S. 2001. 'Pèlerinage, vœux et miracles: une "affaire de femmes"?'. *Archivio Antropologico Mediterraneo* III–IV, no. 3–4: 173–80.

———. 2008. *Des saints nés des rêves. Fabrication de la sainteté et commémoration des néomartyrs de Lesvos (Grèce).* Lausanne: Antipodes.

Scott, J. 1986. 'Gender: A Useful Category of Historical Analysis'. *American Historical Review* 91: 1053–75.

Seraïdari, K. 2001. 'La Vierge de Tinos: le cœur sacré de l'Etat grec'. *Archives de sciences sociales des religions,* no. 113: 45–59.

6

Say a Little Hallo to Padre Pio

Production and Consumption of Space in the Construction of the Sacred at the Shrine of Santa Maria delle Grazie

Evgenia Mesaritou

In Catholic Christianity, officially recognized public cults can only be paid to the dead. Nevertheless, it is very often the case that a dead saint's cult springs from a reputation for sanctity in life. Insofar as they eliminate the need for priestly mediation, living saints pose a problem to the ecclesiastical hierarchy, which fears the development of personalized cults (Eade and Sallnow 1991: 7). The institutional church's attempts to control these saints' charisma are not always successful (Coleman and Elsner 1995: 110) during their lifetime, mainly due to their great popularity. After their death, control is more easily regained, primarily, through sanctification procedures.

The initiation of the canonization process is accompanied by the placing of an increased emphasis on the saint's post-mortem cult in the framework of which control is regained primarily – as Eade and Sallnow (1991) suggest – through a process of 'charisma spatialization'. This process, described as the sedimentation and preservation of a person's power in the power of a place after his death, produces a space charged with religious meaning while transforming the saint into a 'mute, hieratic, domesticated shrine' (8). Nevertheless, the significance and use of the shrine's space does not remain fully under ecclesiastical control. The pilgrimage site emerges as a 'religious void', deriving its power, religious capital and universalistic character not only from its own religious significance, but also from its character as a platform able to accommodate the different and often conflicting meanings and practices that different groups bring to the shrine, according to their background (15).

A result of this pluralism of representations and discourses is the emergence of 'complex relationships between power and resistance, control and freedom of choice, hierarchy and equality' (Eade and Sallnow 1991: 18). In the dialectical construction of the sacred, shrine officials have an advantage over the production of a homogenous discourse and the regulation of ritual practices due to the control they exercise over the organization of the shrine's space and time. Although this limits the pilgrim's freedom, pilgrims are nevertheless able to contest sacred space, as this is defined and bounded by the shrine's managers (11). The ability of pilgrims to contest is to a large degree aided by the pilgrimage centre itself, which, as Coleman and Elsner note, provides the pilgrims with the props with which to enact their own play (1995: 49). Crowded with pilgrims and material props such as icons and holy objects (49), the pilgrimage centre thus appears as 'the stage against which many of the contested views and interpretations' (70) – at once incorporated and constrained by the shrine – are performed.

The idea of the 'religious void' and its 'props' can be combined with de Certeau's theory of everyday practice, finding useful applications in the analysis of the ways in which the sacred is constituted within pilgrimage cults which are characterized by a place-centred sacredness. Such is the case of the pilgrimage cult developed around Padre Pio in San Giovanni Rotondo (South Italy).

In *The Practice of Everyday Life*, de Certeau defines consumption as a 'secondary production hidden in the process of ... utilization' (1988: xiii) and thus, as a form of hidden poiēsis, 'scattered over areas defined and occupied by systems of "production"' (xii). Perceiving consumption as consisting of a set of signifying practices, which he conceptualizes as acts of re-appropriation or 'ways of operating' of the weak against the strong, de Certeau accounts for the oppositional practices of everyday life by using the schema of 'strategies' and 'tactics'. Defining strategies and tactics in relation to a 'proper place', he takes strategies to be the manipulation of force-relationships, which becomes possible when a subject of will and power can be isolated from an 'environment' (xix). He thus conceives them as actions which depend on the establishment of a space of power and which are able to project totalizing systems and types of discourses that can articulate the ensemble of physical places where force is distributed. Taking tactics as calculated actions, which cannot count on a place of power and which always take place in the space of 'the other', he sees them as determined by the absence of a 'proper place' and thus as constituting the 'art of the weak' (xix; de Certeau 1980: 6).

I would like to argue that with the institutionalization and spatialization of a saints' charisma, and the subsequent transformation of a person to place-centred sacredness, 'proper places' are created on the basis of which those who officially manage a saint's charisma can form strategies for the production of the sacred. These same places are, simultaneously, 'spaces of the other' for the saint's devotees who can only act in them through their tactics, consuming and thus re-appropriating and transforming the meaning of the officially produced sacred, the constitution of which appears to involve both its production by the managers of a saint's charisma and its consumption by the saint's devotees.[1] In this light, strategies and tactics are taken to be the ways in which the various groups that come together at the shrine communicate their interpretations and understandings of the meaning of saints and places. Applying this framework of analysis in the examination of the Padre Pio cult, I will here focus on the pilgrimage shrine as one of the 'proper places' described above. Presenting it as a 'religious void' that is being structured in a way that channels the movements and experience of its visitors, as well as providing them with the props through which they can articulate their embodied discourse concerning the sacred, I will see the process whereby the sacred is constituted in relation to the production and consumption of the shrine's spatial structures.

While acknowledging that de Certeau's schema of strategies and tactics may conceal the need to distinguish between those practices which self-consciously 'contest' the site's ecclesiastical control and those practices – which although not sanctioned by religious authorities – are not obviously premeditated, here my interest is not so much in the hermeneutics of the motives underlying the possibly subversive practices of the shrine visitors, but in the practices themselves and their end result. This is often, intentionally or unintentionally, one of creative diversion and contestation.

Making use of ethnographic data gathered in 2004–2005, during fieldwork at the shrine of Santa Maria delle Grazie where Padre Pio's tomb is located, I will explain, firstly, how the shrine is structured and organized by its 'managers' so as to produce an official discourse about the saint's meaning, and, secondly, how it is re-appropriated by its visitors through their 'ways of operating', manifested in their signifying devotional practices. In this manner, I will illustrate the different modalities of action that are manifested at the shrine, showing how, on the one hand, the official discourse about Padre Pio changes diachronically and how, on the other, the pilgrimage practices are differentiated in the shrine's old and new spatial structures.

The Friars and the Strategic Production of the Sacred

As in many cases of saints' cults, the phenomenon of Padre Pio started as local before acquiring national and international dimensions. Born in 1887 as Francesco Forgione, Padre Pio entered the Capuchin order in 1903. Two years after his arrival in San Giovanni Rotondo in 1916, he manifested the stigmata, which were to be a point of controversy in the church and an article of faith for the devotees. The rising devotion towards Padre Pio alarmed the Church, which unsuccessfully tried to suppress the phenomenon through the implementation of a series of restrictive measures. In 1938, Padre Pio set in motion a project for the construction of a clinic, which resulted in the foundation of the Casa Sollievo della Sofferenza. This hospital housed the International Centre of the Prayer Groups, which having been developed around the spiritual children of Padre Pio grew into an international network of devotees. Despite the controversies surrounding Padre Pio and his cult, in 1999 he was beatified and in 2002 canonized.

The death of Padre Pio in 1968, but mainly his beatification and canonization, saw the shrine's landscape transforming through a process of 'charisma spatialization', whereby, 'the aura of holiness which emanated from the person of Padre Pio in life [was] ... being gradually transmuted into a spatial sacredness anchored in the places he frequented and sanctified by his presence' (Eade and Sallnow 1991: 8). The landscape around the crypt where his body lies was imprinted with a sacred geography which consists of the various locations 'which most strongly evoke his spirit' (8), while parts of the churches and the friary where Padre Pio lived were gradually converted into a sort of museum, displaying pictures of the saint and objects he had used (Margry 2002: 99).[2]

Through a process of symbolic investment of the shrine's spatial structures, in the framework of which the saint's figure was extensively inserted in existing representations, a particular way of reading the importance of the saint and shrine is promoted. Being invested with symbolism, the shrine's spatial structures not only visualize particular discourses, but also trigger and guide the religious imagination of the shrine's visitors, nonetheless through the creation of a sense of historical continuity at the site.

As a very important 'way of denying the effects of time, which ordinarily breeds change' (Morinis 1992: 27), historical continuity is both consciously and unintentionally secured at pilgrimage centres, mainly through a process of an 'invention of tradition' (Hobsbawm and Ranger 2002). In the case of the Padre Pio cult such 'invention of tradition' is mainly manifested in the anachronisms, which are created through the appropriation of established Christian symbols with which Padre Pio is associated, and of established Christian narratives into which he is strategically inserted. These symbols and narratives, which present a 'comparable juxtaposition of Pio with central Christian figures' (Margry 2002: 105), are somewhat differentiated in the old and new spatial structures of the shrine. This differentiation, which changes the official discourse about Padre Pio's sanctity and meaning, is marked by and manifested in the new church dedicated to the saint and inaugurated in 2004. The Saint Pio Church, as it so named, has changed through its invested symbolism the past, with which historical continuity is created at the site.

The Sanctuary of Santa Maria delle Grazie: Padre Pio Meets the Franciscan and Local Garganic Traditions

The sanctuary consists of the friary, the 'old' and 'new' church of Santa Maria delle Grazie and an underground crypt, which houses the saint's tomb. What is interesting about the sanctuary is not so much the building styles and spatial arrangements of its structures – both sanctuary churches have the traditional shape of the Roman Cross – but their themes, the symbols in which these are expressed and the narrative that they create.

At the sanctuary, the cult's connection to Franciscanism is emphasized, while the past to be linked with is more of a local past than a biblical one, with Garganic traditions and mainly the shrine's Marian past being referenced extensively. The lunette on the façade of the original friary church may be used to sum up both the themes and symbols prevailing in the sanctuary. Here, the Madonna, depicted with baby Jesus, is flanked by the Archangel Michael and St Francis: the local Garganic tradition, mainly that part of it which relates to Archangel Michael and his alleged appearance at the nearby shrine at Monte San Angelo, meets with the shrine's own Marian past and Franciscan tradition. These themes are also brought together at the crypt, where a reference to the apparitions of the archangel is made through the engravings of the two ancient sets of coats of arms of the bishop of Siponto, on the side supports of the crypt's altar. These coats symbolize, according to the friars' guide, 'the connection between the ancient beginnings of divine manifestations on this Gargano mountain and … the manifestations of Our Lord to Padre Pio' (da Ripabottoni and di Flumeri 1987: 42). In the crypt, references to Jesus and St Francis are also made in reliefs and engravings. Combined with Padre Pio's tomb, these references create 'a trilogy of mystical significance with Jesus, St Francis and Padre Pio' in the crypt (40). Through this trilogy, a discourse concerning the saint is constructed through his parallelization and juxtaposition with these two central Catholic Christian figures.

Another juxtaposition evident in the New Church of Santa Maria delle Grazie is that of Padre Pio and the Madonna delle Grazie, the old devotional centre of the friary and one of the two patron saints of the village. This juxtaposition is most clearly made in the mosaic located behind the main altar of the church. On this mosaic, which originally depicted the particular Madonna with angels, the figure of Padre Pio pointing to her as the way to heaven was later added. The addition of Padre Pio to the mosaic linked the past and present of the shrine by symbolically establishing a connection between the shrine's old and new devotional centres. The establishment of this connection was attributed by Margry (2002) to the fact that Padre Pio's cult, being disapproved of by the Vatican, was publicized under the banner of the original Marian shrine and not as an independent devotion (ibid.: 103). Whatever the reasons for the association of the two figures might have been, the fact is that the Madonna, as an established symbol with its own devotional tradition, lent her symbolic capital to Padre Pio, at least at the initial stages of the cult's formation.

The Saint Pio Church:
Padre Pio Meets the Christian Biblical Past

Built after the canonization of Padre Pio and designed by Renzo Piano, the Saint Pio Church (hereafter referred to as the Church), marks a break with the shrine's tradition not only in terms of aesthetics and architecture, but also in terms of its status and symbolism. Although seemingly one, this new church is in reality a complex of ritual spaces, consisting of the Churchyard, the Superior and the Lower Church and the Chapel of the Eucharist.

Spreading in front of the Church, the Churchyard serves as an uncovered church and a ceremonial arena. Sloping downwards in declining levels, it draws in great numbers of people, gathering them together and guiding them into the Liturgical Hall of the Superior Church. The Hall was designed as semi-circular, promoting the idea of a church that creates a community, and 'diminishing the expression of hierarchy' (Amelar 2004: 188). The Church is invested with symbolism evoking the Christian narrative, resonating with theological themes through the invocation of events recounted in the Old and New Testaments. What is dominant are references to Jesus, who symbolically acquires a new centrality at the site, and to important moments and figures of the Christian narrative, into which Padre Pio is strategically inserted through the construction of what could be called 'theological anachronisms'. Through these anachronisms, the friars are able to produce a discourse that connects the cult, saint and shrine with the wider Christian tradition and to established images and principles, etched in the collective memory of Catholics. In the Church, the past to be linked with is a Christian, biblical past, which although also 'present' at the sanctuary, is so to a lesser degree. Hence this new church serves both as a device providing catechesis, and as a devise of discourse production concerning the sanctity, meaning and importance of Padre Pio.

The story narrated through the Church begins in its Churchyard and is completed in its Liturgical Hall. Its main scenes are the baptism of Jesus in the river Jordan, the Last Supper and the institution of the Eucharist, and the death and resurrection of Jesus. Through the various depictions of these events, the Church symbolizes the main tenets of Christian belief and its important acts of worship: the mass, the sacraments of baptism and the Eucharistic and the Pasqual mystery. For the purposes of this chapter, I focus on the pulpit and the sculpture that is located next to it as together they constitute an example of the 'theological anachronisms' I mentioned above.

The pulpit and the sculpture narrate the events following the crucifixion of Jesus. The story begins at the sculpture which shows Mary Magdalene and Nicodemus supporting the body of Christ after his descent from the cross, and concludes in the pulpit, at the moment where the Apostles are informed of his resurrection. What is interesting in this composition is the replacement of Nicodemus's face by the face of Padre Pio (*Guide to the Church of Saint Pio of Pietrelcina*). Through depictions such as this one, the friars symbolically connect the saint with the death and resurrection of Jesus, thereby inserting him in the most important part of the Christian narrative.

As illustrated in the descriptions provided above, an official interpretation of the saint's 'true message' is literally set in stone in the shrine's churches. Since both the sanctuary and the Church embody a discourse concerning the meaning of sanctity, even though a differentiated one, the analysis of their structures may take the form of an 'archaeology' in Foucault's terms. This archaeology of the sacred that may be practiced by the researcher can reveal ideological shifts and changes in the official discourses produced at pilgrimage shrines. The symbolism of the sanctuary and the Church, different as it is in its emphasis, connects the saint with a different narrative – Garganic and Franciscan in the case of the sanctuary, biblical in the case of the Church. Both ensuring historical continuity, but with a different past, these two complexes present a transition from the religio-historical narrative which is specific to the shrine, the order and the area to the abstract, general and universal Catholic narrative into which Padre Pio is strategically inserted by the friars. This transition effects a change in the official discourse concerning Padre Pio's sanctity and can be viewed in the framework of the friars' attempts to modernize the cult. The new church does more than just stand as a metaphor for the cult's growth and development from a local to an international phenomenon (Margry 2002: 99). By embodying a discourse which incorporates Padre Pio into more established and formal lines, it is designed to express the friars' new vision for the future of the cult: vast, encompassing and modern.

Emotional Investment and the Establishment of the Saint's Presence and Absence through Devotional Practices

While the shrine may be the friars' 'proper place' and a strategic deployment in the production of an official discourse concerning Padre Pio's meaning for the pilgrims and shrine visitors it is the space of the 'other'. Not being able to articulate a strong discourse about Padre Pio, shrine visitors rely on opportunities offered to them by both time and space in order to communicate their view of Padre Pio and insert creativity in the space of the other. Through their practices, which can only be tactical in nature, visitors of the shrine use its spatial structures as props, consuming, re-appropriating and thus transforming the meanings that were ascribed and inscribed on them by the shrine officials. They accomplish this by signifying devotional practices, which are differentiated in the sanctuary and the Church.

One of the primary ways in which the shrine visitors appropriate the shrine is by investing it with memory and emotion. This is particularly the case where returning visitors are concerned, especially those who have personal memories of the saint in the site's specific spatial contexts. Their stories, traversing and organizing the shrine, create a space in the place of the other, acting as spatial trajectories, which, in a way uncontrollable by the shrine managers, 'select and link [the places] together [and] … make sentences and itineraries out of them' (de Certeau 1988: 115). This type of organization of the shrine's place by its visitors is a form of re-appropriation, which influences to a great degree people's responses to the alterations occurring in its spatial and material landscape. Connected to particular experiences, their memory and the feelings they engendered, the various features of the shrine's materiality act as material reminders of past events and are therefore ascribed with sentimental value and personal meaning by the shrine's visitors. Any alterations that disrupt the 'nostalgic re-construction' of the past (McDannel 1995: 39), which denies the present and gives the past 'authenticity of being' (Stewart 1984: 23), are resisted.

The past's 'authenticity of being' can best be ensured in the original context in which this past occurred, and that is the sanctuary. With the whole drama of Padre Pio's existence being set in the sanctuary's structures, people are more capable of remembering or even imagining him there. This transforms the sanctuary into a physical medium through which the devotees connect and communicate with the saint, while also affecting the type of devotional practices manifested there. These practices, which re-appropriate the sanctuary, either by establishing it as a setting for a 'ritualised exchange' (Morgan 1998) with the saint or by using its materiality for the transformation of objects into portable carriers of the saint's and the place's charisma, relate to a feeling of presence of the saint at the site. At the same time, their aim is to construct a relationship with the saint and to ensure his continuous presence in people's everyday lives.

Appropriating the Sanctuary

The 'absent presence' of the saint at the site provokes the contrasting feelings which this oxymoron denotes: while the feeling of absence creates a feeling of loss and nostalgia for the days when Padre Pio was alive and for the contact that people had had with him, the feeling of presence, preserved and promoted by the managers of the site, creates a feeling of well-being, protection and re-assurance.

As noted by Wilson, the belief that 'far from inhabiting any distant heaven, the saint remained present in his shrine' is a common and central motif in the veneration of saints (1983: 11). This belief is expressed by various shrine visitors, who often say that they have experienced the presence of Padre Pio in the shrine and elsewhere in the form of dreams but mainly of sweet odours, and who often talk of their visit to the shrine as if Padre Pio was still alive: 'I came to say a little hallo to Padre Pio', or 'I was in the area and thought of dropping in to greet him'.

Most of all, the feeling of the saint's presence at the shrine is manifested in people's practices. Many of the spots displayed and protected by glass cases, i.e. Padre Pio's confession box in the old friary church, become focal points for people's requests or thanks for graces granted. These places are connected to Padre Pio either because he appropriated them or because they encase his relics. They thus become sites where intimate relationships with the saint are created and maintained, as well as sites of ritualised exchange where money and objects of personal identity, such as photographs of loved ones and letters, are being placed in spite of the prohibiting signs and special boxes provided for exactly this purpose by the friars. Expressing people's petitions or prayers of thanksgiving, these 'tangible traces of the person for whom intercession is sought' (Morgan 1998: 52), act not only as 'means of prompting saintly aid' (54), but also as 'testaments to divine mercy and ... as ... crucial link[s] in the public ritual of intercession and its proclamation' (52).

Forming part of the ways in which people relate to Padre Pio – to the construction of whose sanctity they contribute – the practices involving the placement of these objects at the shrine express a perception of the saint as being present and accessible at the shrine. At the same time, tactical as they are in their nature, these same practices construct the site by registering, through votive offerings, both the intimate and emotional relationship (see Orsi 2005) and the ritualised exchange that people develop with the saint 'in the sacred and public setting of the pilgrimage cathedral' (Morgan 1998: 54). They are therefore both meaningful and signifying practices, which contest the nature and the borders of the sacred as set by shrine officials. And yet they do not openly call the shrine officials' discourse on the sacred in question. Instead, they re-appropriate and re-construct it through personal evocations of and exchanges with the saint and his sanctuary.

As the place where the saint's body lies, the crypt is where one can most easily observe the kind of relationship people develop with the saint, but also people's perceptions and appropriation of Padre Pio's meaning and sacredness. Despite the control exercised by the friars over the access to the tomb, a certain degree of autonomy is retained by people in relation to their practices. Connected as they are to the idea of the saint's presence at the site, these practices reveal a desire to establish a closer, more intimate relationship with the saint. This becomes visible during the hours when direct access to the tomb is possible. During this time, people's practices range from touching to kneeling and kissing. People also place the letters they write to Padre Pio on his tomb, often hiding them under the flower arrangements, despite the special boxes provided for this purpose by the friars.

Another practice in which people engage at the crypt is the unofficial 'consecration' of various commercial religious objects and souvenirs. This 'consecration' is effected by rubbing these objects on the saint's tomb: as people would take rosaries to Padre Pio during his lifetime to be blessed by him, so today, they take a variety of objects to his tomb, blessing them directly and without the institutional intercession of the priest, through the usage of the site's materiality. Rosaries, postcards, handkerchiefs and on many occasions photographs of loved ones, become the means through which people ensure the saint's continuous presence in their everyday lives, as well as the vehicles through which a sort of 'contesting' agency is exercised and channelled.

By re-appropriating objects in this manner, people transform them into a sort of 'sacramental', changing their status from commercial objects into portable carriers of the saint's and site's charisma and efficacy. These objects may later act as evidence of the journey's completion, but also as material links through which the relationship with the saint is maintained and as a physical manifestation of the sacred centre's charisma (McDannell 1995: 41). For if, as Dubisch notes, 'pilgrimage is based on the belief that certain places ... are in some sense ... powerful and extraordinary... [T]his power can not only be experienced by the pilgrim who visits such places; it can also be taken home in one form or another – ... as a physical object imbued with the sacred power of the pilgrimage site' (35).

Escaping the site, objects 'blessed' in this manner diffuse its sacred landscape, 'permeating even the everyday lives of those who have never been ... at the place' (Coleman and Elsner 1995: 6). As demonstrated by the fact that people bring into the crypt plastic bags loaded with objects which they rub on the tomb, either one by one or all together, objects 'blessed' in this manner are not only for personal use but are to be distributed among friends and loved ones upon the pilgrims' return from the shrine. While for the aspiring pilgrims such 'objects provide an imaginative link with a sacred goal which, it is hoped to be encountered in the future' (6), for the actual pilgrims they provide a link with a real past, 'the continuous and personal narrative' (Stewart 1984: 140) which they help create. Serving as traces of the original experience in the power of which they are thought to participate (McDannell 1995: 41), these tokens of the place are therefore more than mementoes and souvenirs, aiding the sacred journey's reconstruction in the imagination (Coleman and Elsner 1995: 6) and acting as indexes of the saint, site and pilgrimage experience. They are integral both to the act of memory and to the pilgrimage practice.

The practices which co-involve material objects link to a perception of the shrine and of the saint's relics and remains that views them as retaining a part of Padre Pio's individual charisma and miraculous qualities. But apart from indicating the perception of the Saint's body and various relics as the materialization and embodiment of his sanctity and charisma, these practices construct them as such: they signify them by reinforcing their perception as retaining the saint's efficacy. Forming patterns over the years, these practices are further transformed from unofficial rituals into routine activities.

Similar practices as the ones manifested at the sanctuary were not manifested at the Church. In its Liturgical Hall people move in a more unstructured way, often taking videos and pictures, most commonly praying or participating in the celebration of Mass rather than engaging in para-liturgical practices as the ones observed at the shrine. This difference may be attributed to the contrasting feelings that this new church provokes: while its aesthetic merits, virtuosity and craftsmanship are acknowledged, its ability to provoke prayer and meditation are questioned. This happens mainly due to the shape and size of the Church and the lack of Padre Pio relics in it.

Appropriating the Saint Pio Church

Having been built according to a modern, unconventional – in terms of church building – design, the Church does not respond to people's expectations on how religious buildings should be. It thus creates a new, almost foreign reality to which people need to adjust, while also appearing to some as a more secular than religious structure. The Church often appears to the pilgrims and the village's inhabitants[3] as too big, too modern, cold and unwelcoming. Feeling unable to pray or express their feelings in this new structure, people often compare it to the sanctuary, which they see as being connected to the saint and thus preferable for the expression of their religious sentiments.

The size, shape and form of the Church affect people's devotional practices in that they minimize the possibilities of the church's spatial re-appropriation. Semi-circular and with a more rigid, formalized, almost ready-made structure than that of the sanctuary churches, the Liturgical Hall of this new church has all its spaces accounted for, hence leaving little space for the alterations and transformative effects of its visitors. Having no corners where people can place objects or flowers and no Padre Pio spaces where people can engage in para-liturgical practices, the Church cannot therefore be creatively consumed by people in the same way as the sanctuary, where slight modifications of the basic structure were inserted by the shrine managers and where little changes initiated by people were tolerated or even approved and ultimately remodelled and reshaped the shrine. The very monumentality of the structure gives it an imposing character (see Miller 2005), which dominates the shrine, making the power and control of the friars over the sanctuary visible. It is both an act and an expression of power. At the same time, this very monumentality is what diminishes its emotional impact on the people who visit the shrine – and thus also its capacity to govern them – not only because it creates a rupture in the shrine's architectural past and tradition but also because it is seen as being opposed to Padre Pio's character, simplicity and even wishes, as these were interpreted by his fellow friars.

By limiting the visitors' freedom to appropriate and reshape it, the spatial arrangement of the new church influences pilgrimage practice and through it the experience of the sacred: a ready-made construction which allows little modification in its structure, the Church is designed to influence the body techniques of its visitors and hence their spatial understandings of the sacred. With its construction, the friars not only have attempted to direct people's devotion to the sacraments, but have also regained control of the site by creating a need for interpretation of the new church's design and theological symbolism.

Apart from the size and form of the new church, there is another very important factor which affects the devotional practices manifested there, and that is the absence of the saint himself from this new structure. The figure of Padre Pio, so ubiquitous in the sanctuary complex, is almost nonexistent in the Church. The sense of Padre Pio's absence in this new structure may easily be explained if one considers the fact that relics have a fundamental role to play in the formation of a feeling of saintly presence on the one hand, and the formation of devotional practices on the other. The lack of relics in the Church translates into a lack of physical mediums through which people can communicate with the saint but it also mutes or rather silences the saint in this structure.

Even though the degree of people's liberty in introducing creative diversions into this new structure is to a large degree restricted by its monumental, almost pervasive character, people are not utterly unable to insert imagination in this space. Coins are tossed in the baptistery or stream's basins. A Padre Pio statue brought and left at the site by a group of pilgrims became, even if temporarily, a devotional focal point for the church's visitors, who started placing and lighting candles around it.

Conclusions

In this chapter, I have looked at the construction of the sacred as a dialectical process that consists of production and consumption practices, in the sense given to them by de Certeau. The chapter was divided into two parts which respectively examined the friars' strategic deployment of the shrine's spatial structures for the production and dissemination of a particular discourse about Padre Pio's meaning, and the shrine visitors' utilization and appropriation of the shrine's spatial structures and materiality, through their tactical uses and consumption of the sanctuary and Church and signifying devotional practices. The analysis of the shrine managers' and visitors' practices in relation to space showed that both the strategic design of physical space and its tactical consumption are constitutive of the pilgrimage site, and both are transformed as a result of changes taking place at the pilgrimage centre and in the institutional framework into which it is incorporated.

Understanding the interactions of the various groups that come together at the shrine allows us to see the ways in which strategic and tactic engagement with a sacred space intertwine. Seen in light of de Certeau's theory, the clergy appear as able to speak officially in the name of religion due to their possession of a 'proper place'. With their perspective of power being the only legitimate one, they thus emerge as the strategic producer of the sacred and its official definition. The shrine visitors, on the other side, having no 'proper place' on which to base a production, appear as tactical consumers, actively engaging with the site through their modes of operating that consist of perceptions and practices which, being manifested in the space of the friars as 'the other', appropriate official interpretations of the sacred as institutional products, redefining and reproducing them. In this light, the different understandings and uses of the sacred space appear as modalities of engagement with a charismatic person and his cult that are at each instance formed and informed by particular and identifiable relations of power.

The boundaries set by the managers of the saint's charisma around space, time, and ultimately the sacred, constrain the extent to which visitors are able to express and realize their desires, making the questioning of official rules almost inconceivable (see Eade 1991: 75). The advantage of the shrine managers over the organization of the visitors' experience, as well as their advantage in the imposition of an official discourse about sanctity, is therefore obvious, at least when one examines officially recognized pilgrimage shrines. Having at their disposition a 'proper place', the managers of a saint's charisma therefore have the means of production of a sacred discourse. Nevertheless, while the expressions of devotion to Padre Pio are constrained by the structures of the shrine and the religious tradition into which this is incorporated, they are never determined by the friars' attempts to govern the pilgrimage. Instead they exist in a mutually influencing relation with officially prescribed ways of devotion. And since visitors are vital to pilgrimage sites, they are of equal importance in defining the sacred. Their agency and the creativity with which they induce the shrine as the space of 'the other' should not be overlooked.

The active role of shrine visitors in the process whereby the sacred is constituted highlights the creative character of the processes which locally construct the sacred as well as the creative character of the interactions which take place at the shrine. These interactions may include tensions, diversions, juxtapositions, resistance, conformity and transformation. The

shrine managers and visitors are not in direct conflict, although their relationship is characterized by tension: the shrine managers sometimes overlook or even tolerate the visitors' practices and diversions, even if trying
to re-direct them, while the visitors are often guided and affected by the
former's view of the sacred, as this is communicated through the site and
the cult's institutions. Furthermore, the shrine visitors do not necessarily intend to contest and while some of their usages are ignored, forgotten or suppressed, others become popular and established. Contrary to de
Certeau's view then, people's tactics are at times able to keep some of what
they win in the space of the other.

Notes

I am grateful to the Cambridge Commonwealth Trust for granting me a bursary for
my PhD, on which this chapter was based. I would like to thank David Lehmann,
John Eade and Simon Coleman. I would also like to thank Hugo Reinert for suggesting I read de Certeau. Previous versions of this chapter were presented, apart
from the EASA conference in 2008, at the conference 'Dimensions of Pilgrimage:
Journey, Meaning and Place", organized by the Canterbury Christ Church University, and at the ASA 2009 conference. I am of course solely responsible for any
of the weaknesses of my argument.

 1. In the cases of pilgrimage cults, officially sanctioned by the Catholic Church
    or aspiring to be so in the future, shrine managers belong to a hierarchical
    chain of production, through which power is distributed. At the top of this
    chain there is the Vatican, which thereby moulds through its production the
    production of all others. In this sense, the status of a shrine's managers is rela-
    tive: they are producers in relation to shrine visitors and consumers in relation
    to the Vatican. Hence, their advantageous position in relation to the former
    but not in relation to the latter.
 2. In 2009, the tomb of Padre Pio was tranferred from the crypt of the new Santa
    Maria delle Grazie Church to the crypt of the Padre Pio Church. This chapter
    describes the devotional practices as they could be observed before the tomb
    was moved.
 2. For research concerning the village's inhabitants see McKevitt 1991.

References

Amelar, S. 2004. 'Against the Profane, the Commercial, and the Mundane, Renzo
    Piano Strives to Create a Spiritual Pilgrimage Site at the Church of Padre Pio'.
    Architectural Record no. 195: 184–92.
Coleman, S., and J. Elsner. 1995. *Pilgrimage: Past and Present in World Religions.*
    Cambridge, MA: Harvard University Press.

da Ripabottoni, A., and G. di Flumeri. 1987. *Guide to the Shrine of Our Lady of Grace and Padre Pio's Friary.* San Giovanni Rotondo: Editions Padre Pio of Pietrelcina.

de Certeau, M. 1980. 'On the Oppositional Practices of Everyday Life'. *Social Text,* no. 3: 3–43

———. 1988. *The Practice of Everyday Life.* Berkley: University of California Press.

Dubisch, J. 1995. *In a Different Place: Pilgrimage, Gender and Politics at a Greek Island Shrine.* Princeton, NJ: Princeton University Press.

Eade, J. 1991. 'Order and Power at Lourdes: Lay Helpers and the Organization of a Pilgrimage Shrine'. In *Contesting the Sacred: The Anthropology of Christian Pilgrimage,* ed. J. Eade and M. J. Sallnow, 51–76. Urbana and Chicago: University of Illinois.

Eade, J., and M. J. Sallnow, eds. 1991. Introduction to *Contesting the Sacred: The Anthropology of Christian Pilgrimage,* 1–29. Urbana and Chicago: University of Illinois.

Guide to the Church of Saint Pio of Pietrelcina. n.d. Chiesa San Pio da Pietrelcina, The Monastery of Capuchin Minor Friars.

Hobsbawm, E., and T. Ranger, eds. 2002. *The Invention of Tradition.* Cambridge, UK: Cambridge University Press.

Margry, P. J. 2002. 'Merchandising and Sanctity: The Invasive Cult of Padre Pio'. *Journal of Modern Italian Studies* 7, no. 1: 88–115.

McDannel, C. 1995. *Material Christianity: Religion and Popular Culture in America.* New Heaven, CT: Yale University Press.

McKevitt, C. 1991. 'San Giovanni Rotondo and the Shrine of Padre Pio'. In *Contesting the Sacred: The Anthropology of Christian Pilgrimage,* ed. J. Eade and M. J. Sallnow (eds), 77–97. Urbana and Chicago: University of Illinois.

Mesaritou, E. 2009. 'The Dialectics of the Sacred: Institutionalization, Power and Transformation of Padre Pio's Charisma at the Shrine of Santa Maria delle Grazie'. Unpublished PhD thesis, University of Cambridge.

Miller, D. 2005. 'Materiality: An Introduction'. In *Materiality,* ed. D. Miller, 1–50. Durham, NC, and London: Duke University Press.

Morgan, D. 1998. *Visual Piety: A History and Theory of Popular Religious Images.* Berkley: University of California Press.

Morinis, A. 1992. 'Introduction: The Territory of the Anthropology of Pilgrimage'. In *Sacred Journeys: The Anthropology of Pilgrimage,* ed. A. Morinis, 1–28. Westport, CT: Greenwood Press.

Orsi, R. A. 2005. *Between Heaven and Earth: The Religious Worlds People Make and the Scholars Who Study Them.* Princeton, NJ: Princeton University Press.

Stewart, S. 1984. *On Longing: Narratives of the Miniature, the Gigantic, the Souvenir, the Collection.* Baltimore: Johns Hopkins University Press.

Wilson, S., ed. 1983. Introduction to *Saints and Their Cults: Studies in Religious Sociology, Folklore and History,* 1–53. Cambridge, UK: Cambridge University Press.

7

Going to the Mulid
Street-smart Spirituality in Egypt

Jennifer Peterson

'This is Islam in Egypt!
– bystander gesturing to ecstatic Sufi *dhikr* at the entrance to the
Al-Sayyida Zeinab mosque during the mulid of Al-Sayyida Zeinab, 2008

'Do you want to watch the soccer game in a café? How about seeing
a calf get slaughtered? No? You only want to watch the mulid?'
– bystander pointing to a group of teenage boys street-dancing
at the mulid of Fatima Al-Nabawiya, 2007

Introduction

Sprinkled, at times heavily, throughout the Islamic and Gregorian calendars, Egypt hosts countless saint festivals across the country every
year. They take place in urban centres, villages, oases, convents, and even
shrines remote from any permanent human settlement, such as that held
for Abul-Hassan Al-Shazli in the arid Red Sea mountains. These events
are called *mawalid* (sg. *mulid*), a word derived from the classical Arabic *mawlid* meaning birthday, although they typically commemorate the
death, rather than birth, of a revered pious figure. In the Islamic context,
which applies to the vast majority of such festivals and is the focus of this
chapter, mulids are hosted in honour of the Prophet Muhammad and his
family (*ahl al-bayt*), as well as a wide array of saints or 'friends of God'
(*awliya'*, sg. *wali*) ranging from Islamic scholars and Sufi leaders to devout ascetics and simple righteous folk popularly deemed saints for their
spiritual purity, closeness to God, and enactment of miracles.

Over the last decade, a grassroots trend of dance music in Egypt has adopted these festivals as its inspiration and namesake. Borrowing musically and lyrically from the Sufi song featured at mulids, the trend has transformed these festivals into a metaphorical motif of boisterous tunes popular at weddings and street parties. In some cases this trend playfully imitates the Sufi ritual and fairground fun found at mulids; in other cases it imparts messages of morality considered to be in line with spiritual teachings. In all cases, however, the mulid dance trend retains a rough and unruly feel suggestive of male youth culture in low-income neighbourhoods. It effuses a back-alley ambience that is down-to-earth and in touch with contemporary urban reality, projecting an attitude that is tough, jaded, irreverent and sometimes seedy, setting it firmly apart from the staid, virtuous and sentimental pop productions identified with the Islamic piety movements.

Upon initially encountering this trend, one might assume aesthetic and moral contradictions in its borrowing from Sufi ritual and festive tradition, and one may doubt that its lyrics so popular with street-smart youth could contain any degree of pious sincerity. As Asef Bayat (2007: 435) has discussed, the Islamist pious movements so intellectually popular now in Egypt show an animosity to fun that is common to most religious and secular frameworks that seek social hegemony, and the mulid dance trend is certainly not an overtly pious one that represents a form of 'controlled fun' (457); it is rambunctious, cheeky, and youthfully impertinent. Yet, as this chapter aims to show, aspects of the trend in fact reflect the everyday spirituality of Egyptian youth who seek to balance both piety and coolness without fully subjecting one standard to the other. Used in the everyday contexts of their streets, their groups of friends, and the celebrations of their family and neighbours, this trend playfully brings together various and sometimes contradictory aspects of their identities and modes of everyday action.

As Michael Jackson (1996: 2) notes in an introduction to phenomenological anthropology that focuses on the everyday and the concept of the lifeworld, or life as lived, 'The knowledge whereby one lives is not necessarily identical with the knowledge whereby one explains life.' In other words, people do not always practice what they preach, and nearly everyone's life at times runs counter to his or her convictions. The mulid, however, serves as a metaphor that allows for the interpretation of multiple kinds of lived experience all enacted under the umbrella of a higher religious authority, and thus lends itself as a model for the kind of moral balancing acts that fans of the mulid dance trend undertake. As such, this chapter aims to show how street-smart youth in Egypt adopt the exceptional, spectacular, all-encompassing festive moments of the mulid as an accommodating framework in which they negotiate both the knowledge that explains their lives and the ways that they actually want to live them.

Worldly Saint Festivals

Mulids are festivals in every sense of the word. Mostly night-time events, they can last from one day to two weeks and spread over entire city districts and cover kilometres of urban and rural space. As their raison d'être is the commemoration of a saint, they always include visits to the mulid's physical and symbolic centre – the saint's shrine, where special prayers are said and invocations made, symbolic gifts from the saint, such as rice pudding or dabs of musk, are distributed, and sessions of Sufi *dhikr,* a ritual 'mentioning' of God, are held. *Dhikr* practised in shrines typically consists of prayers, poetry and singing accompanied by frame drum, the only musical instrument that is widely held as officially permissible by Islam.

Outside the shrine, a primary feature at most mulids are the more ecstatic *dhikr* sessions hosted by Sufi patrons in temporarily constructed spaces – often colourful tents – that are called services. These spaces offer shelter, hot drinks, food, and amplified Sufi music and song called *inshad,* as well as a carpeted area in which to rhythmically sway to the live performance. This movement-oriented *dhikr* ranges from controlled breathing and synchronized swaying, leaps, and gymnastic contortions to highly individualistic and free-form bodily expressions; it is believed to foster the attainment of heightened spiritual states. In contrast to *dhikr* held inside the shrine, the musical accompaniment at services may include reed flutes, tambourines, goblet-shaped drums, finger cymbals, violins, lutes (*al-'ud*), electric keyboards, and, in some very rare cases, electric guitars.

Like at all outdoor Egyptian festivities ranging from weddings to the grand opening of small businesses, the festive atmosphere of mulids is accentuated by strings of flashing coloured lights that are draped over the shrine, mosque, services and streets of the area. The brightly coloured emblematic flags of Sufi orders and the framed portraits of their sheikhs are hung on tents, buildings, poles and even trees. Vendors set up stalls selling sweets, roasted chickpeas and other snacks, as well as toys, party hats, cassette tapes and religious items such as prayer beads and books. A fairground area typically includes swings, shooting galleries, magic shows and games of chance. Families open up their homes to guests and picnic in public parks, while local youth deck out in their most fashionable and stroll about to see and be seen. Groups of boys wildly push their way through the crowds, carousing and harassing girls. Wedding and night club bands perform at outdoor cafés, and youth set up DJ stations in the streets. The overall mood is of joyous and carefree celebration in a festive sphere that allows one to sample an array of amusements and distractions of one's choice.

The overlap of the spiritual and the secular is an intrinsic feature of mulids. The notion of baraka, a type of locally-effusive spiritual energy, is believed to spread from the saint's presence concentrated at the shrine to the entire mulid area, imbuing even material souvenirs with a kind of blessing. Without both the spiritual and the more secular aspects of its celebration, a mulid simply would not be one. Two Egyptian colloquial sayings stress the essentiality of each of these factors – one is '*mulid wa sahibu ghayib*' (a mulid without a saint), which is used as a metaphor for utter chaos with neither rhyme nor reason. The other is '*tili' min il-mulid bi-la humus*' (he left the mulid without any chickpeas) meaning that someone failed to benefit from something obvious or reach a primary goal. It can be inferred from these sayings that mulids are left meaningless if one misses either their saints or their fairground treats and pleasures.

The youthful dance trend that borrows from the mulid milieu builds upon this intrinsic commingling of the spiritual and the secular. It feeds from the logic whereby, according to the quotes introducing this chapter, Islam can be spectacular and exceptional, just as rowdy dancing youth can exemplify a saint festival. It reformulates mulids as noisy expressions of joy and merrymaking that offer a musical means of accessing the out-of-the-ordinary, even in the everyday, and all the while allowing for a mix of thrill-seeking with more pious pursuits. For society's street, where the cacophony of life includes popular music, Qur'anic recitation, the cries of street vendors, fights and laughter, is after all not so far from the concept or reality of the mulid's *saha*, that open space where people and experiences of all kinds converge under the umbrella of spiritual commemoration.[1]

The Popularity of Mulid Dance Songs

Mulid dance songs were first developed in the street-wedding milieu during 2001 when a 24-year-old keyboard player in a low-income neighbourhood of Cairo introduced musical ornamentation to dance songs that was clearly borrowed from Sufi *inshad* melodies. Singer Gamal Al-Sobky soon added lyrics stressing the mulid connection, borrowing text from *inshad* and shouting phrases such as 'Let's go to the mulid!' The trend was then adopted by numerous singers and DJs, featuring in the repertoire of five-star hotel and night club performer Saad Al-Sughayr as well as in the productions of unknown DJs and singers performing in small studios or on the street.

Despite the relative variety found in the source, production, quality and tone of mulid songs, they all fall within the larger Egyptian music genre of *sha'bi* and can be collectively considered a sub-genre of it. *Sha'bi* literally means 'popular' with a focus on the word's sense as being 'of the people', although the Arabic word's other connotations of 'liked by many' and 'folkloric' are also relevant to its description (and *sha'bi* is furthermore used to label much more than music). Music television professional and *sha'bi* fan Yasser Abdel-Latif (2007) describes the rough, working-class realism of the *sha'bi* genre as a kind of urban blues 'whose content revolves around cursing fate and its treachery that destroys pleasure and disperses communities, as well as love concerns of a sensual nature. ... This is in addition to the raw, untamed performance of this sector's singers and their rough voices that pour over music that is a mix of the city's clamour and crowdedness ...' (2007: 223). Fans of *sha'bi* music appreciate what they perceive as an unassuming attitude, simple honesty, and a down-to-earth approach that remains in touch with contemporary urban reality. Although *sha'bi* songs may be exaggeratedly emotional at times, they are still generally deemed more authentic and reflective of mass culture than comparable ballads in corporate-styled pop, for example.

On the flip-side, however, *sha'bi* is regarded by its detractors as lowbrow and vulgar. And within the *sha'bi* genre, mulid songs tend to be associated with its more immediately urban street-level end. They were developed at the kind of street weddings in which beer, hashish, scantily-clad dancers and fights are common, and where the family celebrations thus assume a coarser, more night club-like feel than others. Most of the trend's singers hail from the relatively rough neighbourhoods of Imbaba and Shubra Al-Kheima, semi-informal areas that have developed on Cairo's margins over the last three decades and whose migrant inhabitants are seen as socially rootless and therefore unaccountable compared to residents of the longer established communities of Cairo's central *sha'bi* neighbourhoods. Given this overall context, it is unsurprising then that much of the trend's recorded production has taken place in exceedingly informal circuits – in small, family-owned production companies on the high end and on grubby home computers on the low end. Similarly, the distribution of mulid songs is predominantly facilitated by the bootleg cassette tape industry, internet downloads, and the informal swapping of music files. The marginalized production and distribution of mulid songs, together with the associations of their social contexts, mark the trend with an extremely lowbrow artistic status, identified with its clamourous sound and the sight of young men dancing to it with knife props and erotic gestures.

Mulid dance songs, then, most obviously reflect the 'of the people', or grassroots, character of *sha'bi* music. Yet they are also, roughly a decade since their debut, continuing to maintain a high level of popularity, with the continual production of new songs and the commandment of a persistently high priority at street celebrations. Mulid dance songs are moreover influencing other styles of music by lending ornamentation to *sha'bi* songs that are not so strictly mulid, and even by having portions of their musical and lyrical elements readopted by performers of Sufi *inshad*. And although the mulid dance trend remains purely *sha'bi*, its popularity means that it is also slowly creeping into mainstream media venues, featured in the soundtracks of commercial films (usually in wedding party scenes) and now even boasting professionally directed music videos.[2] Late 2011 saw the launch of a satellite television station devoted to *sha'bi* music videos, and while mulid songs are featured in only a small proportion of the broadcast, the channel is cashing in on the trend's popularity, calling itself "Al-mulid".[3]

Going to the Mulid

When Gamal Al-Sobky first shouted 'Let's go to the mulid!' and this phrase was adopted by the trend he helped to launch, going to the mulid implied many things. Foremost it suggested seeking the out-of-the-ordinary by turning the everyday into an exceptional experience filled with fun, excitement and wonder. It meant being out on the street, where the public space's inherent unpredictability makes one anticipate a certain degree of danger, thrill and adventure. There, in the mulid's *saha* or on the everyday street, real and would-be festival-goers can take their pick from an array of delights, spontaneously celebrating the moment in the style of their choosing. It is this very smorgasbord of celebratory experience that subsequent mulid dance songs have reflected, ranging in tone and content from exuberantly mirthful and hip yet pious to seedily tongue-in-cheek.

The characteristic of the mulid trend that has probably contributed the most to its success is that 'it has a good beat and you can dance to it', danceability being an essential criterion for songs played at all Egyptian festivities.[4] Weddings, where mulid dance songs originated, are called *afrah* (sg. *farah*), occasions of unfettered 'joy' that are essentially deafening dance parties orchestrated from start to finish by a DJ or the MC of a live band. Yet *farah* is a term also used to refer to mulids themselves, where the commemorated death of saints marks their union with God in the afterlife, and where celebrations are largely rhythmically centred, exuberant, and carefree. Thus here a kind of dance party atmosphere also exists; as Michael Frishkopf (2001: 236, 246.) points out, 'the processes of expressive emotion in Sufi *inshad* may appear similar to those of *sha'bi* ('popular') singing. Indeed, Sufi and secular music in Egypt, rural and urban, do share many elements [with regard to shared melodic motifs and] a dance-like ethos.' Rhythmic movement, ecstasy and joyful communality are essential elements of both mulids and the other contexts in which mulid dance songs are featured, explaining in part why inshad has been so easily adopted by this trend.[5]

While most mulid dance songs feature simple musical borrowings from the Sufi milieu, making alterations through repetition, electronic ornamentation and driving *sha'bi* dance beats, others add *inshad* lyrics and Sufi-inspired refrains of spiritual and moral intent that are performed in styles largely faithful to the spirit of their origin. A prominent example are the songs of Mahmoud Al-Leithy, a young *sha'bi* star who made his break in 2005 with a song that draws conspicuously on the lyrics and styles of popular *munshidin* (sg. *munshid*, singer of *inshad*) including Sheikh 'Arabi

Farhan Al-Balbisi of the Delta and Sheikh Yassin Al-Tuhami from Upper Egypt, in addition to borrowings from the Beni Hilal epic, a performance of song and spoken narration considered a pillar of Egyptian folklore. Al-Leithy has since produced numerous mulid-inspired hits, including *'sidi abd al-rahim'* (Saint Abdel Rahim), which incorporates the raspy, rhythmical breathing of *dhikr* participants as a repetitive musical element, and *'mulid fi hubb al-rasul – madad ya dasuqi'* (Mulid in love of the Prophet – support oh [Saint] Dasuqi), in which he sings, inshad-style, 'I am a dervish walking in the light of God. Whoever is with their Lord will never get lost.'

Al-Leithy's focus on the mulid style is partly explained by the fact that he describes himself as emotionally attached to source of inspiration. He nostalgically tells of being raised in the mulid milieu with circus-performer relatives and a grandfather who taught him *madih*, which means praise (of the Prophet) and is generally interchangeable with the term *inshad*.[6] Al-Leithy says that singing *madih* is 'the most beautiful thing in the world. The best speech that comes out, the most sincere, is that singing'. He describes his mulid style as a mission of music with a message, (*al-fann al-hadif*, art with a purpose), one in which he strives to make *madih* chic and its message therefore attractive to youth. Al-Leithy boasts that his style has been approved by Amr Khalid, the multimedia preacher so popular with middle class youth: 'What did Amr Khalid tell them? Mahmoud Al-Leithy is a *sha'bi* singer who has delivered his message in his style, in his own milieu, his *sha'bi* milieu' (Rahhal 2009: 15.03).

Mahmoud Al-Husseiny is another young *sha'bi* singer whose repertoire includes songs of moralistic orientation. While Al-Husseiny maintains a rougher, more rambunctious edge than Al-Leithy does, he likewise speaks of delivering virtuous messages:

> If I were a sermon-giver, it would be the committed who would listen to me. But I want to reach the people who are not committed and tell them to commit. If I stood in a mosque, who would listen to me? Those who pray. Okay, those who don't pray – who speaks to them? Who tells them? The artist. It's a matter of outreach.[7]

Al-Husseiny tells of being contacted by a girl who says she started praying after listening to his sentimental track *'yom al-hisab'* (Day of Reckoning). She is one of several who have relayed to him testimonies of spiritual awakenings, and Al-Husseiny is proud, 'overjoyed,' he says, that his songs have wrought such results.

Despite their relative righteousness, however, mulid songs with the moralistic approach taken by Al-Leithy and Al-Husseiny nonetheless retain a distinctively rough *sha'bi* feel. This street tone is produced through the use of *sha'bi* vocal styles, shifts in the tone of lyrics and music, the ubiquitous use of driving, rambunctious dance rhythms, and ambiguity in the arrangement of lyrics that both celebrate waywardness and make a case for repentance. They are not alone in adopting moralistic or spiritual themes – the production of religiously oriented songs is found in many Egyptian music genres, including the pop scene (such as the religious songs of stars Muhammad Munir and Amr Diab, for example), Islamist *nashid*, and the so-called halal movement that cleans existent songs of what it holds as impious lyrics.[8] Yet in comparison to the consistently staid tone of such songs, which carefully maintain a pristine projection of purity and uprightness, the sound of mulid dance songs shifts between the piously moral and the jadedly tough. In keeping with the realism of the *sha'bi* genre, moralistic mulid dance songs retain and even emphasize a street-smart ambience even as they might earnestly express or negotiate notions of morality and spirituality.

There are certainly mulid dance songs devoid of sincere references to spirituality, however, songs whose main or only reference to mulids is as an object of cheekily irreverent jest. These songs may have an exceedingly rowdy feel or a sleazy ambience to them, making explicit references to drug and alcohol use or employing the affected vocals of assumably disreputable women. Saint veneration, Sufi ritual and the humble forms of entertainment found at mulids are made to seem laughably naïve when placed in juxtaposition to the street-smart or seedy milieus associated with urban back-alleys or cheap night clubs.

One example of this untamed style is a track titled '*mulid karkar 1*' (The mulid of Karkar 1), in which a saucy-sounding woman speaks of the hash dealer downstairs and asks God to forgive him when he doesn't have any marijuana to give her. Another example opens with a moralistic *mawwal* but soon moves on to a driving dance rhythm and a motley array of lyrics all performed in a coarse style, including brazen female vocals that suggestively invite those who don't want to play to watch.[9] This song imitates a boy begging for a party hat at the mulid, innocence crudely mocked through the song's other associations with deviance and vice.

Street-smart Spirituality

The first professional music video for a mulid song, Nasser Saqr's '*lili lili*' (a nonsense word), drives home its moralising message through the use of story-telling visuals.[10] The song bewails self-interestedness and evil, and calls on sinners to repent before the door to God's forgiveness is closed to them (see annex one). The video's visuals alternate between scenes of immorality and vice (gambling, drinking, theft, murder and romancing with multiple women, some of them scantily clad foreigners) and scenes of piety and spirituality (reading the Qur'an, a father kissing a pious son, a mulid featuring stilt-walkers and whirling dervishes, as well as a Coptic priest preaching to children). The singer plays dramatic roles in both the immoral and moral segments, suggesting that the character he portrays experienced wrongdoing and then repented. Although the song and video have a clearly moralistic tone, its *sha'bi* dance elements keep it street-level and anything but stuffy, while the singer's dual role makes the message more ambiguous than it would have been if preached from beyond the underworld. Given its artistic and conceptual appeal to street-smart youth, the humility and assumed realism of this message likely make it more convincing than would have strictly normative preaching.

Yet Saqr's song and video are not the only moralistic mulid dance productions willing to get their hands dirty, as it were. Widely popular songs performed by Mahmoud Al-Husseiny, *'al-'abd wa-l-shaytan'* (The worshipper and Satan), parts one and two, tell similar tales of wild living and repentance. Their lyrics (see annex two) form a dialogue in which Satan tempts the worshipper with a fun-loving, carefree lifestyle and initially succeeds in commanding his following. When the worshipper subsequently regrets the path that he has taken, Satan taunts him to no avail. The worshipper repents, resumes fulfilling his religious obligations, and writes off his past as a lesson to others. Yet by the logic of the song that past did happen, and the song's performance and use suggest a certain glee in this after-the-matter fact. The singer's voice is rough, the music is rambunctious, and the phrase 'drink Johnny Walker' is repeated with a sense of hilarity – with young DJs sometimes looping it in performance, temporarily inverting the song's message.

Fans of mulid dance songs say the appeal of *'al-'abd wa-l-shaytan'* is partly found in the realism of its lyrics. They deem the rhetoric a style that people they personally know would use, while the theme of conflicting desires – of enjoying the world's temptations and yet ultimately being what they consider upright Muslims – is one to which they relate. Most of those interviewed for this research stressed the importance of gaining first-hand knowledge in all realms of experience, including drug use and illicit encounters with the opposite sex. Yet they also spoke of personal religious preoccupations that suggest conflicts between their moralistic ideals and convictions, on the one hand, and their desire for the pursuit of pleasure and worldliness, on the other.

One of the thornier issues these youth addressed was a conflict between their religious beliefs and their passion for music itself. This is a dilemma shared even by music professionals, including Salah Al-Kurdi, the young keyboard player who first incorporated the mulid motif into *sha'bi* dance music. Al-Kurdi believes that music is haram, forbidden by Islam, even as he says, 'but I love this thing, I love music. I'm not doing something bad'.[11] Salah finds no way to reconcile the conflict between his belief that music is haram and the irresistible draw that he feels to listen to and play it other than accepting that both are inevitable givens of his existence: 'The matter [music] is truly forbidden, but this is something that I grew up loving – it's in my blood and in my body. May God forgive me,' he says.

A similar case to Al-Kurdi's is that of Mahmoud, a DJ who is passion-
ate about music but who also believes that it is haram.[12] Despite this conviction, he continues to work in a small DJ business and indulges in the
indisputably haram pleasures this scene makes available – he gleefully tells
of the time vodka cocktails inspired his drunkenly superb performance.
Muhammad, as another example, is a music fan with a 20-gigabyte collection of sha'bi music who tells of once renouncing this passion when he fell
in with Islamists. Fearful of the intelligence agencies, he later reneged on
this path and is again an active music fan – although the spiritual peace he
describes feeling during his Islamist phase suggests the likelihood of his
undergoing further lifestyle fluctuations in the future.[13]

A generation past the spread of sermon cassette tapes, at a time when
Islamic satellite stations are commanding high popularity across social
classes throughout the country, aspects of fundamentalist (*salafi*) thought
have become an intellectual norm in Egypt, and yet still the embodiment
of a strictly *salafi* lifestyle remains the choice of a committed minority.
Rather than questioning *salafi* dictates on religion, it is more common to
find conflicted individuals functioning within an unquestioned and over-
arching religious framework, struggling to find a balance between what
they are convinced they should do and how they actually act. The result
is what Husam Tammam calls a *mazaag salafi*, or a *salafi* 'mood', in which
salafism has become popularized in a light-hearted Egyptian style that allows for a balance between religious commitment and a love for life, an
hour for your Lord and an hour for your heart, as the colloquial Egyptian
saying goes.[14] As opposed to the 1970s and 80s, Tammam says, when spiritual paths and lifestyles were clearly delineated, everything is now mixed
together in Egypt, where you find salafism within Sufism, non-veiled girls
with *salafi* ideas, and even cases such as Salafis hawking shiny emblems
of commercial globalization – heart-shaped balloons that boldly state in
English 'I love you'.[15]

The *sha'bi* youth who constitute the primary fan base of mulid dance
songs thus exhibit an ambivalent relationship with pious practice, not
with religion itself. Openly-declared atheists and even agnostics remain
rare and shunned in Egypt, 'not knowing God' being equated with de-
praved murderers, social deviants with no sense of moral accountability.
In contrast to American Christian rock, the spiritual identity of which
is largely seen as a killjoy force and thus enjoys only a small and highly
religious popular base, the street-smart attitude that the *sha'bi* dance trend
brings to its mulid borrowings only makes more palatable what are already accepted dictates of morality. Some of the practices related to the
use of mulid dance songs illustrate just how inseparable the trend is from
its Islamic milieu: DJs who play mulid and other dance songs at street
festivities typically commence the evening's amplified sound with recorded Qur'anic recitation, usually followed at weddings by a song listing
Islam's 99 names for God. Another practice hard to imagine being cool

in an American Christian context is DJs shouting out encouragement to partygoers along the lines of 'If you love the Prophet, clap your hands!', at which point everyone, including those drinking beer or smoking hashish, does. And in an ingrained show of respect, DJs typically pull the plug when the call to prayer sounds, and may wait until the prayer ends to resume their noisemaking.[16]

Rather than contesting religious frameworks, then, fans of mulid dance songs are negotiating how to have fun in the here and now while still securing their place in heaven. They are certainly not the only youth in the Islamic world to be attempting this balance, however. In their research on Shi'i youth and leisure in Beirut, where middle class youth date at 'halal cafés' and 'some pious individuals find it acceptable to go to the movies as long as they look away from the scenes deemed immoral' and others 'claim to "disengage" from the soundtrack', Lara Deeb and Mona Harb (2007: 14) have found that 'youth practices and discourses of morality are flexible in their deployments, perhaps especially when it comes to ideas about leisure and sexuality, and … this interpretive flexibility works to redefine ideas about sexuality and leisure within a framework of religiosity'.[17] Asef Bayat (2007: 441) writes of what he calls subversive accommodation in Tehran, where 'God existed but did not prevent them from drinking alcohol or dating the opposite sex. The globalising Iranian youth reinvented their religiosity, blending the transcendental with the secular, faith with freedom, divine with diversion'. And the so-called 'lite Islam' of Egypt's middle class youth feeds from and to commercial productions ranging from music videos to talk shows to striking veiled fashions as its followers imbue their cushy, material lives with a neo-Islamic flair.[18]

Yet in contrast to these other youth orientations, the mulid dance trend does not overtly identify itself with Islamic piety movements or claim to reconcile Islamic virtues with cultural globalization. Grounded in the down-to-earth working-class attitudes of its *sha'bi* environs, the mulid dance trend and its fan base are more flexible with regard to religion and spirituality, accepting them as unquestioned givens of local identity even while balancing them with other social paradigms that would seem to undermine them. Samuli Schielke (2009: 166) analyses this balancing act by looking at how people switch moral registers as they negotiate the various demands of everyday life, explaining that 'Morality is not a coherent system but an incoherent and unsystematic conglomerate of different moral registers that exist parallel to and often contradict each other.' In his study of the everyday lives of young men in a Nile Delta village, Schielke (2009: 166–67) identifies seven key normative registers, or 'modalities of moral speech and action' that youth use to make sense of their selves and to justify their (sometimes contradictory) lifestyle choices: religion, respect, good character, family, social justice and rights, love, and success and self-realization. The first two of these are central to the *sha'bi* notions of morality as exemplified by some mulid dance songs, while the last one partially represents and complements the register of being street-smart, an additional standard that the young and male in Cairo's back alleys aspire to. Youth living in *sha'bi* neighbourhoods say they have to be street-smart in order to negotiate the ever-corrupting world around them, even as they stress the importance of not becoming (too) morally corrupt themselves.

This complex equation is successfully embodied by friends Shiko and Mustafa, known for their spectacular knife dancing to mulid music and the toughened street attitudes that it poses. They stress that their performance is a kind of 'respectable deviance' that looks tough and intimidating, but is in fact an innocent, theatrical show, and they condemn the 'true deviants' who arbitrarily impose their might on the weak.[19] Music fan Amr is another example – describing himself as both 'deviant' and 'respectable', he admits to taking drugs and engaging in premarital sex even while making efforts to become ever more religiously committed.[20] Fashionably tough in dark sunglasses, longish hair and leather bracelets, he sprinkles his speech with pious phrases and his trendy cell phone has a religious chant as its ring tone. Anyone who isn't streetwise in his neighbourhood would be eaten alive, he says, forcing him and other youth to balance their moral convictions with a projection of back-alley worldliness.

Conclusion

In his study of extreme music scenes and 'post-Islamism' across the Middle East, Mark LeVine (2008) describes heavy metal fans in the Arab world as, rather than incongruous outcasts, markers of the increasing diversity of contemporary Islam. Of young heavy metal fans in Egypt, he writes:

> Most are able to find space inside their moral and aesthetic universe for rock and religion. For many the dividing line is quite hard to find. 'Look, you can be a metalien [Egyptian for metalhead] and a good Muslim at the same time,' they explained. … Indeed, for them rock, religion and rebellion are all of a piece. Each endeavour supports the other two. (2008: 238)

While mulid dance aficionados share with these metal fans a balancing of coolness with spirituality, the approach of mulid dance fans is closer to 'you can be street-smart, a good Muslim, and not-always-so-good a Muslim at the same time'. Saqr's '*lili lili*' in particular makes explicit the notion that a relative reconciliation of waywardness and piousness is offered through the possibility of repentance, and this recognition implicitly sanctions the enactment of vice. Both '*lili lili*' and '*al-'abd wa-l-shaytan*' mirthfully acknowledge that believers can, and are, easily led astray by their earthly desires, even as they emphasize that this does not 'close the door' to their subsequent embodiment of moral ideals.

Rather than a subversive contestation of religious hegemony or moralistic dictates, however, this light-hearted negotiation of behavioural pulls simply reflects the various, often contradictory standards to which *sha'bi* youth in Egypt hold themselves. Katherine Ewing (1990) describes such oscillations in moral registers as typical of the social human condition: 'The same individual may shift frames of reference from one context to another, even from one moment to the next, and may tolerate considerable inconsistency in his or her own beliefs and opinions, often without realizing it,' (1990: 268) even as that individual may maintain the sense of an overall whole and cohesive identity. Or as Michael Jackson (1996) frames it:

> The lifeworld is never a seamless, unitary domain in which social relations remain constant and the experience of self remains stable. Nor is it ever arcadian: it is a scene of turmoil, ambiguity, resistance, dissimulation, and struggle. ... An empirically faithful concept of experience has first to recognize this multifaceted character of the person – the fact that experience of self, or of self in relation to other, is continually adjusted to and modulated by circumstance. (1996: 27)

Singer Mahmoud Al-Husseiny puts this in terms of what he calls the various mental states of people, states that he says require various aural inputs – romantic or sad songs, sermons, dance music – to suit their mood of the moment and serve their fluctuating existential needs.[21] So when mulid dance songs reflect the juggling of earthly realities with pious ideals, of the attempt to be street-smart and worldly on the one hand and morally upright and faithful to religious conviction on the other, they are in fact simultaneously serving competing needs. Yet another example of *sha'bi* music's realism, this sensitive relevance to the complex subtleties of being young, hip, tough and upright in Egypt today surely explains in part the mulid dance trend's immense popularity.

Annex One:

Translated lyrics of Nasser Saqr's '*lili lili*'

> Allah!
> Oh Merciful!
> Oh Forgiving!
> Oh Creator!
> Oh Lord!
>
> Who aims for the door of the generous, his door is opened.
> Who acts with a pure heart, no door is closed to him.
> Act in time, oh sinner, repent
> before the door is closed on you.

Saint lililililililili….
My beloved lililililililili….

Kindness has long disappeared,
and the people, oh Lord, helped it go.
Even siblings, oh Daddy, have become like wolves.

Saint lililililililili….
My beloved lililililililili….

Allah!

Everyone is after their own interests and that's all;
they aren't interested in anything else.
There are people who are crazy about evil,
and don't take note of anything else.

Saint lililililililili….
My beloved lililililililili….

Allah!

Have mercy on us, oh Lord,
You know us well.
Have mercy, oh Lord, on your worshippers,
and rescue us from what we're in.

Saint lililililililili….
My beloved lililililililili….

Annex Two

Translated lyrics of Mahmoud Al-Husseiny's '*al-'abd wa-l-shaytan*' (The worshipper and Satan), parts one and two:

Translation of Part One:

To begin my speech I pray upon the Prophet
I'll tell stories and lessons,
study me and learn.

Satan told the worshipper,
'All your life you've prayed, and praised God and fasted.

All your life you've been preoccupied with the Eternally Alive.
Why don't you get lively and go to the movies
and play a round of dominoes?
Play ...
The woman living across from you
is distracting you,
so give her your attention, you're about to lose her.'

The worshipper said to Satan,
'Oh enemy of humans,
oh outcast by the Merciful,
among the traditions of our chosen Prophet,
there are several pieces of wisdom, oh Satan, about neighbours.'

Satan told the worshipper,
'If you drank, you lousy fool,
you'd feel like a kid.
With a bottle of cognac,
your worries would leave you.'

The worshipper said to Satan,
'Have you come to laugh at my propriety?
I'm a man, an educated man.
It'd be best for you to leave me,
or else I'll hit you with my cane.
Wouldn't it be shameful for me to stagger,
and roll about in the mud,
and make a scene with my family and neighbours?'

People are such wonders,
they're nothing but a tongue
that speaks nonsense.

Translation of Part Two:

Gogogogogogogogo
Oh Daddy oh Daddy oh Daddy

The first lesson in love:
I called out 'in the name of God' as I sang.
I seek the forgiveness of God Almighty for what happened with me.

Satan told the worshipper,
'I showed you the world in all its colours,

and you sold heaven for me and began to fear leaving the world.
You even forgot your prayer and religious duty.
In the beginning I pulled you,
And due to your weakness I drugged you.
You learned how to lie and play with your neighbour,
and to play …
You started playing poker
and drinking Johnny Walker,
and drinking …'

Gogogogogogogogogo
Oh Daddy oh Daddy oh Daddy

The worshipper told Satan,
'After obeying you
I no longer knew how to live.
You took me to hell and then disowned me.'

Satan told the worshipper,
'Why don't you get up
and go out with some women?
Make a mess of yourself,
spend all you've got.
If you want to rebel,
you're doing a good job.
Why don't you get out your money
and pay some tips,
or are you one of those?
Why don't you light up and smoke some hashish,
or are we in a gas station?'

Gogogogogogogogogo
Oh Daddy oh Daddy oh Daddy

The worshipper told Satan
'I'll leave sinning to you
and go visit the Prophet of God,
and if you come to me
I'll repel you with verses from the book of God.
As long as I go back to praying,
you won't be able to reach me,
and people will learn from all that happened to me.'

Notes

1. For more on the metaphorical travelling of mulids into dance music and spaces, see Peterson 2008b.
2. The majority of mulid dance song videos are home-made productions in which mulid tracks are played over typically unrelated images, such as footage taken from European television of people dancing in nightclubs, or cell-phone videos of Egyptian and Arab women in nightgowns dancing suggestively in private homes. These videos are uploaded on the internet and commonly distributed through cell phones.
3. Al-Mulid and Sha'biyat, another *sha'bi* music video station that debuted at the same time, were predecessed by satellite television stations broadcasting uninterrupted sha'bi music to static screen images.
4. Quote by Amber von Tussle in the 1988 John Waters film *Hairspray*.
5. For more on *mulid* dance music and weddings, see Peterson 2008b.
6. Interview with Mahmoud Al-Leithy, Imbaba, 25 April 2007.
7. Interview with Mahmoud Al-Husseiny, Al-Matariyya, 18 September 2009.
8. *Nashid* is etymologically related to the term *inshad* and implies religious anthems and hymns, ranging from the militant to the modern and romantic (see also Frishkopf 2000).
9. A *mawwal* is a traditional form of lamenting sung verse that is often used as an opening to songs. The song referred to here is a variant of *'al-'abd wa-l-shaytan'* (The worshipper and Satan) apparently performed by Gamal Al-Sobky.
10. An earlier video was produced for Saad Al-Sughayr's *'naruh al-mulid'* (Let's go to the mulid), but this song was part of a movie soundtrack and the clip consisted almost entirely of film segments, serving as promotion for the film (*lakhmat ras* – A Mixed up Head, Ahmed Al-Badri, Cairo: Al-Sobky Film, 2006).
11. Interview with Salah Al-Kurdi, Al-Waily, 18 November 2009.
12. Interview with DJ Mahmoud, Sayyida Sakina, August 2008.
13. Interview with Muhammad in Al-Mazallat, August 2008.
14. Lecture titled *"id al-hubb: qira'a fi al-jadal al-thiqafi wa al-dini bi-misr"* (Valentine's Day: A Reading of Cultural and Religious Debate in Egypt) given at the Centre d'Études et de Documentation Économiques, Juridiques et Sociales (CEDEJ) in Cairo on 23 February 2010.
15. Reference to Salafi man selling heart-shaped balloons related by Samuli Schielke, February 2010.
16. For more on the relationship between religious frameworks and the mulid dance trend, see Peterson 2008a.
17. This final quote is from the abstract of their paper titled 'Piety and Pleasure: Youth Negotiations of Moral Authority in Al-Dahiya (Beirut)', presented at the Bahithat 14 Workshop on the Cultural Practices of Youth in the Arab World, Beirut, 12 December 2009.
18. See Haenni and Tammam 2003 and Kubala 2007.
19. Interview with Shiko and Mustafa, Al-Darb Al-Ahmar, August 2008.
20. Interview with Amr, Imbaba, August 2008.
21. Interview with Mahmoud Al-Husseiny, Al-Matariyya, 18 September 2009.

References

Abdel-Latif, Y. 2007. 'musiqa al-shari'', in *Amkenah: ta'ni bi-thaqafat al-makan*, Book 8, Alexandria, 232–37.

Bayat, A. 2007. 'Islamism and the Politics of Fun'. *Public Culture* 19, no. 3: 433–59.

Deeb, L., and M. Harb. 2007. 'Sanctioned Pleasures: Youth, Piety and Leisure in Beirut'. *Middle East Report: The Politics of Youth* 245, no. 4: 12–19.

Ewing, K. P. 1990. 'The Illusion of Wholeness: Culture, Self, and the Experience of Inconsistency'. *Ethos* 18, no. 3: 251–78.

Frishkopf, M. 2000. 'Inshad Dini and Aghani Diniyya in Twentieth Century Egypt: A Review of Styles, Genres, and Available Recordings'. *Middle East Studies Association Bulletin* 34, no. 2: 167–83.

———. 2001. 'Tarab ('Enchantment') in the Mystic Sufi Chant of Egypt'. In *Colors of Enchantment: Theater, Dance, Music, and the Visual Arts of the Middle East*, ed. S. Zuhur, 233–69. Cairo: The American University in Cairo Press.

Haenni, P., and H. Tammam. 2003. 'Chat Shows, Nashid Groups and Lite Preaching: Egypt's Air-conditioned Islam'. *Le Monde Diplomatique*, English ed., September. http://mondediplo.com/2003/09/03egyptislam (retrieved 13 April 2010).

Jackson, M. 1996. 'Introduction: Phenomenology, Radical Empiricism, and Anthropological Critique'. In *Things as They Are: New Directions in Phenomenological Anthropology*, ed. M. Jackson, 1–50. Bloomington: Indiana University Press.

Kubala, P. 2007. 'Satellite TV and Islamic Pop Culture in Egypt'. *ISIM Review*, no. 20: 60–61.

LeVine, M. 2008. 'Heavy Metal Muslims: The Rise of a Post-Islamist Sphere'. *Contemporary Islam: Dynamics of Muslim Life* 2, no. 3: 229–49.

Peterson, J. 2008a. 'Playing with Spirituality: The Adoption of Mulid Motifs in Egyptian Dance Music'. *Contemporary Islam: Dynamics of Muslim Life* 2, no. 3: 271–95.

———. 2008b. 'Remixing Songs, Remaking Mulids: The Merging Spaces of Dance Music and Saint Festivals in Egypt'. In Dimensions of Locality: Muslim Saints, their Place and Space, *Yearbook of the Sociology of Islam* 8, ed. S. Schielke and G. Stauth, 67–88. Bielefeld: Transcript Verlag.

'sha'bi'. 2009. Documentary film by Ahmed Rahhal, 21:47, Alexandria.

Schielke, S. 2009. 'Ambivalent Commitments: Troubles of Morality, Religiosity and Aspiration among Young Egyptians'. *Journal of Religion in Africa*, no. 39: 158–85.

8

Capitalist Ethics and
the Spirit of Islamization in Egypt

Samuli Schielke

A Post-revolutionary Preface

As this chapter goes to press in early 2012, Egypt is in a state of transition following the January 25 revolution. Some of what is written in the present tense in the following pages already belongs to the past. I have decided not to rewrite the chapter (originally written between 2008 and 2010) to make it up to date. Things are still changing too quickly to do that. The reader should therefore bear in mind the historicity of this chapter, describing not a lasting condition but rather a unique momentum in a changing world.

What can already be said with certainty, however, is that the situation I describe in this chapter has been one of the grounds of the revolutionary uprising. As Walter Armbrust has pointed out in an early analysis (2011), the January 25 revolution was directed against the frustrating conditions of life that had emerged through the neoliberal entrenchment of economy and politics since the 1970s. At the same time, however, the Egyptian revolution has not been an anti-capitalist one. While directed against oligarchs, corruption and everyday frustration and humiliation, it is firmly grounded in expectations of economical growth, material well-being, and a vision of Egypt as a God-fearing society. If things go well, some of the problems that this chapter describes – such as nepotism and corruption – may become a little less pressing. But the pressure of a future so characteristic of both capitalism and revivalist religiosity, will remain. One thing the revolution will not bring to Egyptians is contentedness.

The Presence of Religion

In contemporary Egypt, Islam is omnipresent in daily life. This has not always been so. Although a visible and deep attachment to either one of Egypt's two prevalent religious traditions – Islam and Christianity – has a long history in Egypt, the current turn to religion that began in the 1970s is in many ways novel. Unlike in earlier times when the significance of religion could be perhaps best described as a constant presence of God in daily life, today Muslims have increasingly come to understand their faith as a perfect and objective system that is at once the definite guideline of daily life and external to it. Based on the aim to learn and implement this system, Muslims' attempts to imagine and live a good life have thus become strongly characterized by an ideal of purity and perfection. At a closer look, however, this pursuit of perfection turns out to be a very complex matter. As I have argued elsewhere, it does not exclude other, partly contrary, and yet equally perfectionist pursuits such as love (Schielke 2009). More importantly perhaps, and this is the issue I pursue in this chapter, the very aim of religious perfection itself is part of a complex social experience and cannot be understood separately from parallel aims and experiences. Many, albeit not all, of them are intimately linked with the outlook of living under conditions of advanced capitalism.

The Islamic revival emerged in Egypt at a historical moment that also witnessed another significant historical turn: the reintroduction of capitalist economy and the introduction of neo-liberal governance after a period of Arab socialism. Since the 1970s, Islamic revival and economic liberalization cannot be thought of separately. Wealthy businesspeople who have often made their first fortune in the Arab Gulf states promote religious dress and behaviour by donations and company practices. Speculative investment in housing involves the increased investment in mosques which carries the double virtue of pious deed and tax benefits. Countless small businesspeople and vendors make a living from selling religious commodities, which in turn become a main medium of religious mobilization. Women's religious dress is a major fashion industry. The spread of private satellite channels has opened the way for Salafi-oriented religious channels to spread their messages to the same living rooms which have been furnished with much effort to match a modern middle-class life style that has become the aim of almost every Egyptian since the influx of imported goods and migrants' remittances that began in the 1970s.

The ubiquitous presence of religion in the time of the Islamic revival is to a significant extent due to the commodity form it has taken. At the same time, the commodity form and the logic of consumption has become an equally ubiquitous feature of almost all parts of daily life. In this chapter, I look at this alliance of the Islamic revival with contemporary capitalism and the complications that result from the everyday practice of living under conditions where capitalism provides a key sensibility of livelihood and better future and revivalist Islam provides a key promise of moral righteousness and existential trust.

What characterizes these complications is the centrality of often unpredictable daily moves, uses and adaptations that compel us to think about 'capitalism' and 'Islam' not as something substantial and given, but as something that emerges in daily interactions. This is a perspective that cannot be framed in terms of either structure or agency. Instead, it shows human interaction as limited but manipulative and thus indirectly constitutive of its own limitations (de Certeau 1984). It also shows human action as tragic rather than either free or determined: the same actions and possibilities that provide hope and a possible way out are also the things that cause anxiety and block alternative paths (Orsi 2005). It is this aspect that I especially wish to highlight in this chapter, emphasizing that capitalism is not only a configuration of relations of production and consumption, but is also inherently accompanied by an ideology, promises and ends of its own, which is why it can never be reduced to a simple instrument in pursuit of an independent purpose, such as religious mobilization.

Living Capitalism

People in contemporary Egypt live in a time in which their society is going through a transformation from a nation-state-based economy with strong socialist leanings towards a globally oriented capitalist one, and a time in which mass-produced and mass-mediated consumer goods such as cassette tapes, booklets, televisions and computers have become central media of religious messages. The logics and moral messages of the different technologies and ideologies (in this case notably revivalist Islam, socialism, and capitalism) involved do not exist separately from one another, and just like there are major (and successful) efforts of creating (niches of) Islamic markets and finances, so also the logic of markets, finances, production, profit and consumption becomes part of Muslims' religious experience and beliefs.

One feature of capitalism that has made it so successful and dynamic around the world (aside, of course, from its exceptional capability to generate profit) is its peculiar dual face of a value-neutral, even amoral technology that can and must be 'filled' with moral content, and of a moral order that privileges innovation, initiative, self-responsibility, competition, and success as core characteristics of being a good human being. The first face makes capitalism and movements of religious revival natural allies, as proselytization can become a profitable source of living, consumption an ethical means to a religious purpose, and a religiously inspired notion of morally responsible action the normative framework to guide the search for profit. At the same time, this alliance is troubled by the second face of capitalism as an ideologically grounded practice that carries notions of morality and humanity of its own, paradigms of human action with a powerful dynamic to transform all social practices – including religious ones – according to a logic of investment, profit and consumption. This is not to say that the logic of capitalism now dictates everything. That would be a very hurried and false conclusion. What I want to argue is that it, in part, shapes the aims and practice of revivalist religious and moral commitment in complicated and unpredictable ways.

Here, caution is needed, because one part of the power of the metaphors of capitalism is that 'capitalism' appears as something clear, solid and globally unified while in reality it, too, is complex, dynamic and embedded in idiosyncrasies and cultural specificities: 'In turning one's gaze to the systemic features of world capitalism, it is easy to lose track of the specificity of particular capitalist niches' (Tsing 2000: 340; see also Ho 2005; Kingfisher and Maskovsky 2008). So in order to understand the formative influence of capitalism as a mode of subjectivity and sociality, again we need to take a detour in order to properly understand the problem at hand. In this section, I therefore focus on the specific features of capitalism in contemporary Egypt, in order to look at how revivalist religiosity today seems to be appropriating some of the virtues that are central to capitalist experience.

To start with, a key feature of capitalism at the turn of the millennium in Egypt is its uneasy coexistence with traces of Arab socialism. In the 1950s, Egypt's growing sector of private industry and trade, to a significant extent owned by foreign nationals residing in Egypt, was largely nationalized in the course of the Gamâl Abd an-Nâsir's socialist experiment. In the 1970s, his successor Anwar as-Sâdât initiated the *infitâh* (open-door) policy of gradual privatization and economic liberalization. Although government subsidies have since been dramatically reduced and a large part of state-owned companies sold, rent income from oil, gas, Suez Canal and political alliances allows the Egyptian state to continue maintaining some of its socialist structures, notably a very large and unproductive public sector workforce. Despite the bad salaries, people with lower incomes especially rely on public-sector jobs because of the security and social status they continue to be associated with, not to mention the social insurance and pension benefits they include. Despite the neo-liberal policies of privatization of some parts of the functions of the state, an Arab socialist image of the public sector as the responsible institution to solve societal and economical issues of all kinds prevails.

Much of the expansion of investment and consumption since the 1990s has been made possible by generous credits of different scales, with the result that both individuals and companies base their spending on large-scale debt. Even the lowest levels of economic transactions in small village shops are based on payment in instalments, guaranteed by blank cheques. Such reliance on debt is not necessarily a problem from a macroeconomic point of view (although it can be if the amount of debt exceeds people's capacity to pay and the value of their guarantees – whether this will be the case in Egypt remains to be seen). On the contrary, the 'commodification of the future' (Appadurai 1996: chapter 4), implied in the way consumption is financed – and in fact made possible – by credit and payment in instalments, is necessary for the growth and expansion of a capitalist economy. From a practical, everyday perspective this means that the pressure of debts and instalments has become one of the most present issues in people's lives as they accumulate consumer goods such as apartments, furniture, televisions, satellite dishes, mobile telephones, computers and fashionable clothing with money they yet have to earn.

While the rapid expansion of consumption and the commodification of the future have nurtured high expectations for the good life, these expectations are accompanied by another, more troubling and uncertain face of capitalist economy. Policies of structural adjustment and the relative dependence of Egypt on imports have lead to a dramatic gap between growing pressure of consumption and credit, while the income of low-income families is stagnating or even declining. This gap is especially strongly felt in regard to the interlinked issues of marriage and housing, where the inflationary growth of the cost of marriage and of housing standards have made marriage an increasingly difficult task for young people.

Another major cause for frustration and uncertainty is that the great aspirations inspired by the socialist legacy and the capitalist promises can seldom be realized in the ways promised because the actual workings of educational, administrative and economic institutions significantly differ from their official, legal shape. These institutions are governed by informal logics and structures that in most cases make 'other considerations' (*hisâbât tâniya*) based on family relations and clientelist allegiances (*wasta*), bribes, and other informal transactions that bypass formal qualifications and legal entitlements (see Rabo 2006). Also the socialist sectors of the economy have been transformed by an informal version of the privatisation of public services. School diplomas with high grades are almost impossible to get without private tutoring which can be a very lucrative business for teachers – a profession otherwise severely underpaid. Government jobs that include the possibility of significant income in bribes are either distributed on the basis of *wasta*, or sold for high prices. The police can be hired to extract private debts. Allegedly, even inclusion in the national football selection is influenced to some degree by considerations of *wasta*. Largely due to these clientelist relations, Egypt in the early twenty-first century emerges as a strongly stratified class society where paths of success are extremely dependent on family background and the ability to pay for private high-quality (preferably English-medium) education (de Koning 2009).

Given the scarcity of reliable legal paths to success for people without *wasta*, illegal or semi-legal means to success appear as necessary and even acceptable in the face of a feeling that anyone who has money must be a thief anyway, or the heir of a thief. Although people often stress the legality and legitimacy of income (especially in the religious sense of that income being halal), economic practices have not been influenced by the Islamic revival to the degree that, say gender relations, dress and drinking practices have been. The expectation that Muslims, by the virtue of their faith, would be more moral and responsible economical actors is not met by the practice of everyday economic transactions in Egypt. While Islamic legal norms for contracts and obligations are an important part of everyday economical interactions, so are various tricks, shady deals, bribes and outright swindle and theft. Even interest (*ribâ* in the religious terminology, but euphemistically renamed to *fâ'ida*, 'profit,' in the language of modern banking), the most central issue of Islamic economics, is far from absent in the Egyptian economy. While traditional money-lenders have come to face significant opposition in their communities for religious reasons (and probably because they have never been very much liked in the first place), payment in instalments routinely involves interest, as do bank accounts which are becoming increasingly popular especially among small entrepreneurs.

It is important to highlight that even for people who hold to a socialist set of beliefs in regard to economic policy or who end up being at the losing end of the redistribution of wealth, capitalism is never merely a menace. Wealth, which today is measured primarily by the capability to consume, equals a promise of good life and happiness, and it is the issue Egyptians I know spend most energy and time on. Conditions of poverty only make this promise of wealth stronger. It would be misleading to attribute this aspiration for a good life in wealth and security to capitalism only: The drive for wealth quite certainly precedes capitalism, and the wider promise of progress – of cumulative improvement in all aspects of life in both qualitative and quantitative terms – also draws on other sources. But what definitely can be attributed to capitalism is the way growing and conspicuous consumption has become the most important marker of wealth and good life. The capability to consume has developed into the primary aim of people's economic activities and is the key register in which people judge various social relationships, most notably marriage and social standing.

The moral notion of respect – a key virtue for being a full-fledged member of a community – is especially heavily dependent on the ability to consume conspicuous goods and to serve debt. This importance of consumption for respect and recognition is at the same time very powerful and very controversial. People take it very seriously, harshly judging people who fail to perform the (rapidly growing) economic obligations involved in gaining respect, and at the same time complaining that respect has become an empty virtue based entirely on money rather than character, justice or religiosity:

Ismâ'îl: One wants to live as a respected (*muhtaram*) person one day, to plan for the future so as to have a decent and respectable life when one is forty. The older one grows, the stronger the pressure. And when one has lived in poverty, it is very important for one.

Samuli: What makes one respected in the village?

I.: That it is primarily measured by wealth. Having stable income, money, a good house, etc.

S.: Is respect not measured by friendship, love, moral integrity, religiosity etc.?

I.: No, all that really matters is wealth. People respect my cousin because they think he is a millionaire, works in the Gulf since fifteen years, invites everyone in the café and lives lavishly, not because of his personal qualities.

S.: What about if one's wealth is based on bribes or drug trafficking?

I.: It has become irrelevant, it no longer plays a role where your money comes from as long as you have it.

Disillusioned and critical of what he perceives as an ethos of materialism, Ismâ'îl nevertheless works hard in order to become respected on these terms. Such critique of materialism should not be understood as an opposition to the promises and pressures entailed in consumption but as an expression of the ambivalence they cause. The ability to spend money on conspicuous commodities has become a virtue in itself, and even when people express their discontent about it being so, in their daily judgements about the qualities of other people as respectable or disrespectable, it counts. This is a real and serious moral pressure, and it makes conspicuous consumption an aim that concerns not only the goods one can buy and the girl one can marry – to refer to a male perspective (Masquelier 2005) – but also the kind of personality one wants to portray to other people and oneself.

The modes of subjectivity entailed in consumption do not only concern respect, which is essentially an intersubjective virtue of performing proper social relations. They also entail an ideal of reaching happiness. Furthermore, they emphasize success as a virtue and a key condition of happiness. The intertwined pursuits of happiness and success may be phrased together under the keyword of aspiration, the pursuit of a better life that is understood in terms of increasing material well-being and advancement in terms of income, skill and experience. Capitalist aspiration is not only an issue of how many square metres one's apartment has and how much the furniture costs; it also presents a particular and powerful way to understand all kinds of human actions and relations in terms of investment, accumulation, consumption, and success.

In the age of (re)-emerging global capitalism along with traces of Arab socialism, economy dominates people's lives, sometimes as a promise, sometimes as a threat. In such a chaotic, unpredictable mixture of dramatic hardship, grand promises, sudden wealth and shady deals, religion can appear as precisely the kind of firm hold and straight path that is needed to make things a little clearer. But when we look at the actual ef-. fects of capitalist economy, we see that this is easier said than done. Capitalist economy and consumption entail a proper ethics of subjectivity that cannot be subsumed under a religious regime. More than that, as I show in the next section, capitalist ethics themselves infiltrate the promises and practices of religion.

Profit and Reward

Consumption is never simply a neutral means for the ends of a religious movement, as Martin Stokes reminds us:

> Consumption-based strategies can never take everything into account. The commodity form is never simply amendable to ideological control. The commodity fetish, as Marx constantly reminds us, leads its own life – it 'thinks us', no matter how much we like to believe we are capable of 'thinking it'. (Stokes 2002: 331)

A striking case in point is perhaps the similarity and affinity between the capitalist ethics of consumption, success and profit, and the Islamic revivalist framing of reward as the central paradigm and motivation for religiosity. While the religious discourse disseminated both by the religious establishment and the countless individual preachers of the Islamic revival focuses heavily on *iltizâm*, the commitment to a pious and moral discipline as a means to forge a character willingly obedient to God, many Muslims are actually much more concerned with collecting reward (*thawâb*) that can be obtained by praying, fasting, invoking God, doing pious and good deeds, and the like. These are not mutually exclusive discourses: They co-exist as two key notions of religious practice both in the sermons of preachers as well as in the discussions among ordinary Muslims. The focus on reward is intimately connected to the heavy emphasis of the Islamic revival on death and the afterworld. But although the striving for reward and the pursuit of self-formation both belong to a shared project of cultivating an emotional habitus of stern, God-fearing adherence to religion as 'facts', they can, nevertheless, present somewhat different emphases of piety: the one based on a holistic discipline, the other focussed on maximizing divine reward for the sake of maximal pleasure in the afterworld.

The focus on reward has become a key issue of Muslim religiosity in the age of the Islamic revival for two reasons. One is the way preachers of the Islamic revival have very successfully mobilized the afterworld, especially the fear of hell and the Punishment of the Grave,[1] as a key religious sentiment (see, e.g. Mahmood 2005: 140–45; Hirschkind 2006). The daily concern for punishment and reward has proven to be a very powerful way to persuade people to desire a stricter religious commitment. Booklets and sermons that detail the terrible tortures of the Punishment of the Grave are among the most widely circulated.

This is not to say that Muslims would not have believed in reward and punishment, heaven and hell, before – they certainly have, and yet it seems that concern for the fine details of maximizing reward has not been quite as central before as it is now. In my earlier fieldwork in the Sufi milieu (note that Sufi notions of piety used to be hegemonic in Egypt until recently) I never encountered people discussing the issue of reward in such an explicit and elaborate manner. Many people wanted to convert me to Islam because they wanted to save me from hell, but for them the issue was very straightforward: non-Muslims go to hell, Muslims go to paradise. Rather than trying to maximize reward in the afterworld, people in the Sufi milieu were much more concerned with a spiritual progress to higher states of religious experience, and with searching for the assistance of the friends of God (that is, Muslim saints) in their worldly problems.

The way a middle-class urban mother, who had come to the *mulid* festival of as-Sayyid al-Badawî in Tantâ in order to take her children to see the rides and fair, interpreted the meaning of a Sufi gathering is telling of the shift. She argued that the Sufis engaged in an ecstatic *dhikr* (collective meditation to music) were misguided in their attempt to gain reward that way. I have actually never heard followers of mystical Islam claim that participation in *dhikr* would be a way to gather reward, but unlike for the Sufis, for her reward clearly was the paradigmatic, if not the only, motivation to be involved in a religious ritual.

A second reason for the privileging of reward is related to a more general vision of the human condition that privileges profit as a paradigmatic motivation and outcome of action. Take, for example, the countless little prayers and invocations that circulate on the Internet, invariably carrying some variation of the promise that they will bring huge 'mountains of *hasanât*' (points of reward) to whoever reads, speaks out and forwards them. One such invocation that circulated on Facebook in 2008 declares: 'Send this to 15 [others] – in an hour you will have gained [the reward of] 15 million blessings for the Prophet in your accounts, God willing. Don't be arrogant towards God by saying you don't have time. This is a million points of reward which you certainly need.'

Such hyperbolic promises of millions of points of reward and thousands of angels praying for one are very common, and very telling of the way the fear of punishment and the drive for reward has become a key motivation for religiosity in a way that does not automatically imply a sense of flawless commitment. This is in fact a rather utilitarian notion of religion where saying a prayer and forwarding it to friends is an easy and accessible way to balance one's account: a million points one certainly needs. This is not to say that the issue of religious commitment would be absent: it is present through the very fear and anxiety that make people so eager to circulate such messages. But the hyperbolic promises of easy reward are motivated by a sensibility that is in a significant way different from the ideal of committed personality. In the prayer posts on the Internet, what is central is concrete, direct reward (and punishment) rather than developing the ethical sensibility to fear and obey God. And this reward is just a click away.

Such messages, which come in handy posts and pictures, often written in an informal colloquial style similar to that of advertisements, are one of the many successful means of a religious revival initiated but no longer controlled by groups of religious activists with the aim of proselytizing a movement of comprehensive religious commitment. But by virtue of the life experience and expectations shared by the people who write and read them, the rhetoric of persuasion they employ, and the sensibilities to which they appeal, they, too, become influenced by ideals and logics other than the one they were ostensibly designed to proliferate. When people who share the logic of profit, success and consumption as metaphors of human relations and as modes of subjectivity come to act in religious terms, they bring their horizons of expectation and modes of action along. In short: Religion, too, gains a flavour of capitalism (and vice versa).

This was first pointed out to me by Layla, a woman in her mid-twenties who works as a consultant for an international company in a very elevated and exclusive social milieu that has only been reached by the latest wave of the Islamic revival after 2000. Returning to Egypt after studying abroad for five years, she expresses her surprise and dislike about the wave of religiosity that has reached the upper and upper-middle classes. She complains about one of her colleagues, a very religious person who prays regularly. She ends up doing much of his work because he, rather than praying in the office or at the mosque next door, always walks to a mosque further away because every step he takes to walk to a mosque for prayer brings him more reward.

> I think it has something similar with the work itself. At my work, we work by the hour. The hour is paid well in dollar, and it means that I have a very high pressure to optimize my use of time, to work as much and as efficiently I can in that hour. My colleague does the same in religion. Just like I count at work: How much have I done in my working time? – he thinks: How much reward have I gathered, how many points do I have, am I falling behind in points? He thinks about religion exactly the same way he thinks about money and work. And religion for him is not about peace of mind, about the feeling in his heart; it's all about gathering points. All life shrinks to just making profit for the afterworld. The women with *higâb* really suffer in hot weather under their clothes, but they say: it's OK, I do it all for the afterlife. They think about religion in a completely capitalist way.

This is evidently the point of view of a person who finds collecting reward a misguided form of religiosity. Layla probably underestimates the peace of mind and sense of direction that intense involvement in ritual practice may often offer. But aside from her normative judgement, she makes an important observation: There is a clear similarity, even affinity, between the capitalist logic of profit and the revivalist logic of reward. This is particularly obvious in the elite milieu of an international company where high income is justified by high standards of productivity. But the focus on wealth and profit does not necessarily mean a 'Protestant' work ethic; on the contrary, the unpredictable and chaotic nature of global capitalism in a post-socialist economy makes both wealth and poverty often appear sudden, unpredictable, even miraculous.[2] In fact, very much like the Internet posts that promise huge loads of reward (often much more reward than is entailed in performing major religious obligations like the pilgrimage to Mecca) for reading a short prayer, stories and promises of dramatic and sudden wealth due to the green card lottery, lucky breaks, shady deals, and alliances of politics and trade monopolies of the kind of the steel oligarch Ahmad 'Izz,[3] circulate among Egyptians from less privileged milieus.

The religious promise of the good life in this and the afterworld does not remain untouched by this capitalist paradigm of the good life, and yet this does not mean that revivalist Islam could be reduced to the capitalist sensibilities it addresses. Just like the ubiquitous presence of religion makes religious considerations important without making them the single dominant mode of people's everyday behaviour, so also the ubiquitous presence of capitalist economy makes economic considerations of the consumerist kind important without replacing other considerations. Neither revivalist religion nor global capitalism exist as conclusive systemic wholes but rather as complex everyday practices and discourses that partly influence and partly contradict each other.

This is not a matter of simple causality. In the final instance both Islam and capitalism are processes and outcomes of human action, and as such they cannot be ascribed causality in any direct way. What we have at hand are affinities or resonances between different practices that are undertaken by people who 'share a spiritual disposition to existence' (Connolly 2008: 42; see also Weber 1979). The notion of points of reward (*hasanât*) and points of punishment (*sayyi'ât*) has a long tradition in Islam, and so have trade and profit. But the particular, contemporary capitalist shape of consumption and profit – especially profit of the sudden kind – does favour notions of religiosity that highlight reward because they appeal to key sensibilities that have developed into master metaphors of subjectivity and social practice in the course of the re-introduction of capitalism in Egypt: the necessity of consumption as a key to happiness, the capability to consume as key ideal of subjectivity and social status (thus not really a choice, albeit commonly framed in terms of choice), profit as the main aim and motivation of action, and the often sudden and miraculous appearance of profit and conspicuous consumption.

Most importantly perhaps, profit and consumption, reward and the afterworld share a deeper layer of a shared sense of temporality that really makes revivalist religion and capitalist consumption so closely connected in such complex and unpredictable ways. In a time of global capitalism, religion may sometimes appear as an alternative to the seemingly materialist tendency of capitalism, and more often it appears as the moral content that is needed to fill and guide the pursuit of wealth and consumption. But in daily practice, the attempt to instil capitalism with Islam and to promote religion within the logic of an expansive market of consumer commodities, has much more complex consequences. The attempt to saturate capitalism with Islam also saturates Islam with capitalism, and one of the key moments where this takes place is in the way the temporality of everyday life is increasingly dominated by the future.

One of the most widespread and powerful moments of Islamic religious life in both past and present has been the ideal of contentedness (*ridâ*) with the will of God. Also today Muslims often emphasize that in the end, praise is due to God in good and bad times alike. But this emphasis often is made in the middle of bitter complaints and agitated anxiety about one's share in life. And the heavy emphasis of revivalist sermons on cultivating anxiety about one's share in the afterlife does not make things easier in a situation where people face and cultivate the two contrary affects of contentedness with the present and anxiety about the future. My friend Mustafa had been bothered by this for a few days as we met in a café in downtown Alexandria. He had recently started his career as a salesman in an import-export company, and he was making good progress establishing business contacts, but he could still sense nothing but pressure to go ahead:

> It's a strange thought I have had in the last days. I think that *qanâ'a* (conviction/contentedness) is all a lie. Everybody talks about it, but nobody is really content. Sure, faith (*îmân*) should be about contentedness with what our Lord gives us. I'm sure that in the age of the Prophet people were content. When you read the Qur'ân it praises the grain, the dates – but it doesn't talk about chicken or meat. In those days people could be content with the simple gift (*ni'ma*) our Lord gave them. But I don't see anybody today really having that; everybody is under pressure, never content, always looking for something better. You can never stop and be happy with what you have reached. If I make 700 pounds (ca. 100 EUR) I am already worried about where I can get more. The only way you can stop and be content is to surrender like a beggar, stretch out your hand and let things happen to you.

This combined sense of religiosity and aspiration in the age of Islamic revival shares a key sense of temporality with capitalist production and consumption: both are based on the constant production of a sense of shortcoming, of a perpetually under-fulfilled aspiration. Both profit and reward involve a sensibility of living in the future tense, which exerts continuous pressure and anxiety for the present moment, and posits fulfilment always in the future, almost but not yet within reach. The actual moments of satisfaction they do provide – the sense of peace and certainty that religious practice often offers, the sense of satisfaction that the successful acquisition of goods often brings along – are characteristically transient. After a prayer, new sins are accumulated, and need to be overcome by the next prayer. With life being full of little and big shortcomings, there is no certainty of one's status of reward. After new goods have been bought, the instalments are yet to be paid. And as soon as they are paid – or even before – even newer, better goods have to be purchased.

Conclusion

While ending this chapter on such a pessimistic note, I do not, however, aim to argue that people would be victims of structural constraints under which both their religious and worldly aspirations offer little more than false comfort. Critically appropriating the approach of Michel de Certeau (1984; see also Mitchell 2007) on the tactics of the weak versus the strategies of the powerful, I instead argue that the power of both capitalism and the Islamic revival is at once established and circumvented through everyday tactics as people try to make the best out of the powers, expectations and pressures they face (see also Jackson 1998: 26–27). Rather than as a duality of the powerful and the powerless, I suggest that we should understand these tactics as the very condition under which people live their lives while at times trying to develop and to enforce theoretical, ideological and theological grand strategies. Just as tactics are not necessarily of the weak, strategies are not necessarily of the strong, as we can clearly see when we look at the articulations of perfectionist religious ideology, a textbook case of a grand strategy that is yet often undertaken by people in marginal and precarious situations, and vice versa: the complex workings of economical desires, pressures, transactions, tricks and detours are a tactical business in which the elites are involved as much as the poor are. This is not to deny that there are winners and losers, powerful and weak. But in order to understand what it means to act and live under given circumstances, it is important to avoid too much dualism, and instead highlight the general, existential concerns that motivate people's acts.

The race to built better homes on credit and the hope invested in a prayer that makes one's account in the afterlife overflow with points of reward are both practices which allow people to make their life bearable, manageable and hopeful. The tragic catch of these attempts is that they also constitute the pressures and powers which people face when every potential groom tries to outbid others in standards of housing and every attempt to strive for reward reminds one of the punishments that await behind every corner. This is a power which no grand strategy could ever accomplish. At the same time, this power is never absolute, and is always the outcome of particular actions that can be changed, even if only slightly. In this sense, the coming together of economical aspiration and religious hope is a source of direction and optimism as much as it is a source of anxiety and constraint (Orsi 2005). It is in this sense that it may be useful to think about human lives and experiences less in terms of structure and agency, and more in terms of the hopeful and the tragic.

Notes

1. Analogue to the Christian belief in purgatory, the Punishment of the Grave is understood to be a punishment which believers must undergo for their sins before they are granted entrance to paradise.
2. I am indebted to Jan Beek for this point.
3. Incidentally, Ahmad 'Izz became one of the first leading figures of the Mubarak regime to be arrested in the wake of the revolution.

References

Appadurai, A. 1996. *Modernity at Large: Cultural Dimensions of Globalization.* Minneapolis: University of Minnesota Press.

Armbrust, W. 2011. 'The Revolution against Neoliberalism'. *Jadaliyya*, 23 February. http://www.jadaliyya.com/pages/index/717/the-revolution-against-neo-liberalism (retrieved 24 February 2011).

Connolly, W. E. 2008. *Capitalism and Christianity, American Style.* Durham, NC, and London: Duke University Press.

de Certeau, M. 1984. *The Practice of Everyday Life.* Trans. S. Rendall. Berkeley: University of California Press.

de Koning, A. 2009. *Global Dreams: Class, Gender and Public Space in Cosmopolitan Cairo.* Cairo: American University in Cairo Press.

Hirschkind, C. 2006. *The Ethical Soundscape: Cassette Sermons and Islamic Counter-publics.* New York: Columbia University Press.

Ho, K. 2005. 'Situating Global Capitalisms: A View from Wall Street Investment Banks'. *Cultural Anthropology* 20, no. 1: 68–96.

Jackson, M. 1998. *Minima Ethnographica: Intersubjectivity and the Anthropological Project.* Chicago and London: The University of Chicago Press.

Kingfisher, C., and J. Maskovsky. 2008. 'The Limits of Neoliberalism'. *Critique of Anthropology* 28, no. 2: 115–26.

Mahmood, S. 2005. *Politics of Piety: The Islamic Revival and the Feminist Subject.* Princeton, NJ: Princeton University Press.

Masquelier, A. 2005. 'The Scorpion's Sting: Youth, Marriage and the Struggle for Social Maturity on Niger'. *Journal of the Royal Anthropological Institute* 11, no. 1: 59–83.

Mitchell, J. 2007. 'A Fourth Critic of the Enlightenment: Michel de Certeau and the Ethnography of Subjectivity'. *Social Anthropology* 15, no. 1: 89–106.

Orsi, Robert A. 2005. *Between Heaven and Earth: The Religious Worlds People Make and the Scholars Who Study Them.* Princeton, NJ: Princeton University Press.

Rabo, A. 2006. 'Aleppo Traders and the Syrian State'. In *The Role of the State in West Asia,* ed. A. Rabo and B. Utas, 115–27. Swedish Research Institute in Istanbul, Transactions: 14. London and New York: I. B. Tauris.

Schielke, S. 2009. 'Ambivalent Commitments: Troubles of Morality, Religiosity and Aspiration among Young Egyptians'. *Journal of Religion in Africa* 39, no. 2: 158–85.

Stokes, M. 2002. 'Afterword: Recognizing the Everyday'. In *Fragments of Culture: The Everyday of Modern Turkey,* ed. D. Kandiyoti and A. Saktanber, 322–38. London: I. B. Tauris.

Tsing, A. 2000. 'The Global Situation'. *Cultural Anthropology* 15, no. 3: 327–60.

Weber, M. 1979. 'Die protestantische Ethik und der Geist des Kapitalismus'. In *Die Protestantische Ethik: Eine Aufsatzsammlung.* Vol. 1, ed. J. Winckelmann, 9–277. 5th rev. ed. Gütersloh: Mohn.

Afterword

Everyday Religion and the Contemporary World

The Un-Modern, Or What Was Supposed to Have Disappeared But Did Not

Robert A. Orsi

> The world—the time has come to say it, though
> the news will not be welcome to everyone—has
> no intention of abandoning enchantment altogether.
> —Roberto Calasso, *Literature and the Gods*

The modern world was not supposed to look the way it does in this book. Modern men and women were not – still at this late date (which means this many years from the European Enlightenment[s]) – supposed to be finding saints beneath the soil of a Greek island, or bringing their needs to a deceased southern Italian holy figure who had for years soaked his sacerdotal clothing with blood from miraculous wounds in his hands, feet and side (cloth cherished now by his devout as precious relics), nor were they supposed to be dancing in the alleys of Egyptian cities to boisterous pop music first composed for celebrations at the tombs of Muslim saints (to cite three examples of contemporary religion from this collection of essays). This sort of religion – and it is the assumption of the contributors to this volume that these different examples of contemporary religiosity share characteristics that warrant organizing them under the single rubric of 'everyday religion' – was fated to be outgrown by the world's cultures, beginning with the West (specifically northern Europe) and then spreading across the globe, to be succeeded by a modern liberal faith sanctioned by (and providing sanction for) law, political theory, epistemology and science. Let me briefly review this history of the making of religious obsolescence here, because I think the notion of 'everyday religion' as developed in this collection is usefully viewed in relation to this story, as it offers an important alternative perspective, another angle of vision, on modern and contemporary religion.

The intellectuals and divines of the European seventeenth century, weary of endless internecine religious terrorism and war, imagined a 're-ligion' free of local particularities, a faith that all reasonable people, un-less corrupted by priests, would be naturally inclined to share. Modern religion was to be an interior and personal matter, freely assented to, not compelled by priests or magistrates, and it was to be independent of the nation-state (although emergent modern Western nationalisms were heavily dependent on religion). This 'religion' addressed itself to a sane and singular divinity who did not seek human sacrifice, as the old god had (during the Saint Bartholomew's Day massacre in 1572, for example, when the Seine flowed red from the blood of hundreds of brutalized Prot-estant bodies thrown into it as it flowed out of Paris into the countryside), but order, peace and human flourishing. Modern religion was about ethics and belief, not about kissing the relics of a dead saint. In the eighteenth century this vision of a universal, inwardly focused and tolerant religion – tolerant, that is, except for the religions featured in the chapters of this book, which were seen by liberal theorists such as John Locke as so ir-remediably out of step with and hostile to the coming age as not to be protected by guarantees of toleration – underwrote new ideas about the organization of society, about freedom of conscience, and about human nature and identity. It also condoned chattel slavery and soon provided the moral rationale for empire (as well as contributing to slavery's end and challenging imperial pretensions).

By the end of the nineteenth century – we can take 1871, the date of the publication of Edward Burnett Tylor's *Primitive Culture* (in two volumes: *The Origins of Culture* and *Religion in Primitive Culture*) as a crucial marker here – this notion of 'religion', with its origins first in violence and exhaustion and then in the repression and sublimation of the memory of violence in liberal political theory, an amnesia fundamental to the self-understanding and self-regard of the modern nation-state, had also become the theoretical foundation of the new science of religion.[1] So when we talk about modern religion we are referring to at least three things: (1) the subject of academic inquiry, as in religious studies and the anthropology of religion, where "modern religion" is an analytic category that attempts to name a distinct and universal dimension of human ex-perience; (2) a normative discourse about religion and the self that has been developing from the seventeenth to the twenty-first centuries and that proposes how persons ought to live and how states ought to be orga-nized, with northern European and American Protestantism as exemplary forms; and (3) the lived practices of modern men and women since the eighteenth century. The phrase 'modern religion' has always entailed both descriptive and prescriptive dimensions; it inscribes one way of being re-ligious as 'religion' itself.

Between the seventeenth and the nineteenth centuries, modern 'religion', in the social world and in scholarship alike, served as the ground of cultural hierarchies (more advanced societies practiced the higher, more modern forms of religion, free of archaic residue; lesser societies practiced religion of the sort evident in this volume) and as a metric for distinguishing among kinds or levels of human consciousness (primitive or infantile consciousness vs. the mature, enlightened mind); and it was mobilized as a political and legal mandate. Modern understandings of 'religion' also told a story about time: certain ways of being religious belonged inherently to past times and would inexorably be discredited and discarded. When Americans set out to explain and justify the decision to go to war against Iraq they conflated all these inherited certainties, thus unleashing anew the violence and intolerance latent in modern notions of 'religion' and contributing (together with their counterparts in Muslim societies) to bringing the world back full circle to the sixteenth century (this time around with new and deadlier weapons). This resurgence not simply of 'religion' but of religious war has led to what social theorist Arjun Appadurai identifies as 'the odd return of the body of the patriot, the martyr, and the sacrificial victim into the spaces of mass violence' (2006). We seem to have entered upon another age like that of the Thirty Years War.[2]

Modern religion turned out not to be stable and singular, however. Over the centuries, it generated out of itself alternative religious sensibilities and practices (religious 'enthusiasm', for instance, and the varieties of pietism). One of the most recent of such variants, which is central to contemporary conversations about global 'religion' and politics, is what was until a decade ago called 'fundamentalism'. The term is of recent vintage. Americans introduced it in the early twentieth century to describe a group of highly educated Protestant Christians who rejected modern liberal Christianity, which at that time was at the pinnacle of its prestige and power in the United States and in Western Europe. Doctrinally, fundamentalists believed in the infallibility and inerrancy of scripture (against the new Biblical criticism), in the literal reality of Jesus' miracles, in the superiority of conservative Protestant Christianity over all other religions, and in the moral depravity of humans, which necessitated the disciplines of religion. Fundamentalists emphasized clerical authority; they tended to be socially conservative, rejecting the allure of modern culture. By the end of the twentieth century 'fundamentalist' had expanded to include religious practitioners of whatever faith who were at odds with liberal modernity generally and specifically with its religious and political expectations.

Fundamentalists of all sorts were said to share a common set of family resemblances. They took their sacred texts literally, both as history and as moral legislation; they stressed male clerical authority over individual lay choice; they created social and political structures that would insure religious conformity and orthodoxy as they saw it; and they expected the self-effacement, if not the subordination, of women. Because modern 'religion' is also the subject of an academic discipline, religious studies contributed to the construction and elaboration of the term 'fundamentalism' and to its status as an atavism in the modern world. This is why the discipline was not immediately prepared to understand the world after 9/11, when it became clear that 'fundamentalism' was not, in fact, a retrograde religious form, but an integral, inescapable and possibly permanent part of modernity itself (see, e.g. Gray 2003).

After the events first of 1989 and then of September 2001 (and the subsequent wars), the word and concept 'fundamentalism' lost salience. 'Fundamentalism' is no longer much in use, having been replaced by religious 'terrorism' in the minds of anxious citizens, but also among sympathetic observers by the more neutral and even positive terms 'conservative' religion, political religion, political theology (which assumes the fundamental interconnectedness of the political and the religious, often in a spirit of advocacy, e.g. this is the way it ought to be), or traditional piety. The rise of Islamism was paralleled by the deepening political confidence in the United States of conservative evangelical Christian coalitions, who likewise called for a rethinking of the independence of the political sphere from religion. The liberal state, with its separation of the civic and the religious, was no longer the only acceptable political form of modernity. In the United States these days, as among the clerical ruling circles of Iran, for example, you are not 'religious' unless your religion includes political ambitions and agendas. A politics free of religion has come to seem naïve and old-fashioned, and with this has come an insistence on the singular, coherent and authoritative nature of religious traditions. Among the 'world religions' everywhere there are 'heightened demands for a unitary profession of the faith', in anthropologist Robert W. Hefner's words, pervasive 'homogenizing pressures', and a widespread 'drive to make the state an instrument of religious standardization.' The phenomenon once called 'fundamentalism', imagined as the antithesis of modernity, has become an alternative modernity, one of multiple modernities; as Hefner's comments suggest, it has become the new modern. The poles of religious possibility in the contemporary world, Hefner writes, appear to be 'separation' (the old modern) and 'conquest' (the new modern) (1998: 92, 95, 99).

The religious practices and practitioners discussed in this book have very little to do with all this; they appear to be off to one side of the spectrum of modern religion, off-modern rather than an instance of the multiple modern. Does this mean that the practices of everyday religion are 'survivals', traces of the past in the present? It is the case that the religious idioms described here illustrate the multiplicity of temporalities that coexist within the modern and contemporary, especially in religious contexts, the simultaneity of the unsimultaneous (to borrow Ernst Bloch's famous phrase). I will develop this idea further towards the end of this chapter. But the 'modern' has been thoroughly deprived of its teleological inevitability and I see no justification for reinstating it as a lens for viewing and assessing everyday Muslim and Catholic practices. So then where do we locate these religious forms on the landscape of the contemporary global religious scene? How are the everyday religious idioms described and studied in this collection part of contemporary global reality and contemporary religion? If we do not find a place for 'everyday religion' in the conversations underway about secularization, political theology, modernity and post-modernity, scholarship of the sort evident in this book will be consigned to irrelevance, having nothing to offer the most urgent questions of our historical moment.[3]

That the everyday seriously matters in the contemporary world is perversely and tragically evident in the rage such religious practices and attitudes cause political and religious elites and in their determination to harass and suppress them. Everyday life, its pleasures and its pieties, are fiercely monitored by the various guardians of sacred public order on the planet, secular and religious, or more often some combination of the two. Nothing so provokes religious moderns of all sorts as religious idioms independent of their controlling orthodoxy and scrutiny, of their political agendas and moral rigidities. Yet the way of being religious described in this volume, organized under the rubric of 'everyday religion', is how most of the world is religious today, from the alleys of Egypt to the new religions of African and Asian cities, to the shrine culture re-emerging across Southeast Asia; in the plethora of religious improvisations in the United States; and in the resurgence of devotions to the saints across the former Soviet space.[4]

So what is everyday religion? The term 'everyday' has had, in the words of a scholar who has carefully traced its history, a very 'troubled career' (Highmore 2002: 1). It has been used (inconsistently) as a vehicle for examining and critiquing capitalist modes of consumption, the allure of the commodity, and the routinization of ordinary life, as well as a designation for spaces and times free from capitalist disciplines. The concept of the everyday, as developed by European and American historians after World War II, opened a window onto working-class culture. It has been a useful lens for tracing relationships between the global and the local. But 'the everyday' has never been a stable category.

The meaning of 'everyday' when used to modify 'religion' seems at first glance to be self-evident: it refers to how men and women appropriate for themselves the dominant religious idioms of their cultures. The phrase implies an opposition: 'everyday religion' as opposed to ... 'Everyday religion' is not solely or primarily what happens in specially designated and consecrated sacred spaces, under the authority of religious elites, but in street and alleys, in the souvenir stalls outside shrines, and in bedrooms and kitchens; 'everyday religion' does not happen at times determined by sacred calendars or official celestial computations, but by the circumstances and exigencies of people's lives. The everyday religious is not performed by rote or in accordance with authority; it is improvised and situational. Everyday religion takes place at (and contributes to the making of)

> those moments in social life when the customary, given, habitual, and normal is disrupted, flouted, suspended and negated, when crises transform the world from an apparently fixed and finished set of rules into a repertoire of possibilities, when a person stands out against the world and, to borrow Marx's vivid image, forces the frozen circumstances to dance by singing to them their own melody. (Jackson 1989: 20)

But this dichotomy between the frozen and the fluid, the orthodox and the popular, does not work well as a way of thinking about everyday religion. For one thing, the religious person who enters a particular life moment or crisis does not come to it free of all memory, relationships, embodiments, desires, fears and inheritances (unlike the archetypal existential man of phenomenological anthropology, who appears to arrive always without a story or a past and without any relationships, making him an avatar of the modernist fantasy of the unencumbered and radically individual self). This cannot be true in religious contexts. Religion situates practitioners in webs of relationships between heaven and earth, living and dead, and in rounds of stories; religious practices are always embodied and if they are forgotten in the mind they are remembered in muscle and sinew. The religious person (by which I do not mean a hypostasized entity but simply a man or woman using religious idioms in engaging their lived circumstances) comes to no life occasion free of connections and entanglements. Moreover, the two ways of participating in a religious world sketched out above, e.g., church/street – corresponding to the famous distinction sacred/profane – are obviously not distinct. Everyday religion understood from one perspective may be viewed as the most intimate (if not the most insidious) site of the intrusion of religious institutions, doctrines and authorities into the secret places of personal experience. The everyday religion of the Catholic women of Quebec in the nineteenth and early twentieth centuries, for instance, kept them bound to a sacred and sacerdotal regime that required them on doctrinal grounds to bear children well beyond the strength of their bodies and the capacities of their families to feed them, and they did (see Gauvreau 2005). The problem of 'everyday religion' remains.

What makes the example of the woman calling on Santo Pio's assistance an instance of everyday religion, as Samuli Schielke and Liza Debevec introduce the term in this collection, is not that the woman is praying at home rather than in church, but that her prayer arises at the point where 'daily practice and grand schemes come together'. The key here is the word 'everyday'. Giovanna Bacchiddu writes later in the volume that the practices of everyday life are 'irreducible' to the category 'religion'. Religion, says Bacchiddu, 'surfaces in everyday activities and practices'. The 'everyday' is more capacious than the 'religious'. Inquiry into everyday

religion, consequently, begins not with specific religious traditions, in order to trace the indigenous appropriation and reinvention of particular elements, but with the 'manifold paths of daily life', in a phrase of Schielke's
and Debevec's. 'Equally if not more important' than the religious tradition
in question, they write, is 'to inquire what it means, in a specific situation,
to live a life.' This is an empirical matter. The central question in the study
of everyday religion is 'how to account for the relationship [between] articulations of a coherent world-view and the practice and knowledge of
living a life?'

It is in the interplay of religious practices and understandings with the
circumstances of everyday life that religion is experienced as really real,
indeed that religious phenomena become real – meaning that they acquire
an 'objective, external quality', an 'objective power' – in the experiences,
imaginations and practices of men and women in relation to each other and
to their gods. The really realness of the two great poles of contemporary
religion – liberal modern/fundamentalist modern – comes from commitment to doctrinal orthodoxy; from the alignment of religion with national
or regional identities imagined as static, ancient and singular; or from adherence to a particular leader or to a political agenda. But this is not the
case with the religious practices described in this volume. In everyday religion, at the juncture of the exigencies of daily life with inchoate religious
inheritances, religious reality acquires a life apart from practitioners, in the
world. People meet their gods as present and real before them; the gods
(and ancestors, ghosts, demons, saints, and so on) take their places within
necessary circles of relationships. Religious idioms become 'things [and, I
would add, living beings] that people approach, use and do', as Schielke
and Debevec put it. As a result of this objectivity, externality and realness,
religious idioms that arise within and exist in response to the exigencies
of everyday life are not ever completely or securely under the authority
either of the persons using them or of religious or political authorities. In
an important phrase from the introduction, everyday religious practice is
'embedded in traditions, relations of power and social dynamics, but it is
not determined by them.'

The 'circumstances of everyday life', moreover, include religious doctrines and rules, as well as the official limits to practice and imagination.
'Everyday religion' is not premised on the dichotomy of religious elites/
ordinary practitioners, which was so crucial to scholars of 'popular' religion. Santo Pio, for example, as Evgenia Mesaritou shows, becomes real
in the contradictions and contests among his devout (who include, in any
case, many priests, nuns, bishops, even cardinals and one pope, John Paul
II) and church authorities (architects, bureaucrats, the officials of the local
Franciscan order) determined to direct and control the devotion. It is by
manipulating the spaces of the shrine – spaces which have been designed
and organized by the caretakers of the devotion precisely in such a way as
to shape what can and cannot take place with them between the saint and

his devout – that Santo Pio's devout have access to him. Everyday religion, in other words, does not exist apart from religious tradition and authority, either in religious spaces or at home. As American sociologist Nancy Ammerman puts it, to study everyday religion 'requires both an attentiveness to unconventional practices and an ear for the pervasiveness of traditions' (2007: 8). To return to my example of a woman praying to Santo Pio in her kitchen, it is the powerful sanction of the church and the fact of this woman's having been formed from childhood by the disciplines of a particular Southern Italian Catholic religious and social world that endows her with the capacity to deploy the devotion in order to (freely?) do what she must do within the limits of her social world (see Apolito 1998). There is no absolute distinction between freedom and authority in everyday religion.

Everyday religion is also thus the practice of a great refusal – the refusal to be excluded from religious traditions construed as normative and singular by government officials, religious elites, or scholars of religion and religions. As Graw writes of West Africa, 'Diviners usually perceive of themselves as opening within, not outside, the realm of Islam', rendering impossible any absolute distinction between '"popular" or "official" varieties of Islam.' Perhaps it is better to say that everyday religion is the practice of varied strategies of a great refusal. The men and women Debevec spoke with in Burkina Faso, for example, laid claim to their identities as 'good Muslims' first by establishing and recognizing the (impossible) ideal of perfect adherence as defined by the authorities (this is what the really good Muslim does) and then by marking their distance from this (alas, this is not what we do), a kind of participation by conscious inversion. Knowing what they are not doing is what makes them good Muslims. Or as Peterson says of the street-smart Egyptian mulid revellers, they struggle 'to find a balance between religious commitment and a love for life', or in a local popular expression, 'an hour for your Lord and an hour for your heart.'

Religion in everyday life, then, refers to the places and times where the ordinary and daunting, the exhilarating and joyful realities of human experience are taken hold of, by men and women in the company of their gods, and where other discourses (nationalism, for instance, or political fearfulness) are most intimately encountered and engaged. Here these other discourses do not dominate, or they do not always or simply dominate. In everyday religion men and women (and children), holding the multiple media of their traditions in their hands – relics, songs, images, stories, memories, beads, candles and so on – show themselves as being adept at cordoning off without actually denying – even while affirming – religious requirements that otherwise would keep them from living life the way they want to live it or the way they need to live it. 'Street-smart youth in Egypt adopt the exceptional, spectacular, all-encompassing festive moments of the mulid', Peterson tells us, 'as an accommodating framework in which they negotiate both the knowledge that explains their lives and the ways that they actually want to live them', finding a path between 'what they are convinced they should do and how they actually act'. The 'everyday' offers a theoretical framework for the study of religion that points beyond the catalogue of antinomies in human experience that have long oriented religious scholarship – discipline/freedom; authority/agency; choice/determination; resignation/hopefulness, to cite just some of them – while at the same time keeping in clear sight the realities of political power, social hierarchies and cultural formations.

In addition to such experiential dichotomies, the study of religion has also been historically shaped by a number of key conceptual or analytical antinomies, famous pairs of opposites that have fundamentally constituted how we understand the 'religious'. Attending to religion in everyday circumstances offers the theoretical resources for developing the study of religion beyond these as well. One is, as already noted, sacred/profane. The chapters in this volume confirm that sacred and profane are never distinct or never distinct in an absolute way, but are braided in people's everyday experience. We no longer speak of sacred or profane but of a helix, a twisting of sacred and profane around each other through the movement of people's days, the contingencies of their social circumstances, and the dynamics of their relationships. This is not to say that the problem Clifford Geertz identified as one of the most vexed in the study of religion – that is, how people move back and forth between modes of thought or experience (as a nurse, for example, in a modern hospital who is also a devout of Santo Pio, whom she understands as present to her throughout her rounds, goes between her medical duties and her relationship with the saint and prayers for the sick) – is simply solved. It especially does not mean that in particular circumstances the transition between sacred and profane might not be jarring, disorienting or disruptive. But it undermines the assumption that the two are absolutely divergent registers of experience and being (Geertz 1973: 119).

The second essential pairing of oppositions in the making of religion is us/them. Theorist of religion Jonathan Z. Smith identifies this as the most fundamental and necessary of all the opposites that have contributed to the making of modern notions of 'religion' (1982: 6). Religious practitioners of the sort who appear in these pages – who have recourse to diviners in times of confusion, unsatisfied desire, and stress, for example, who dream of saints, who seek ways of securing Santo Pio's 'continuing presence in their everyday lives' – were again precisely the ones destined to disappear, in Europe and around the globe, according to the normative timeline of religious theory. Their ongoing presence in the contemporary world is taken as anomalous, even bizarre, exotic and risible; within the hierarchy of religious evaluation their behaviours are judged delusional, infantile and escapist. What modern person looks with equanimity on a woman kissing the bloody cloth relic of a dead miraculous healer? But the existential and phenomenological orientation of the contributors to this collection – an orientation that fundamentally shapes the understanding of 'everyday religion' that emerges in these pages – restores the common and recognizable humanity of religious practitioners. (In the academic and theoretical context, that is. Their humanity was not necessarily in need of restoration in other contexts or among other interlocutors.) The notion of 'everyday religion' as developed here undoes the radical otherness of men and women practicing these forms of religion by acknowledging that they (who were once called our 'subjects') and we, the scholars who study them – us/them – are contending with similar life challenges and that all of us equally must deal with the inevitable doubleness of being both agents of our own lives and experiencing ourselves as powerless and determined, of having chosen and of having no choice.

Knut Graw puts this most eloquently and clearly when he writes, 'An anthropological study of divination as a cultural field of hope and prospect shows that divination is neither exotic nor part of a primordial cultural past but a complex and highly topical cultural practice of understanding and empowerment. Such a perspective on (Islamic) divinatory praxis highlights, in other words, its existential significance, not its otherness.' Otherness is not the same as difference. Scholars of religion can, and I believe that they must, attend to the existential, political and cultural differences between themselves and the men and women whose religious practices they study. But this does not mean rendering these men and women so different – so alien – as to make them virtually members of another species, finding no common ground between their lives and ours. This impulse of othering is unfortunately too common in the study of religion, where others and women at work on their worlds in the company of their gods are viewed as 'data' or 'fair game' for theorizing (see Orsi 2004).

The third and final foundational dichotomy in the study of 'religion' that the concept of 'everyday religion' radically calls into question is presence/absence, in particular the presence/absence of the gods (a synecdoche for the whole host of 'imaginary' beings of different religious worlds, among them ghosts, saints, ancestors and spirits). This is the most vexed oppositional pair in the modern history of the study of religion and also the most mandated, the most authoritative, and the most consequential for religious practitioners; dissolving it, consequently, is the most theoretically challenging, even explosive, contribution of the study of everyday religion as proposed in this collection to the broader study of religion.

'There was a time', says literary critic Roberto Calasso, 'when the gods were not just a literary cliché, but an event, a sudden apparition' (2001: 23).[5] But that was then and this is now. Although we know enough today not to say that the modern world is 'disenchanted', in Max Weber's famous word (there are plenty of enchantments among both modern secularists and religionists), religious practices oriented to presence of the gods in particular things or particular times and places – touching the gods, kissing them, punishing and entreating, speaking to them, feeding and anointing them, dressing them – which included the understanding that the gods were there, really present, to be dressed, fed, kissed, and so on – were taken by modern religious theorists as evidence of the most 'primitive' and 'savage' level of religiosity, among other peoples and among the Western industrial working class. 'Good' modern religion did not include real presences. Modern religious elites sought to expunge practices of presence; at the extreme, such behaviours were classified as pathological. 'Religion', as it developed as an analytical category in northern Europe, England and America, banished the gods; the most influential modern definition of religion, Clifford Geertz's 1973 essay on 'Religion as a Cultural System', makes no reference to special beings. Philosopher Charles Taylor refers in his history of the making of modern consciousness to this understanding of supernatural presence, what I am calling 'real presence', (rather than, for example, symbolic or metaphorical presence or the doctrine God's providential agency in the movement of history) as 'the old model of presence'. Real presence is the clearest indicator of the premodern. Other forms of religiosity, including (especially, as I have argued) 'fundamentalism', were congruent with the modern. But real presence was just what modern people were expected to grow out of in time (see Taylor 2007: 447–48).

Most of the chapters in this book describe practices of presence, so we can say that everyday religion, as a theoretical category as well as lived practice, becomes those occasions when humans in the mundane circumstances of their lives engage and are engaged by the gods along with all the media (things, stones, grottos, tombs and so on) of real presence. This identification of the everyday with the real or literal presence of the gods runs throughout the chapters of this book. According to Bacchiddu, everyday religion embodies and enacts 'relations between humans and supernatural entities'; in everyday religious practices 'God and the saints are "socialized", brought into an active social relation and experienced as interlocutors.' Severine Rey speaks of 'the profound feelings of closeness felt by the villagers for the saints.' By means of rosaries, prayer cards, and other objects, writes Mesaritou, 'people ensure the saints' continuing presence in their everyday lives.' Peterson says that according to the devout, the saint's presence extends to the entire mulid area, imbuing material objects there with blessings. Debevec describes women, who are otherwise so assiduous at postponing the requirements of piety, negotiating with God to give them husbands.

As the contributors to this collection make clear, furthermore, the experience of presence is not a matter solely of the vertical, but the horizontal too. Men and women engaging and being engaged by the gods are also at the same time in relationship to other persons, in their families, states, communities and social worlds. These others include the dead and the absent, as Alison Marshall shows in her discussion of the religious practices of Chinese immigrants to Manitoba, Canada. Religion in everyday life is abundantly intersubjective and relational. Inevitably, then, the currents that flow through the spaces and times of everyday religion include unconscious or unacknowledged desires, fears, and hopes (as well as conscious ones). The identities of the gods and persons present to each other amid the realities of everyday experience are multiple and intertwined: to borrow language from object relations theory, they include desired and feared, possible and rejected embodiments of practitioners' selves as well as of their significant circles of others (which always include the gods). Padre Pio may be one's longed for father, feared mother, the love one needs or cannot bear, or some combination of fragments of these inner realities. This makes everyday religion an especially dynamic, unstable and highly fluid psychological and social reality; the intersection of the horizontal and the vertical has consequences for both the gods and humans. Identities and lives are transformed, for better and for worse, by the presence of the gods and humans to each other.

'For better or worse' is key here. There is nothing necessarily 'good' or 'bad' about everyday religion; it is neither nourishing nor harmful, simply. Everyday religion does not liberate people from 'the continuum of the present' (in David Harvey's description of Henri Lefebvre's idea of the 'everyday') nor does it suture them more tightly to it. Either/or is not the appropriate register for the critical study of everyday religion. But as people move in and out of healing sites, as they enter the company of diviners and visit the shrines and tombs of saints, bringing their lives into these venues of presence and then bringing things touched to or taken from these places and holy persons back to their homes and workplaces, the givenness of the real is no longer stable or singular. Everyday religions are, in Graw's phrase, 'cultural technolog[ies] of hope and prospect.' This is what makes the sites and practices of everyday religion irritating and dangerous to religious and political authorities, however much they may sanction, tolerate, or authorize them.[6]

The study of contemporary religions has begun to seem increasingly claustrophobic to some of us. As one of my students, who plans to study the lives of a small community of vowed Catholic women in the middle of the United States, said in exasperation, 'how do you escape the trap of the modern?' She was frustrated because almost everything she was reading about contemporary religious women in various traditions around the world viewed them inevitably in some relation to 'the modern', however much this term is said to be contested. Contemporary religious are modern, anti-modern, alternately modern, one of a multiple of moderns, or (less often) pre-modern; but they are always defined in relationship to the modern (which includes the fundamentalist modern, in Hefner's words, the party of 'conquest'). Discourse about modernity and secularization theory (and its inadequacies and limitations) has become like a woven finger-trap toy, impossible to extricate oneself from, especially the harder one tries. The conclusions are given from the start: the nuns my student wished to study were already destined to be located theoretically somewhere along this continuum of variations of the modern.

But with this growing frustration has come an interest in finding and developing theoretically what Hefner more than a decade ago identified as 'a third option for a refigured religion', a religious practice that is neither separation not conquest, religiously liberal modern or religiously orthodox modern. Many others have come to share this aim. 'Objects, sites, practices, words, representations – even the minds and bodies of worshippers', Talal Asad has written, 'cannot be confined within the exclusive space of what secularists name religion' (1999: 192). At the end of her study of the ways that American Christianity (including Catholicism) is being reformulated to bring it into alignment with state limitations on religion in the public sphere in order to legitimate the presence of Christian programs in state institutions, American legal scholar Winnifred Fallers Sullivan refers as an alternative to contemporary religious idioms and practitioners (she is speaking in particular about Asia and the Middle East) that 'seem to be taking charge of their own lives through re-appropriations of traditional religions in ways that appear to reject both Enlightenment epistemologies and traditional hierarchical structures of religious authorities' (2009: 178). She is pointing here to what I understand Hefner to mean by 'subaltern religious experiences' within traditions. So then what is this third way that is distinct from the two megaliths of modernity/anti-modernity, the parties of separation and conquest, this way of thinking about our world that is not exhausted either by liberal religious modernity or anti-secularist orthodoxies and political theologies?

At the same time, many of us who work on people's everyday relationships with gods, demons, angels and other such figures – those of us who work on real presences in people's experience in history and contemporary culture – have begun to feel restless with the limitations modern social science and historiography impose on what may be said about these figures, about what happens in the interactions between them and the humans who are in relation to them, of their bonds with humans, and about the social and historical import of these relationships that exist between heaven and earth. Modernity – and the critical tools to study the modern world – situates the human at the centre of things; reality exists only as it is for the human. But it is a central contribution of the study of everyday religion that the gods (to remind readers: I use the word as a synecdoche for the plethora of special beings in relation to humans and more broadly still for religious imaginings of reality) are encountered in the circumstances of everyday life as objective, really real, there apart from the human imaginations and bodies out of which they arise. If we do not find a way of studying such experiences of really realness then, as Michel de Certeau has written, they will 'sink into a hidden "underside"' of the world as lived, and we will fail to understand much of human life (1988: 128).

'Everyday religion', as the category is introduced and developed in this collection, offers just such a theoretical framework for thinking through these issues with new insight. The religious practitioners described herein make no claims on the nation-state. They do not aspire to establish social and moral orders, to compel obedience, or to institute religious hierarchies; if anything, they are wary of religious authorities and deft in their avoidance and outwitting of them. They are flexible in terms of doctrine and authority. Their primary allegiances are local and they derive their moral codes from families and communities (rather than from clerically authorized readings of sacred texts). This does not mean that they are isolated and withdrawn; the evidence is that they are fully engaged with the modern world, certainly with its idioms of popular culture, opportunities for travel, and communications media. They are focused on life's existential challenges, but they do not mandate a single path to human fulfilment and well being, even for themselves. Everyday religion as it appears in these chapters is certainly not immune from the planet's ubiquitous political violence or from politically and religiously motivated terror, but practitioners do not attempt to harness either for their own ends.

The everyday religions described are neither liberal modern religion (as this developed from the seventeenth century forward) nor fundamentalist modern (in its recent variants); they belong neither to the party of separation nor to the party of conquest, in Hefner's terms. Rather, they are the religions that were supposed to have disappeared by now. It is precisely as such, as the un-modern, as the remembered, inherited, reinvented fragments of ancient religious worlds that long pre-date the modern, that never went away, but that were explicitly excluded from the normative self-construction and self-representation of the modern at its inception – recall here that the two religions exempt from enlightened toleration, as proposed by John Locke, were Catholicism and Islam – that 'everyday religion' becomes the third way of being religious in the contemporary world that many of us have been looking for, the way out of the finger-trap.

I feel urgency in developing this idea of the third way and moving it closer to the centre of our discussions about contemporary religions. Arjun Appadurai and other social critics speak of the increasing abstraction of modern experience; of the intimate and dreadful local consequences of the invisible movements of global finance; of the increasing militarization and massive arming of the planet; the ecological disaster that is already upon us; of the manipulation of fear by nation-states to justify repression within and wars beyond their borders; and the exacerbation of local conflicts and assault against minorities and human dignity. Radical religion has been one response to these circumstances; radical secularism was another. But the majority of the planet's people are contending with the world as they find it in the practices of everyday religion as described in this volume. The un-modern, the religions that were supposed to have disappeared but did not – even in those parts of the world, such as the former Soviet Union, where there was a sustained, politically authorized, and well-organized assault against Islam, Orthodoxy, Catholicism, Tibetan Buddhism, and so on – pries open a theoretical space in the nearly hermetically sealed conceptualization of contemporary religion as organized around the two poles of separation/conquest and allows us to think new thoughts and raise new questions about religious practice in a troubled world.

Notes

1. On forgetting the violent religious past in the making of tolerant modern nation-states, see Marx 2003.
2. For insight into the new seemingly endless religious wars of our time, see Filkins 2008.
3. My first attempt at taking up this question was 'Is the Study of Lived Religion Irrelevant to the World We Live In?' Presidential Plenary Address, Society for the Scientific Study of Religion, Orsi 2003.
4. Two recent novels that powerfully explore the threat of the everyday to religious authorities in two different contexts are Hannaham 2009 and Mandanipour 2010.
5. The epigraph to my chapter is on page 23.
6. David Harvey is cited in Highmore 2002: 116.

References

Ammerman, N. T. 2007. 'Introduction: Observing Modern Religious Lives'. In *Everyday Religion: Observing Modern Religious Lives,* ed. N. T. Ammerman, 3–19. Oxford: Oxford University Press.

Apolito, P. 1998. *Apparitions of the Madonna at Oliveto Citra: Local Visions and Cosmic Drama,* trans. W. A. Christian Jr. University Park, PA.: The Pennsylvania State University Press.

Appadurai, A. 2006. *Fear of Small Numbers: An Essay on the Geography of Anger.* Durham, NC: Duke University Press.

Asad, T. 1999. 'Religion, Nation-State, Secularism'. In *Nation and Religion: Perspectives on Europe and Asia,* ed. P. van der Veer and H. Lehmann, 178–96. Princeton, NJ: Princeton University Press.

Calasso, R. 2001. *Literature and the Gods,* trans. T. Parks. New York: Vintage Books, 2001.

de Certeau, M. 1988. 'The Inversion of What Can Be Thought: Religious History in the Seventeenth Century'. In *The Writing of History,* trans. T. Conley, 125–46. New York: Columbia University Press.

Filkins, D. 2008. *The Forever War.* New York: Alfred A. Knopf.

Gauvreau, M. 2005. *The Catholic Origins of Quebec's Quiet Revolution, 1931-1970.* Montreal and Kingston: McGill-Queens University Press.

Geertz, C. 1973. 'Religion As a Cultural System'. In *The Interpretation of Cultures,* 87–125. New York: Basic Books.

Gray, J. 2003. *Al Qaeda and What It Means to Be Modern.* New York: The New Press.

Hannaham, J. 2009. *God Says No.* San Francisco: McSweeney's Books.

Hefner, R. W. 1998. 'Multiple Modernities: Christianity, Islam, and Hinduism in a Globalizing Age'. *Annual Review of Anthropology,* no. 27: 83–104.

Highmore, B. 2002. *Everyday Life and Cultural Theory: An Introduction.* London and New York: Routledge.

Jackson, M. 1989. *Paths Towards a Clearing: Radical Empiricism and Ethnographic Inquiry.* Bloomington: Indiana University Press.

Mandanipour, S. 2010. *Censoring an Iranian Love Story,* trans. S. Khalili. New York: Vintage Books.

Marx, A. W. 2003. *Faith in Nation: Exclusionary Origins of Nationalism.* New York: Oxford University Press.

Orsi, R. A. 2003. 'Is the Study of Lived Religion Irrelevant to the World We Live In? Presidential Plenary Address, Society for the Scientific Study of Religion'. *Journal for the Scientific Study of Religion* 42, no. 2: 169–74.

———. 2004. 'Fair Game'. *Council of Societies for the Study of Religion Bulletin* 33, no. 3–4.

Smith, J. Z. 1982. 'Fences and Neighbors: Some Contours of Early Judaism'. In *Imagining Religion: From Babylon to Jonestown,* 1–18. Chicago: The University of Chicago Press.

Sullivan, W. F. 2009. *Prison Religion: Faith-Based Reform and the Constitution.* Princeton, NJ: Princeton University Press.

Taylor, C. 2007. *A Secular Age.* Cambridge, MA: Harvard University Press.

Contributors

Samuli Schielke received his PhD in 2006 from the Faculty of Social Sciences at the University of Amsterdam. His research interests include festive culture, morality, religiosity, and aspiration and frustration in contemporary Egypt. He is currently a research fellow at Zentrum Moderner Orient in Berlin where he directs the junior research team working on the topic "In Search of Europe: Considering the Possible in Africa and the Middle East." He teaches visual anthropology and social and cultural anthropology as an external lecturer at the Free University of Berlin.

Liza Debevec holds a PhD in social anthropology from University of St Andrews (2005). She has been doing research in Burkina Faso since 2000 and in Ethiopia since 2010. Her research interests include food, Islam, every day life, gender, water, policy analysis, and natural resource management in Africa. She was a research fellow at the Scientific Research Centre of the Slovenian Academy of Sciences and Arts between 2005–2013 and a Visiting Assistant Professor at the Department of Social Anthropology at Addis Ababa University between 2010–2013. She is currently working as a researcher at the International Water Management Institute in Addis Ababa, Ethiopia.

Knut Graw teaches social and cultural anthropology at the Catholic University of Leuven (KUL) and is associated researcher at the Zentrum Moderner Orient (ZMO) in Berlin. His research concentrates on local hermeneutic practices such as divination and dream interpretation in Senegal and Gambia, and the situation of Senegalese migrants in Spain. His theoretical interests span from ritual studies and phenomenology to globalisation studies and political economy. At the Catholic University of Leuven he works at the Institute for Anthropological research in Africa (IARA) and the Interculturalism, Migration, and Minorities Research Centre (IMMRC).

Alison R. Marshall is Professor of Religion at Brandon University and Adjunct Professor in the Department of Women's and Gender Studies at the University of Winnipeg. A China specialist, Marshall works in the areas of Chinese Canadian religion, history, foodways, and gender. She has published many articles, including "Everyday Religion and Identity in a Western Manitoban Chinese Community: Christianity, The KMT, Foodways and Related Events," *The Journal of the American Academy of Religion* 77, no. 3. She is the author of *The Way of the Bachelor: Early Chinese Settlement in Manitoba* (UBC Press, 2011) and a forthcoming book under contract with University of British Columbia press titled *Confucianism and the Making of Chinese-Canadian Identity in Manitoba and Saskatchewan.*

Giovanna Bacchiddu studied anthropology in Italy (Cagliari), London (LSE) and at the University of St Andrews, where she received her doctorate. She is the author of several articles on religion, sociality and kinship in Apiao, Chiloé, where she did extensive fieldwork. She is currently working on a postdoctoral research project, investigating a case of international adoption and studying perceptions of parenthood, kinship, memory and identity in Italian adoptive parents and Chilean adoptees. She is a lecturer at the Pontificia Universidad Católica in Santiago de Chile.

Séverine Rey currently teaches anthropology and research methodology at the University of Health Sciences (HESAV) in Lausanne, Switzerland. She was previously a lecturer in anthropology at the University of Lausanne. After completing a study on sainthood-making in Greece, her current research topics focus on gender and health professionals, and on image and technology within the radiological practice.

Evgenia Mesaritou obtained a PhD in sociology from the University of Cambridge. Her doctoral thesis was an ethnographic study of the shrine of Santa Maria delle Grazie (San Giovanni Rotondo, South Italy) which examined the construction of the sacred within the pilgrimage cult of Padre Pio. She is currently lecturing and working as a researcher in Cyprus. Her main research interests concern religion, pilgrimage, space and material culture.

Jennifer Peterson is an independent researcher and filmmaker residing in Cairo, Egypt. She holds an MS in Arabic language, literature and linguistics from Georgetown University.

Robert Orsi is Professor of Religious Studies and History at Northwestern University in the United States. He has previously taught at Indiana University and Harvard University, where he was chair of the Committee on the Study of Religion (2003–2007). Orsi is the author of a number of books on religious history, and theory and method in the study of religion, most recently *Between Heaven and Earth: The Religious Worlds People Make and the Scholars Who Study Them.* He is editor of the *Cambridge Companion to Religious Studies* (2012).

Index

www.ingramcontent.com/pod-product-compliance
Lightning Source LLC
Chambersburg PA
CBHW060042030426
42334CB00019B/2450